Critical Academic Writing and Multilingual Students

Michigan Series on Teaching Multilingual Writers

Series Editors
Diane Belcher (Ohio State University) and
Jun Liu (University of Arizona)

Available titles in the series

Peer Response in Second Language Writing Classrooms
Jun Liu & Jette G. Hansen

Treatment of Error in Second Language Student Writing
Dana R. Ferris

Critical Academic Writing and Multilingual Students
A. Suresh Canagarajah

Critical Academic Writing and Multilingual Students

A. Suresh Canagarajah

Baruch College
City University of New York

 Michigan Series on Teaching Multilingual Writers

Ann Arbor
THE UNIVERSITY OF MICHIGAN PRESS

Copyright © by the University of Michigan 2002
Published in the United States of America by
The University of Michigan Press
Manufactured in the United States of America
◎ Printed on acid-free paper

2005   2004   2003   2002   4   3   2   1

A CIP catalog record for this book is available from the British Library.

Library of Congress Cataloging-in-Publication Data

Canagarajah, A. Suresh.
  Critical academic writing and multilingual students / A. Suresh
Canagarajah.
      p.   cm. — (Michigan series on teaching multilingual writers)
  Includes bibliographical references and index.
  ISBN 0-472-08853-X (acid-free paper)
    1. English language—Rhetoric—Study and teaching. 2. English language—
Study and teaching—Foreign speakers. 3. Criticism—Authorship—Study and teaching.
4. Academic writing—Study and teaching. 5. Multilingualism. I. Title. II. Series.
PE1404.C33   2002
808'.042'07—dc21   2002006435

For Wiroshan

Contents

Series Foreword

Critical pedagogy has offered us a number of provocative critiques of by now traditional approaches to the teaching of second-language (L2) literacy. Yet, while many of us in the field of TESOL (teachers of English to speakers of other languages) have been intrigued by the theory and stances of critical pedagogues and by their discussion of the shortcomings of much current classroom practice, we have also wondered exactly how the ideological positioning of critical pedagogy would actually play out in the L2 writing classroom. In *Critical Academic Writing and Multilingual Students,* Suresh Canagarajah presents one of the most comprehensive answers to this question provided in print so far. We feel fortunate that so accomplished a spokesperson for critical pedagogy as Canagarajah has chosen to address this topic for our series—a topic that any series on teaching multilingual writers would be remiss not to include, for the critical approach to L2 writing is arguably one of the most significant recent developments in L2 writing pedagogy.

In an era when English language teaching is increasingly perceived as fraught with "imperialistic implications," as Canagarajah puts it, we who teach this global and globalizing language undoubtedly have an obligation to revisit our assumptions and reconsider the impact of our pedagogical actions. Canagarajah's volume should facilitate such self-reflection and, at the same time, enable readers to better understand the motivations and pedagogical implications (especially for L2 writing) of the more openly ideological approach espoused by many in the TESOL field today. Readers will likely feel, thanks to this volume, much better equipped to decide whether or not they want to make a commitment to teaching

critical academic literacy, after having envisioned, with Canagarajah's help, what such a commitment might look like from
a number of different vantage points—of form, self, content,
and community—and what it might accomplish in the L2
writing classroom. Canagarajah's own wealth of experience as
a critical pedagogue in the privileged and less privileged inner and outer circles of the English-speaking world, as well as
his eloquence and remarkable accessibility as a critical writer
himself, seem to us to make him ideally suited to guide any
writing teachers who wish to embark on a journey toward increased critical awareness of the role they play, or could po-
tentially play, in the lives of their students.

Diane Belcher, Ohio State University
Jun Liu, University of Arizona

Preface

As I am a former ESL student, my learning experience in writing classrooms has shaped the orientation to pedagogy and rhetoric in this book. My later professional life of shuttling between the academic communities in Sri Lanka and the United States helped me develop a distance from the dominant discourses in both circles, facilitating a critical perspective on academic writing.

During my early education in Sri Lanka, there was no formal teaching of writing in our schools. In our essay assignments, in both L1 and L2, all that we received from our teachers were comments on expressive matters. I was shocked, therefore, to find an obsession with "the product" when I came to the United States for my graduate studies. It seemed petty when my instructors penalized me for not placing my quotation marks outside the punctuation, for not leaving two carriage spaces following periods, or for mistakes resulting from my first experience typing. What I expected was an engaging discussion on the intricacies of my argument or the subtleties of my thought development. Though I was thankful that their scrupulous editing helped me develop a sensitivity to the text as a finished product, I resisted when instructors faulted my logic or organization. During my very first semester here, when a zealous young professor used his red ink liberally on my essay to point out contradictions, deviations, and redundancies, because I didn't have the expected topic sentences and thesis statements (or because the ones he treated as mine didn't make sense), I knew that things had gone too far. I spent an hour with him in his office to explain that I was writing "a different kind of essay." I pointed out that my topic was implied in the paragraphs, that my thesis was evolving, and that my argument was embedded in the consecutive examples. Thankfully, he conceded that I was adopting a different logic of development (although neither of us had the language at that time to talk about "front-weighted" and "end-weighted" structures or "low-involvement" and "high-involvement" presentations). The fight was not that easy on many other occasions.

Though my research interest was in sociolinguistics, I was sufficiently fascinated by the institutional emphasis on and scholarly interest and economic investment in composition (nonexistent in the British-influenced educational contexts I was familiar with) that I decided to register for an elective in "Rhet/Comp." This was the time when the "process movement" of Flower and Hayes was generating a lot of excitement. My dissatisfactions with what appeared to be an overly mentalistic orientation to writing by this school found support in a recently published article that was not part of our required reading for the course—Lester Faigley's (1986) "Competing Theories of Process." For my final project, in a prescient move, I undertook to salvage Kaplan's much-maligned contrastive rhetoric in light of the emerging social process perspective in L1 composition (see Canagarajah 1987). Fortunately, Alice Heim-Calderanello (the instructor for this course) had a background in social activism to appreciate my position. When I moved from Ohio to Austin for my Ph.D. in applied linguistics, whom should I bump into but Faigley himself? Soon, meeting others like Linda Brodkey in the English department, I developed an interest in merging my sociolinguistics with composition research. I thank these scholars for shaping my orientation to critical writing.

Returning soon after my doctoral research to Sri Lanka, I had to adjust to ESL teaching, though I had taught mainly L1 students in the United States, and found myself at home in the ideological radicalism and theoretical exuberance of the L1 composition scene. Thankfully, I met colleagues in the ESOL scene who brought with them the advantages of interdisciplinary orientations to writing. Dwight Atkinson, Diane Belcher, Sarah Benesch, Ulla Connor, Tony Dudley-Evans,

John Flowerdew, Ryuko Kubota, Ilona Leki, and Vai Ramanathan have influenced my thinking in diverse ways. Presenting with them in conferences and/or participating in writing projects, I have benefited from their expertise.

I thank Diane Belcher and Jun Liu for inviting me to write
this book. This project has given me a chance to integrate different strands of work I have been developing during my
teaching and scholarly career before my unruly mind gets
drawn to other areas of research. Diane and Jun offered useful advice as this book evolved. I am also indebted to Vai Ramanathan for taking the time to read the manuscript closely.
Kelly Sippell of the University of Michigan Press has helped
me patiently at different stages of this project. Needless to say,
the limitations remain mine.

I acknowledge a grant-in-aid from the National Council of
Teachers of English (grant no. R98:38) that helped me conduct
a classroom ethnography of writing at Baruch College/CUNY.
Data and research experience from this study proved useful
in writing this book.

As always, my family life has proven inseparable from my
academic life. This book took shape as we prepared for the
birth of our son, delivered him, and assisted his growth for the
next eight months. Knowing the type of world Wiroshan is
taking his first steps in, I am even more convinced that we
can't orientate to literacy in a noncommittal and detached
manner but must engage critically for changes in the institutions around us.

New York City
11 September 2001

Chapter 1
Understanding Critical Writing

So what happens to writing when you attach the word *critical* to it? Does anything happen at all? Is this another newfangled label that promotes a novel pedagogy or method for purely commercial reasons or other ulterior motivations without substantially affecting the writing activity? Or, on the other hand, is too much happening—far too much for our liking—shifting our attention to things unrelated to writing? Is this label bringing into composition something extraneous to the writing activity, such as political causes and social concerns that are the whims of one scholarly circle or the other? We in the teaching profession are rightly suspicious of anything that claims to be new, fashionable, or revolutionary nowadays.

For me, the label *critical* brings into sharper focus matters that are always there in writing. It develops an attitude and a perspective that enable us to see some of the hidden components of text construction and the subtler ramifications of writing. We gain these insights by situating the text in a rich context comprising diverse social institutions and experiential domains. In doing so, the label also alerts us to the power—and dangers—of literacy. Texts can open up new possibilities for writers and their communities—just as illiteracy or ineffective writing can deny avenues for advancement. Writing can bring into being new orientations to the self and the world—just as passive, complacent, or mechanical writing parrots the established view of things (which may serve the unfair, partisan interests of dominant institutions and social groups). Indeed, the text is shaped by such processes of conflict, struggle, and change that characterize society. By connecting the text to context (or the word to the world), the critical perspective enables us to appreciate the complexity of writing and address issues of literacy that have far-reaching social implications.

Defining the Critical

Before I spell out how *critical* redefines writing, we should consider briefly the currency of the label itself. We have by now come across critical theory, critical thinking, critical pedagogy, critical ethnography, critical linguistics, critical discourse analysis, and even critical classroom discourse analysis—just to mention a few.[1] We can of course go on attaching this label to any field we want because there is something predictable and distinctive that happens when we do so. It is natural for us to think of *uncritical* as the opposite of this label. But it is unfair to say that those who don't practice a critical approach are choosing to be apathetic or naive. There are good reasons why someone may choose to adopt an alternative approach. Indicative of these more serious motivations are terms like *objective, detached, disinterested, pragmatic, formalistic,* and *abstract.* These adjectives are less pejorative antonyms for the term *critical.*

To understand the ways these terms relate to each other, we need to take a brief detour through history. The Enlightenment movement of seventeenth-century Europe has much to do with the values attached to these terms. Taking pride in adopting a more rational, systematic, and scientific approach to things, the movement initiated radical changes in many domains of inquiry. Its effects are still there in certain traditions of the study of writing. In order to understand writing, the movement would have said, we need first to identify and demarcate the object of our analysis—the text. We should separate the "text-in-itself" from other related activities and domains so that it can speak for itself. For example, the writer's intentions, feelings, values, and interests should be separated from the text. Neither is the text the reader's processing of it in terms of his or her intentions, feelings, values, and interests. Also, the scholar must see to it that he or she doesn't bring any biases or predisposition to the analysis. This disinterested attitude was considered favorable to letting the object speak for itself. At its best, the study of the text could be undertaken without any involvement of the scholar by employing predesigned procedures and methods. As a culmination of the Enlightenment tendency, Structuralism took the scholar further inside the isolated text. It claimed that if one entered the core of the text, cutting through the superficial clutter of content, meaning, and surface structural variations, one would discover the basic underlying rules that account for the text's universal laws of production and reception. This attitude encouraged an abstract and formalistic approach. Schools as diverse as New Criticism in literature, text linguistics in discourse analysis, and the "current traditional" paradigm in rhetoric display such an approach today. Literacy instruction, influenced by this tendency, has been formalistic, skill driven, and product oriented.

The cultivation of such an empirical perspective on texts was certainly productive in many ways. It brought a clarity, discipline, and rigor to the descriptive activity. Getting the predisposition of human subjects muddled in the analysis, or getting distracted by superficial variations, can be misleading. The approach certainly generated important insights into certain general properties of textuality and literacy. But there is also something lost in this type of approach. For the sake of analytical convenience we are deliberately simplifying the disposition and implications of texts. The text becomes more and more isolated, detached, abstract, and generic. The values that inform its structure and form are ignored. It becomes empty of content, losing its complexity and depth. With the decontextualized approach, the influences of social conditions and cultural diversity on text construction are lost. The ways in which texts are shaped by, and in turn shape, sociopolitical realities are obscured. Much of this happens because the text has become static, passive, and one-dimensional. Writers and readers themselves become automatons who employ predesigned formal procedures with detachment to generate texts. All this amounts to adopting an innocence and complacency toward the literate activity. As a corrective, the critical approach grounds the text in the material world to orientate to its troubling social functions, the value-ridden nature of its constitution, and the conflicting motivations behind its production and reception.

Now let's return to our original question: how does the critical orientation redefine writing? We may summarize the shifts in perspective in the following manner.

- *From writing as autonomous to writing as situated.* The production of texts is not an end in itself. We don't write simply to produce a text—and leave it at that. We produce texts to achieve certain interests and purposes. Furthermore, after a text is produced, it gets used in unanticipated ways. Launched into the public world, it takes a life of its own and effects results and processes totally unanticipated by the writer. Therefore, texts not only *mean* but *do.* Their functionality goes to the extent of reconstructing reality, rather than simply reflecting reality. We need to inquire what the word does to/in the world.
- *From writing as individualistic to writing as social.* For many of us, the stock image of writing is that of the lonely writer locked away in his small apartment (in crowded New York City) or a cabin (in the quiet woods of New England) pouring his thoughts on paper under mysteriously received inspiration. But writing is not a monologue; it is dialogical. One has to take account of the audience (implicitly or explicitly) while writing. This may involve a set of intended audiences, but it also involves an ever-expanding unintended audience (stretching limitlessly across time and space). In constructing a text, a writer is conducting a conversation with all this diversity of readers. This process is different from the definition of it we get from communication theory—which is often diagrammed as follows: writer→text→reader (or speaker→words→listener). Writing is not a one-way

transmission of ideas, nor are constructs like *writer* and *text* autonomous. The writer's "intentions" and "thoughts" are considerably influenced by the expectations, norms, and values of the audience (or community). The text itself then becomes a *mediated* construct—one that is shaped by the struggle/collaboration/interplay between the writer, reader, and the community for thought. We have to become sensitive to how the text embodies the influences of this social interaction.

- *From writing as cognitive to writing as material.* For many, writing is a purely mental activity of putting down on paper the relevant ideas, words, and information that one has the capacity to generate. They view writing as a play between the mind and the text for meaning, order, and coherence. But there are many material resources required to do writing. At the simplest level, one needs a pencil, pen, typewriter, or computer to compose one's thoughts. Which of these one uses is often decided by one's economic status. Each of these instruments presents different levels of advantage to the writer. Furthermore, one needs to be privileged to devote the time required for writing. Writers also need the means to tap necessary resources from publishers, libraries, media industries, and the market. The text is shaped out of a negotiation of these constraints and resources. How these material factors impinge upon the text requires examination.

- *From writing as formal to writing as ideological.* Another commonsense assumption is that one only needs grammar, structure, and rules to construct a text. These are treated as abstract, value-free features of textual form. But writing is more than language or structure. It is also a representation of reality, an embodiment of values, and a presentation of self. Form itself is informed by diverse conventions of textuality, values of appropriacy, and attitudes to style. If writing is not just rules but how to use those rules—that is, for what purpose and with what attitude—then this is a contentious area of cultural difference and ideological preference. One has to consider what values are implied by the form and whether textual norms can be modified to represent alternate values.

- *From writing as spatial to writing as historical.* For many, the text (once produced) is an inert object that occupies a space. It is how words populate five pages, structured in a seamless manner, that is treated as the concern of writers and readers. But the text has evolved through time. While the writing was being done, the writer took care of many other responsibilities in his or her everyday life. There were many false starts and failed attempts. There were many visions and revisions of what the writer wanted to say. There were collaborations and conflicts around the evolving text. The changing social conditions of the community and the personal fortunes of the writer also shape the text. After being produced, the text continues to live in history, being decoded differently according to differing social conditions. The text then is not a seamless whole that stands static through reading and writing. How it is shaped by the disjunctions, fissures, struggles, and conflicts during its construction and reception needs attention.

If we can summarize all these differences in one simple slogan, the shift is from writing as an *object* to writing as an *activity*. In integrating the text into the flow of sociohistoric currents and understanding it as one more purposive activity we do in everyday life, writing becomes not a product but a practice. It is in perceiving writing as a situated, mediated, dynamic social activity that the work of critical practice begins. We cannot stop with charting the internal linguistic structures and rhetorical patterns of the text. We have to also interrogate the values and ideologies that inform the text; the ways in which the external contexts of production and reception shape the text; the prospects for human possibilities to be limited or expanded by the text; and the ways in which the unequal status and differing identities of writers (and readers) affect the constitution of the text. In short, we begin to see how writing is implicated in social conflict, material inequality, cultural difference, and power relationships. In critical writing, students would become sensitive to these factors. They would wrestle with textual constraints, tap the available material resources, and negotiate the conflicting discourses in their favor to communicate effectively. In teaching critical writing, instructors have to make students aware of these diverse constraints and possibilities as they strive for a representation of knowledge that is emancipatory and empowering.

The orientations listed earlier differ from the perspectives of some other current schools of thinking that may employ similar constructs in their definitions. For example, that writing should be contextualized is widely held by many schools these days. But for some, contextualizing the text means seeing the specific details/words/images in terms of the total framework of the text. Or it can mean seeing the details in terms of rhetorical/genre conventions. But this sense of context is still "internal" to the text. I have articulated an ever-widening context that expands beyond the writer/reader and the community to historical and social conditions. On the other hand, even when social context is acknowledged by some schools, it is treated as lying outside the text; it doesn't affect the text's very constitution. Furthermore, theorizing the politics of writing has become fashionable in many circles today—especially among those influenced by poststructuralist and postmodernist perspectives. However, here again, politics is defined in terms of discursive and linguistic issues only, leaving more recalcitrant material factors out of consideration. This orientation explains the trend in Western academic circles toward celebrating the rhetorical activity of interpreting the tensions within the text to show how ideological struggle is manifested there. The poststructuralist schools perceive language as one of the tools that sustain inequality and domination at the microsocial level; therefore, deconstructing the written text to expose the tensions therein is treated as equal to bringing the whole unfair social edifice crumbling down. Though I acknowledge the importance of language and discourse in reflecting/sustaining/enforcing inequality, I still feel that the historical and material dimensions of power have to be addressed in their own terms. Therefore my perspective on writing brings together text-internal and text-external factors, discursive and historical forces, linguistic and social considerations.

Orientating to the Multilingual Writer

I have been talking of the writer in very generalized terms up to this point. It is time now to give flesh and blood to the type of writers this book is concerned with. The pedagogical context assumed in this book is the teaching of English for speakers of other languages (ESOL). The ESOL student community includes those who are learning English as a second language—in other words, those living in former British colonies such as India, Nigeria, and Jamaica and those linguistic minorities living in the traditionally English-speaking countries of Canada, the United States, and Britain, all of whom actively use English as an additional language in social and educational life. These are largely bilinguals. Included in this group are speech communities for whom English has become considerably "nativized." Through a long history of interaction, English has now become locally rooted, accommodating lexical, grammatical, and discoursal features from native languages. While some of these speakers would consider English their native language (i.e., speaking English as their first or sole language), they will still face challenges in using the "standard" English dialects (of the Anglo-American variety) treated as the norm for academic writing. Therefore they should also be considered bidialectals who have to shift from one variant of English to another in their writing.

These groups (largely ESL) differ from those who learn English as a foreign language (EFL). In many parts of the contemporary world, English is an indispensable auxiliary language for a variety of specialized purposes. In addition to being proficient in the vernacular, and perhaps in some regional or colonial languages (French in Vietnam, Dutch in Indonesia,

Portuguese in Brazil), students from these communities will still have some competence in English. This circle is largely multilingual, speaking English as a third or fourth language. However, the traditional distinction between EFL and ESL contexts is becoming fluid these days as English attains the position of a global language.[2] It is becoming indispensable for almost everyone in the postmodern world to hold some proficiency in English and use it for a variety of purposes in their everyday life. Despite the varying levels of linguistic competence possessed by the different ESOL subgroups identified earlier, in practicing academic writing in English they have to all acquire new discourses and conventions and represent their identities in novel ways.[3]

Do these students require a different teaching approach from those used for L1 students? To address this question clearly we have to first ask how ESOL and L1 student communities are different. (By "L1 students" I am referring here to those who are "traditionally native" in English, largely monolinguals, coming from the former colonizing communities that still claim ownership over the language.) It has become pedagogical common sense to distinguish these groups in terms of linguistic difference. ESOL teachers have treated multilingual students as strangers to English and thus aimed to develop their grammatical competence in order to facilitate their academic writing. But this approach is misdirected. We must note that many of these students have some competence in one or more dialects of English—sometimes speaking their local variants of English "natively." There is also widespread proficiency in specialized registers in English—such as the language of computers, technology, academia, and the professions (e.g., legalese, journalese). Moreover, writing involves not just grammatical competence. Therefore, different pedagogies are not warranted based purely on differences in grammatical proficiency.

Teachers have also focused on the cultural difference between both student groups. Apart from the larger differences in beliefs and practices, there can be more specific differences related to literacy. The genres and styles of communication, the practices and uses of literacy, and the attitudes and processes in composing can be different. The popularity of approaches like contrastive rhetoric explains the importance given by teachers to cultural differences in text construction. But even this mustn't be exaggerated too much. After the colonial experience, European culture has left an indelible mark on many local communities (see Canagarajah 1999c; Pennycook 1994). The general trend of globalization in the contemporary world has also resulted in the spreading of Anglo-American values and institutions worldwide. More relevant to our discussion, literacy has spread to such levels that we don't have any "pure" oral communities to speak of today. Even the communities that didn't have a written script have developed one through the help of missionary enterprises (though some of this resulted from the motivation of teaching the Bible).

In general, it is becoming more and more difficult to "essentialize" students in ESOL—that is, to generalize their identity and character according to a rigidly definable set of linguistic or cultural traits. We are unable to define them in ways that are diametrically opposed to the language and culture of L1 students. ESOL students are not aliens to the English language or Anglo-American culture anymore. The hybridity that characterizes communities and individuals in the postcolonial world complicates some of the easy distinctions teachers are used to making about ESOL students. In fact, it is difficult now to speak of uncontaminated "native" cultures or "vernaculars," as many communities have accommodated foreign traditions and practices through a history of cultural interaction and adaptation (see Appadurai 1996). Students in ESOL bring with them a mixture of local and Western linguistic/cultural characteristics, and we shouldn't assume that they all require an "introduction" to the English language and Anglo-American culture.

These qualifications don't mean that ESOL students are not different from L1 students but that "difference" has to be redefined in more complex terms. We have to move away from easy stereotypes about them. The fact that ESOL students display hybrid multicultural, multilingual tendencies doesn't make them the same as L1 students. Hybridity doesn't preclude questions of sociocultural uniqueness. These students may display conflicting attitudes toward the various cultures that make up their subjectivity. They may in fact suspect—and resist—their "Anglo-American" legacy, which has the potential to dominate or suppress their more "indigenous" side. They may also display a different subject position in terms of cultural identity. Their preferred choices of community solidarity and cultural identities have to be respected. While most ESOL students occupy a largely unequal status, as colored individuals from periphery communities, L1 students occupy a privileged position. The latter's cultural identity enjoys the power of dominant communities from the geopolitical center, providing a head start on the linguistic and cultural capital necessary for success in the contemporary world. Hybridity shouldn't be taken to mean, therefore, that issues of power and difference are irrelevant in today's world. Some postmodernist scholars have mistakenly assumed that the reality of cultural and linguistic mixing has defeated the designs of imperialistic forces. Nor should we assume that trends toward hybridity and globalization lead to a homogeneous world where difference doesn't matter anymore.[4] In fact, these trends have inspired minority communities to celebrate their differences and develop their local knowledge and identities. Therefore, despite certain obvious signs toward homogeneity through forces of technology, multinational companies, market forces, and the media, we cannot say that difference has been eradicated altogether. Issues of power and difference have simply become more subtle and dispersed.

The more important consideration in critical writing is not difference per se but the attitudes we adopt toward difference. We have a long history in our profession where the linguistic/cultural difference of multilingual students has been treated as making them limited and deficient in their writing ability. Their distance from the English language and Anglo-

American culture has been treated as depriving them of many essential aptitudes required for successful academic literacy practices. Some have gone further to stigmatize multilingual writers as illogical in thinking and incoherent in communication, by virtue of their deficient L1 and native culture. Consider a summary of the many differences discovered between L1 and L2 writers from empirical studies by Silva (1993).

> "L2 writers did less planning, at the global and local levels" (661).
>
> "L2 writers did less goal setting, global and local, and had more difficulty achieving these goals" (661).
>
> "Organizing generated material in the L2 was more difficult" (661).
>
> "Transcribing in the L2 was more laborious, less fluent, and less productive" (661).
>
> "Pauses were more frequent, longer, and consumed more writing time" (662).
>
> "L2 writers wrote at a slower rate and produced fewer words of written text" (662).
>
> "L2 writing reportedly involved less reviewing" (662).
>
> "There was evidence of less rereading of and reflecting on written texts" (662).[5]

We shouldn't be surprised that L2 students fall short when L1 writing is treated as the norm or point of reference. It is important therefore to examine the assumptions and attitudes with which our research is conducted. Though it must be acknowledged that ESOL students would practice English academic writing in the L1 context and cannot escape from the norms of the dominant linguistic circles, we must still ask: How would our interpretation differ if we understood the composing strategies of ESOL students in terms of their own cultural frames and literacy practices?

Adopting a perspective that takes the students' own frames of reference seriously is the *relativistic* orientation, distinct from the *normative* approach described earlier. It is important to take the students' own explanations and orientations into

account, situated in their own cultural and linguistic traditions, to explain their writing practices. This way we are
able to understand that there are good reasons why they do
what they do. Although this attitude is more egalitarian,
differing from the "deficit" perspective described earlier, it
doesn't go far enough in providing dignity to multilingual
students. Their perspectives are seen as being shaped by
their respective cultures and languages, requiring inordinate
effort to reorientate to other discourses. Even well-meaning
scholars sympathetic to minority cultures sometimes theorize
the competence of ESOL students in condescending terms.
For example, some have argued that since students from
Asian communities prefer nonlinear styles of thinking, they
shouldn't be imposed upon to adopt the explicit forms of logic
and reasoning of Anglo-American communities (see Fox
1994).[6] If these students fail in English literacy, this is explained as resulting from the fact that they are strangers to the
established discourses of the academy. (And, displaying a
trace of ethnocentricism, these scholars judge literacy skills
according to Anglo-American rhetorical traditions anyway.)
Such an attitude is to orientate to difference as a problem all
over again. Sometimes this can take a deterministic bent. The
cultural uniqueness of students is treated as *preventing* them
from becoming successful writers in English, trapping them
into their respective cultural/linguistic worlds.

If *difference-as-deficit* and *difference-as-estrangement* are
somewhat limiting perspectives on multilingual writers, an
attitude that gives them more complexity is one that I call the
difference-as-resource perspective. Multilingual students
do—and can—use their background as a stepping-stone to
master academic discourses. Their values can function as a
source of strength in their writing experience in English, enabling them to transfer many skills from their traditions of
vernacular communication. Even in cases where the connection is not clear, it is important for teachers to consider how
the vernacular influence can be made beneficial for their writing experience rather than functioning in negative, unpleas-
ant, or conflictual ways. Such an attitude will involve teach-

ers orientating to their students differently. We should respect and value the linguistic and cultural peculiarities our students may display, rather than suppressing them. We should strive to understand their values and interests and discover ways of engaging those in the writing process. In doing so, we should be ready to accept the ways in which academic texts and discourses will be creatively modified according to the strengths brought by the students. Academic literacy should adopt a bilateral process—in other words, not only should students be made to appreciate academic discourses but the academic community should accommodate alternate discourses. It is such an attitude that characterizes my orientation to composition research and pedagogical practice in the chapters to follow.

Having examined our *attitudes* toward the linguistic/cultural difference of multilingual students, we have to briefly consider the *approach* we should adopt to relate their background to academic writing practice. It is not surprising that the attitudes discussed earlier have brought forth different approaches to teaching writing. There is no need to discuss the unfairness of the *conversion* approach, informed by the deficit attitude, which posits that multilingual students have to permanently move away from their indigenous discourses to superior English-based discourses. An approach that has been more respectable in this regard is what I call the *crossing* model, informed by the relativistic attitude. According to this approach, teachers attempt to build bridges to help multilingual students move from their local literacy practices and cultural frames toward academic/English discourses (and vice versa). Though students may shuttle between academic and home settings, in this approach there is a clear-cut difference between the academic and vernacular literacies. Students have to keep their discourses from home at home and enter into academic discourses with a new sense of self and reality. Students are asked to adopt different roles and identities as they move between the home and school. They have to remember that in each context (or community) there are differ-

ent values, knowledge, discourses, and styles practiced. So
they have to develop the facility to switch discourses in con-
textually relevant ways as they cross boundaries.

Although this approach devises a way to develop respect for
both the academic and nonacademic discourses, there are certain problems with it. It creates an either/or distinction between academic and vernacular literacies. Text construction
in both traditions is treated as mutually exclusive. It also imposes a split subjectivity on multilingual students—they are
asked to be different persons in different communities/con-
texts. However, there is an increasing body of research that
suggests that minority students don't want to suppress or
abandon their vernacular cultures when they practice academic writing.[7] They want to bring their preferred values, ideologies, and styles of writing into English literacy. Students
cannot be expected to leave behind their identities and interests as they engage in the learning process. What I call the *negotiation* model requires that students wrestle with the divergent discourses they face in writing to creatively work out
alternate discourses and literacies that represent better their
values and interests. In some cases this means appropriating
the academic discourse and conventions in terms of the students' own backgrounds. It can sometimes mean a creative
merging of conflicting discourses. It shouldn't be surprising
that the texts of multilingual students are somewhat different—they are embodiments of the unique voices and identities of the students. This approach also tackles some of the
power conflicts experienced by multilingual students. Practicing academic discourses according to the established conventions (as defined by the dominant social groups) would involve endorsing the values and interests these conventions are
informed by. If these values are unfavorable for multilingual
students, or if they don't favor emancipatory interests, these
writers are going to give life to the oppressive ideologies of the
dominant groups. Appropriating academic discourses in their
own terms would enable students to reconstruct established
textual practices and infuse them with oppositional values
and meanings. This is a way of eventually resisting the domi-

nant ideologies and interests that inform academic literacy. There is therefore a critical edge in the negotiation model, while the crossing model (at its best) simply takes the established conventions and knowledge of each context/community for granted in a noncommittal way. Teachers and students who practice the negotiation model would tend to subscribe to the difference-as-resource attitude articulated earlier.

Writing in an Imperialistic Language?

Before I conclude these preliminary statements of intent, I need to adopt a position on one more matter that will nag us in the following chapters. This is the question of the English language. To the extent that we are talking about academic writing in English, there are issues of linguistic imperialism that need to be addressed. Is it proper to encourage and facilitate the use of a language that is tainted with a history of global domination, colonizing other languages and communities with its values? There is no need to prove here that the English language does have a domineering status in the academy and society.[8] What is important, once again, are the attitudes and approaches to be adopted toward this language.

There is an important strand of thinking among some third world scholars that local communities should have no truck with English. We may call this the *separatist* orientation.[9] Treating languages as embodying partisan values, these scholars hold that English will condition our thinking and limit the meanings we may want to express in our writing. They would therefore think of English as muting any oppositional perspectives one may bring to knowledge creation in academic writing—and, in fact, as leading to the reproduction of Eurocentric values and thinking in the local communities. For them, the medium is the message. Opposed to them are the *universalists,* who believe that language is simply a neutral medium that one can use for whatever messages one may want to convey.[10] For the latter, the mind of the writer transcends language to freely employ any grammatical system desired. Some in this camp go further to argue that English has attained the position of a universal language that has accommodated values from different communities and lost its imperialist character.[11]

I hold that while each language is indeed ideological in representing partisan values and interests (being by no means neutral), it is not impossible to negotiate with language to win some space for one's purposes. It appears to me therefore that while the separatists are a bit too cynical, the universalists are complacent. While the former are too deterministic, the latter are romantic. Though we are all ideologically conditioned, human subjects do enjoy some relative autonomy from social institutions and discourses to conduct critical, independent thinking. English itself is becoming hybridized, embodying grammatical features, lexical items, and discourse conventions from a variety of communities. Through such processes of nativization, formerly colonized communities are appropriating the language and making it their own—thus making English a suitable medium for their values and interests. Consistent with my view expressed earlier on culture, the so-called alien language can also become a *resource* for oppositional and critical purposes. It is possible in critical writing for multilingual students to tap the resources of English and use it judiciously to represent the interests of their communities. An uncritical use of the language, on the other hand, poses the threat of making the individual and the community prone to domination. I would give this critical approach the same label I gave earlier for dealing with cultural difference—the *negotiation* model.[12] ESOL writers have to be made reflexively aware of the medium they are using, developing a critical understanding of its potentialities and limitations as they appropriate and reconstruct the language to represent their interests.

On Adopting Ideological Commitments

There are important reasons why I am stating my position up front on some of the controversial questions affecting ESOL writing. It is the view of critical theorists that there are no positions of absolute neutrality available for anyone on any issue. Everything is value ridden and ideological. It is important therefore to be frank about the position one holds on social and educational matters. Making one's assumptions explicit can help one to examine one's ideological positions critically and adopt stances that favor more emancipatory, egalitarian, and empowering interests. Practicing a critical pedagogy would involve instructors being similarly clear about their values, positions, and interests as they engage in teaching writing. Apart from adopting emancipatory agendas in their teaching activity, this would also enable them to examine and refine their ideologies in relation to the conditions confronted in the classroom and the challenges posed by the students. Pretending to be neutral or hiding one's ideological stances is counterproductive, as such practices will lead both to surreptitiously imposing one's values on the students and to limiting one's own development into deeper social awareness.[13]

Needless to say, all this doesn't mean that any ideology is acceptable in the classroom. The purpose of acknowledging one's ideological stance is to frankly examine whether it furthers the interests of justice and equality for all. If teachers recognize that their ideological leanings lead to unfair outcomes, they should have the integrity to revise their beliefs. Even in cases where one may be convinced that one's ideology is the most liberating system of belief, one should have the humility to respect the values of students, engage with them frankly, and negotiate differences in favor of developing beliefs and practices that ensure the well-being of everybody.

Acknowledging one's values shouldn't be taken to mean that one holds rigidly to one's position in the face of conflicting evidence and deepening political understanding. One should be open to developing more humane and progressive positions based on increasing knowledge and changing social conditions. Adopting a critical orientation doesn't mean being dogmatic. It is possible to admit one's tentative position on something while being open to further developing one's awareness. In fact, what is "politically correct" in writing pedagogy has been changing over time, based on new research knowledge and social awareness. For example, during the 1980s the relativistic positions articulated earlier—that is, the difference-as-estrangement attitude and the crossing model—were held by many critical pedagogues (including me) as offering the best recourse for the conflicts faced by multilingual students.[14] This was certainly a more enlightened perspective compared to the deficit approach, as it respected the vernaculars and indigenous cultures of minority students and acknowledged their right to maintain them. But with additional research showing the dissatisfaction of minority students in adopting a split personality as they switch discourses and identities, and the understandable social consequences stemming from the complacency of a relativistic orientation, we have had to adopt more critical positions. Moreover, acknowledging one's position on some of these fundamental theoretical issues doesn't solve all the pedagogical questions one has to face in the classroom. Similarly, how one's positions are to be realized in writing will take different forms in different rhetorical contexts. There are many different methods and strategies that may be adopted to achieve the negotiation model and the difference-as-resource orientation articulated earlier. As we will see in the following chapters, between holding a standpoint and practicing it in the classroom (or practicing it in writing) there is a huge divide that needs to be imaginatively bridged.

The Challenge

Given the general orientation to multilingual students and their writing activity articulated earlier, how can we summarize the challenges we face in teaching critical writing? Here are some of the concerns that will be addressed in the chapters to follow.

- Whereas students are generally taught to take the established genre rules and literacy conventions for granted in constructing texts to suit different rhetorical situations (often with the assumption that these are value-free rules or neutral frameworks that we can use to articulate any message we want), critical writing involves examining the values and interests assumed by these rules. We should teach students not to treat rules of communication as innocent or indisputable but to negotiate for independent expression by reframing them in suitable ways. They have to ask: How did these rules come into being? Whom do these rules favor? What possibilities and limitations do these rules pose for critical expression? What alternatives are available?

- Whereas students are generally taught to use established knowledge already available in texts, critical writing involves interrogating received knowledge and reconstructing it through the writing process. All knowledge should be treated as "interested." Multilingual students have to question the dominant knowledge constructs in the academy, in addition to critically engaging the knowledge traditions they bring from their local communities as they make a space for oppositional knowledge that favors wider emancipatory and democratic interests.

  Whereas students are generally taught academic writing as a detached activity of expressing publicly verifiable knowledge in a balanced and logical way through conventional rules, critical writing encourages a personal engagement in the writing process. One should reflexively explore one's identity, consciousness, and values during text construction not only to make a textual space for one's voice but also to challenge dominant knowledge constructs according to one's personal location.

  Whereas writing is generally taught as an acquiescent activity of assuming a preexisting reality within which the text takes its place, critical writing involves interrogating the dominant conception of reality and changing it to create more democratic possibilities. In order to do so, students have to be taught to treat texts as not only reflecting but constituting reality. Apart from being instrumental in transforming realities, texts may themselves represent new realities.

- Whereas students are generally taught to treat the language of written communication (including registers, styles, and codes of that genre) as an abstract structure or system, critical writing involves interrogating the language for the ways in which it represents its own values and sometimes suppresses divergent messages. Students have to negotiate the ideologies informing the English language as they appropriate it to represent their interests and values in their writing, using language in creative new ways to struggle for alternate expression. Bilingual writers have the further task of finding appropriate ways of accommodating the strengths they bring from their nativized Englishes and vernaculars as they struggle for a voice that suits their values and interests in academic texts.

In one sense, these are perhaps the common issues facing all students in academic writing. But since multilingual students bring with them identities, values, and discourses from multiple communities, the challenges they face in practicing this writing are more complex. Their acquaintance with oppositional intellectual traditions and worldviews can also function as an advantage. These traditions hint of alternate ways in which knowledge and society can be reconstructed.

Conclusion

In the chapters to follow, I discuss current research and teaching practice in ESOL writing from the positions articulated earlier. Throughout, I adopt a special focus on academic writing in higher-educational contexts, acknowledging that ESOL students may engage in many other genres of writing—including professional, creative, and biographical in different social sites—as part of their repertoire. In the next chapter, I will examine the dominant schools in writing pedagogy to explicate *their* assumptions and ideologies. Often their research claims and pedagogical successes mask the underlying assumptions behind their practices. In the four chapters that follow the next, I take up pedagogical issues according to the different foci of writing—that is, issues of form, the writer, content, and audience. It should be noted that this organization is purely based on convenience. Writing involves an integration of all these components—and more—in the composing process. The separate treatment of issues related to these components should not be taken to mean that our pedagogies can be based on developing a single component in isolation from the rest. In the final chapter, I examine the changing faces of global communication and new imperatives in postmodern literacy, concluding with a discussion of the practices and values that should inform teachers in striving for a truly multilingual and multicultural educational environment.

Chapter 2

An Overview of the Discipline

It is important to understand the disciplinary tradition of teaching ESOL writing and examine the potential our professional knowledge may have for facilitating a critical pedagogy. In this respect, it is necessary to interrogate the dominant pedagogical assumptions, values, and practices in our field. Since these concerns are implicated in the professional identity, status, and "culture" of writing teachers, I will begin by exploring how the field of ESOL composition is constituted.

The Community of Writing Teachers

ESOL writing teachers have so far enjoyed an uneasy relationship with the two communities that most matter to them professionally—that is, their immediate family of applied linguists (comprising TESOL professionals) and their extended family of composition specialists (composed largely of L1 teachers). To some extent, they have been marginalized in both circles. There are many reasons for this situation. Within the applied linguistics circle, there is the well-known structuralist bias that spoken language is primary. Therefore pedagogies for ESOL students have largely featured oral interactions. There is also the professional wisdom in our discipline that writing is the last of the four skills that should be developed, long after laying the foundation of grammatical competence through speech and the two receptive skills (i.e., listening and reading). Those who teach writing from the TESOL community have therefore lacked the motivation and opportunities to develop a distinctive professional identity as specialists of composition. It is sometimes mistakenly assumed that *any* ESOL professional can teach writing by virtue of their expertise in applied linguistics, perhaps as part of their classroom experience of developing proficiency in the four skills. Even teacher-training programs in TESOL are influenced by these assumptions, providing little or no place for courses in writing pedagogy.[1]

This unfortunate condition has been exacerbated by the institutional marginalization of ESOL writing in higher education. Often ESOL students are placed in the composition classes of L1 students and taught by professionals without any expertise in teaching multilinguals. While this arrangement is often motivated by economic expediency, there is also the assumption that no special expertise or knowledge is required for teaching multilingual writers. Some do believe that composing processes are universal and that multilingual students have to be brought to the position of displaying the same skills as L1 students. Or the marginalization of ESOL writing may take an alternate route: ESOL students are defined as "remedial" and segregated in non-credit-bearing, intellectually unengaging grammar classes. (The term *remedial* is a misnomer, as ESOL students are not remedying a lack but adding new communicative skills to the rich linguistic repertoire they already have.) Here adjunct staff, usually those with TESOL or linguistic training, will be asked to handle the classes. The implication is that these students are so poor in their grammatical proficiency that they are not ready for the higher-order rhetorical and discursive instruction L1 students are provided in their writing classes. Like the students, ESL faculty are often treated as second-class citizens in English departments, perceived largely as classroom practitioners skilled in grammar instruction but lacking theoretical or research competence. This professional neglect has prevented ESOL writing teachers from constructing an impressive body of knowledge deriving from their classroom experience. They have adopted a dependent/receiving relationship with L1 composition scholars, borrowing theoretical and research knowledge for their instructional purposes, contributing little that is original to the theory and practice of writing/literacy.

This unequal division of labor in the teaching of writing (i.e., composition specialists teaching L1 students and applied linguists teaching ESOL students) has led to some striking differences between the professional communities. The "culture" of L1 and ESL composition teachers has been characterized according to the following dichotomies by a scholar: critical theories/scientific theories, rhetoric/linguistics, radical/conservative, and ideological/pragmatic (see Santos 1993). It is true that ESOL writing teachers sometimes conceive of their task as a pragmatic one of teaching value-free grammatical features or form-related aspects of essays to their students. Rhetorical and ideological issues are considered irrelevant to students' practical needs of learning another language for utilitarian purposes in educational and professional life. While L1 teachers have found it fashionable to indulge in theoretically and politically sophisticated discourse on writing, ESOL teachers have confined themselves to clinically circumscribed classroom-based empirical research on their students' linguistic and cognitive development. While they develop their paradigms largely from linguistics, L1 compositionists are more interdisciplinary, drawing from fields as diverse as rhetoric, literature, and the social sciences.

To some extent, the division of labor has been a blessing in disguise. It has enabled a closer observation of L2 writing by TESOL practitioners. In recent times there has developed a body of research on the unique characteristics of ESOL students in composing. For example, we have deeper insights into the differences in rhetorical development, cognitive processes, and composing practices of ESOL students (which will be reviewed in chap. 4). But, shaped by the limiting assumptions of our professional culture, such research has been more focused on narrow textual, linguistic, cognitive, and classroom features. The overwhelming bias is toward product-oriented studies on linguistic and textual structures or process-oriented studies on the cognitive strategies of text production. We haven't adequately explored the rhetorical and discursive issues of writing, situated in a broader context of social and cultural conditions. We need to understand the strategies multilingual students adopt to negotiate conflicting discourses and values in writing in authentic settings as they struggle for voice. In a state-of-the-art paper on ESOL writing research, Tony Silva (1993) makes the important observation that research on L2 writing has been oriented toward local concerns, ignoring macrolevel issues of literacy. Due to this lopsided nature of our research enterprise, we haven't made substantial contributions to the theorization of writing and literacy in general. Our research findings serve only very narrow classroom needs. In short, our professional culture shapes our research, and our research shapes our teaching—in a vicious circle.

But we must realize that ESOL teachers are well positioned to undertake the types of situated macrolevel research that will enable us to make a critical contribution to literacy theory and practice. ESOL classrooms are rife with politics. We have the most culturally diverse student population, of individuals from economically underprivileged communities learning a then-colonial language as they develop academic literacy.[2] To ignore these realities is to lose the richness and complexity of our work in classrooms. If only we could address the intense conflicts experienced by our students in the everyday life of our professional activity, we could make a more critical contribution to the poetics and politics of writing. Given such classroom conditions, it is indeed ironic that the field of L1 composition should be considered ideologically sophisticated and ESOL composition should be treated as politically innocent.

To develop an independent and critical orientation to writing we have to relate to our professional activity differently. To begin with, we have to develop a more bilateral interaction with L1 composition circles, where we not only borrow constructs from them but also critically examine those in terms of our unique classroom contexts and contribute to the theorization of literacy independently. To do this, we must develop a reflective knowledge that helps us both theorize our immediate work as TESOL professionals and have insights into the general conditions of literacy. We do have a lot of things in common with L1 compositionists. Despite the linguistic difference that the L1 student population is largely monolingual and "traditionally native" in English, there are similarities at the discourse level. Both student groups have to negotiate the genre conventions, knowledge, and values of academic writing to struggle for voice. It is not impossible to think of many areas in which the professional knowledge of ESOL teachers can make a significant contribution to the work of L1 compositionists. While engaging so with L1 composition scholarship, in what has been called a "symbiotic" relationship (see Matsuda 1998), we need some space to theorize with critical detachment the unique challenges concerning our student groups. It is in this manner that we will develop a grounded knowledge about our specific professional responsibilities.

In order to develop this kind of professional knowledge, there are at least two changes required in the way ESOL teachers practice their teaching. First, we have to develop an interdisciplinary awareness. There are other fields of study that provide useful insights into the challenges facing multilingual writers. For example, anthropology informs us about literacy practices in other communities; sociology informs us of the ways in which texts at the microlevel can reflect and shape macrosocial processes; political economy informs us of ways in which literacy is implicated in ideological and material inequalities; history informs us of the changes in oral and literate traditions of communication from premodern times. This doesn't mean that we should become experts in each of those disciplines—a superhuman feat indeed! We should simply be alert to borrowing information and scholarship from other disciplines (available sometimes in popular publications) and connecting them to matters pertaining to ESOL writing. We have to be curious enough to at least read articles in our own professional journals that employ knowledge from other disciplines. In the chapters to follow, I demonstrate how such an interdisciplinary awareness can help develop a critical orientation to our professional knowledge. In the very next section in this chapter I give a more immediate example of how other disciplines—such as the sociology of education and the history of ideas—can help us critique the main schools of writing in ESOL.

A second requirement is that we become researchers, not just remain practitioners. There are interesting ways in which we can fuse our activity as teachers and researchers. Approaches like action research and classroom-based participant research make this marriage possible.[3] There are some special advantages in merging both roles—our teaching helps the research; our research helps the teaching. For example, the access our teaching provides to the writing and views of our students, and the intense daily engagement it entails in their pedagogical and social struggles, help generate in-depth and reliable data. Similarly, the critical detachment, defamiliarization, and reflective attitude our research imposes on our teaching are healthy for our classroom practice. We engage in our teaching with greater awareness and creativity. (There are of course special challenges we face in combining the teacher/researcher roles—which I will discuss later.) In the chapters to follow I will indicate the types of observation and inquiry that will enable us to theorize ESOL writing from the bottom up. I will show how such grounded knowledge can enable us to develop a critical perspective on research findings and professional practices theorized by "experts" from outside the classroom.

In fact, to teach critical writing we have to radically reorientate to our professional roles. We are not just skilled technicians but theoretically informed professionals who must exercise considerable independence, creativity, and control over our pedagogical activities. That is to say, we don't passively adopt theories and pedagogies formulated by experts or blindly implement methods we have been trained to use. We critically inquire about the needs and challenges of our students according to our ongoing experience, interpret them in terms of the theoretical developments in multiple disciplines, and reformulate established professional constructs to suit our specific classroom purposes. More importantly, we don't conduct instruction to satisfy the goals set by society and administrators according to predetermined social expectations and norms; we inspire students to be critical thinkers and writers who may interrogate the assumptions and practices of the social world in order to change it. Writing instructors should be "transformative intellectuals," to use a phrase popularized by educationist Henry Giroux (see Aronowitz and Giroux 1985, 160). Both words in that formulation hold equal importance: we are intellectuals, not technicians; we are transformative, not conformist.

The Dominant Pedagogical Approaches

We turn now to examining the approaches that constitute ESOL writing pedagogy. Since composition textbooks and methods (and sometimes research on writing) are influenced by these approaches, it is important for teachers to be able to recognize their assumptions and practices. More importantly, we have to interrogate the philosophies and ideologies these approaches may be influenced by. Since their underlying assumptions are not always made explicit, teachers may not be able to adopt a critical orientation toward their strengths and limitations. Pedagogical methods and materials shouldn't be treated simply as value-free instruments to achieve practical classroom goals. These are informed by the values and interests of those who fashion them, posing the possibility of shaping the perspectives of students in predefined ways—hence the need to deconstruct these writing approaches for their hidden ideologies.

In a state-of-the-art essay on L2 writing, the dominant approaches have been grouped around four foci: form, the writer, content, and the reader (see Raimes 1991). Though teachers usually integrate all these elements of the text in their pedagogical practice, many still tend to emphasize one focus or another based on their philosophies of writing and teaching. The form-focused approach orientates pedagogy toward the finished product. It therefore conceives of writing as the mastery of correct grammatical and rhetorical structures that shape the text. Typically, exercises in sentence combining, cohesion and coherence, and cloze writing are adopted for grammatical proficiency at the suprasentential level. Exercises in identifying/constructing topic sentences, thesis statements, and transition sentences, together with exercises in paragraph formation, paragraph combining, and the imitation of model essays, are undertaken to develop rhetorical proficiency. Although this approach is nowadays considered old-fashioned, many teachers still practice it widely. Those who treat writing as a mastery of surface-level textual patterns, or those preparing their students for strictly timed/controlled assessment procedures (e.g.., a five-paragraph in-class writing test, graded for grammatical accuracy and paragraph organization), tend to use this approach heavily. The writer-focused approach attends to the thought processes and cognitive strategies that go into generating the finished text. For this reason, it is better known as the "process" approach, to contrast with the "product" orientation of the previous school. Exercises in planning and outlining, generating and developing ideas, and engaging in serial drafting and revising are typical classroom practices. This approach informs in some way nearly all the composition materials and methods today and has passed into professional common sense. The next approach, focused on content, ties academic writing to the knowledge constructs that inform the respective disciplines. Writing instruction is linked to the specific courses followed by the students, often integrating reading and writing, to provide access to the relevant language and information characterizing disciplines. This approach is popular in academic writing programs today, partly because administrators feel that tying writing to the specific academic and professional needs of students is more purposive, practical, and productive. Lastly, the reader-focused school perceives writing as influenced by the values, expectations, and conventions of the discourse communities addressed by the students in each discipline, following pedagogical practices similar to those of the preceding approach. The difference between the two is that the former is a bit more product oriented in focusing on the information, genre conventions, textual features, and registers characterizing disciplinary writing. The latter is more interested in initiating students gradually into the process of knowledge making, shaped by the styles of thinking, interaction, and discourse typical of the disciplinary community, so that they can address scholars as relative insiders of a particular circle. This approach is also more socially and culturally sensitive to the transitions students have to make from the discourses of their "native" community to those of the academy.

Despite the general opinion among practitioners that these four approaches constitute the ESOL disciplinary "tradition" (see Raimes 1991), they in fact have a history of development in L1 composition. To some extent, these approaches have been the dominant paradigms in the L1 field at various periods before being imported to the ESOL context. Although subsequent research in ESOL has typically endorsed the relevance of these approaches, such research activity smacks of influences from the bandwagon. The form-focused approach has its roots in the "current traditional paradigm" that was dominant in the mid-1960s and early 1970s in L1 circles (see Hairston 1982). The paradigm is so named because it is a revitalization of the classifications and structures offered by classical (Greco-Roman) rhetoricians. The writer-focused approach stems from cognitive process theory in L1, which was made fashionable from the late 1970s by Linda Flower and John Hayes (1981) of Carnegie Mellon University, who employed empirical research methods like the "think-aloud" protocol to distinguish the thought processes of skilled and unskilled writers. This orientation was complemented by the expressive process approach, which emphasized creativity, originality, and sincerity of expression in the place of rhetorical rules and formulas. The origins of the content-focused approach may appear less clear. Although some attribute the development of this approach to Bernie Mohan and his associates in the ESOL context (see Raimes 1991), this too had prior development in L1 circles as a version of the writing across the curriculum (WAC) paradigm (see Emig 1977; Beach and Bridwell 1984; Fulwiler 1982). McCrimmon's (1984) notion of "writing as a way of knowing" had already developed an emphasis on content within the L1 process paradigm in the early 1970s. This orientation had further developments more indigenous to ESOL in movements like needs analysis, English for Academic Purposes (EAP), and English for Specific Purposes (ESP) (see Spack 1988, 34–36; Johns and Dudley-Evans 1991, 299–301). The basis of the content approach on a "common cognitive/academic component manifested in discourse across cultures" (Mohan and Lo 1985, 516), and its pedagogy of helping students with "the language of the thinking processes and the structure or shape of content" (Mohan 1986, 18), show that while it benefits from the process paradigm, it also smacks of a product-oriented view of content. To move to the reader-focused approach, this was anticipated by the social process school in the L1 context from the mid-1980s (see Bizzell 1982). This movement began as a corrective to the cognitive orientation of the process movement by adding a social component to writing. The notion of the discourse community was used to explain how writing involves transitions from the values, conventions, and thinking of one's "native" community to those of the disciplinary community in addressing members of the academic circle. My attempt here to point out the "parent" movements in L1 circles shouldn't be treated as a criticism. It is no sin to borrow common insights into writing from L1 scholars. But we have not always developed a critical perspective on this knowledge inspired by the unique characteristics of multilingual students in ESOL classrooms. We have to guard against the danger of lacking a body of "local knowledge" based on grounded theorizing from the everyday experience of our own teaching contexts.

Not only do these approaches lack deep roots in ESOL classroom practice, but they draw from philosophical assumptions and intellectual traditions that have been the dominant discourses at different periods in the West. The form-focused approach, to begin with, is undergirded by American linguistic structuralism and behaviorist psychology—hence the focus on form at the exclusion of meaning.[4] This influence explains, also, the focus on the surface structure of syntax and rhetorical patterns in the written product, ignoring the deep structure of cognitive strategies and processes that generate the text. These abstract structures are "drilled" into students through controlled exercises in order to cultivate habit-motivated skills. But the process paradigm, which looks at composing as a dynamic cognitive activity that is recursive, generative, exploratory, and goal oriented, finds inspiration in the Chomskyan revolution of transformational generative grammar and the related rise of humanistic psychology. The trappings of scientificity and empiricism that accompanied this paradigm (distinguishing it from the prescriptive tendencies and deductive approaches of traditional rhetoric) were acquired from emergent disciplines like developmental psychology, cybernetic theory, and the cognitive sciences (see Faigley 1986, 531–34). The content-focused and reader-focused approaches generally share the discourses of sociolinguistics, ethnography, and communicative competence in linguistics and research methods that are naturalistic or situational (reacting against the narrowly cognitivist discourses and controlled experimental procedures of the writer-focused school)—hence the conception of writing as meaningful, communicative, and situated in the knowledge claims and discourse conventions of specific communities. However, the reader-focused approach is more egalitarian and relativistic than the content-focused approach, as it respects the discourses brought by the students from their native communities and sympathizes with their conflicts in making a transition to academic discourses. It is able to do this because it holds the social-constructionist view that knowledge and discourses are collaboratively constructed and that the different knowledge paradigms represent the sense of reality of the respective discourse communities.

With this background in mind, we can now explore at some depth how these writing approaches orientate to the wider contexts of academic writing. What do they have to say about the social and cultural background of multilingual students? The form-focused approach is normative in considering a specific discourse and rhetorical structure as the accepted/correct form of academic writing. As such, teachers who adopt this approach ignore the rhetorical differences displayed by non-English students, considering them sometimes as illogical, undisciplined, sloppy ways of thinking and communicating. With the motive of stamping out "errors," teachers can stifle the different rhetorics and discourses of the students. In fact, since form and structure are considered value free in this approach (analogous to abstract grammatical structures), sociocultural and political issues are treated as falling outside the strict domain of writing. The sociocultural differences of students that could surface in writing are brushed aside in favor of developing the abstract formal structures of the text in everyone's writing. Moreover, since the acquisition of these structures is considered a matter of habitual automatic skills, in line with behaviorist pedagogy, students are expected to master these textual structures through constant practice and imitation. However, by eschewing thinking and feeling in literacy, writers are asked to be passive, lacking agency and individuality. The students are thus prepared for mechanical, thoughtless, formulaic writing (perhaps the type demanded by bureaucratic institutions in a technological society). Thus, by failing to problematize writing skills and textual structures, this approach not only ignores issues of inequality or cultural difference affecting those with atypical discourses but by default makes normative the textual structures and rhetoric of the dominant social groups. Similarly, by refusing to address content, it encourages the uncritical use of established knowledge paradigms. Disarming resistance by defining writing as value free, it can subtly impose the discourses of dominant social groups on unsuspecting students.

To consider the writer-focused approach next, its descriptive and empirical orientation provides it much potential to understand the unique challenges confronting multilingual students. However, its overriding cognitive tendency limits its scope, preventing it from addressing the sociocultural, material, and institutional pressures that impinge on writing. This tendency has also influenced scholars in this orientation to insist that there is a set of universal cognitive strategies that generate effective writing. Those who display such strategies are considered "skilled" writers and those who don't, "unskilled." In considering cognitive strategies as unmediated by situational factors, teachers ignore the type of sociocultural differences that can influence the production of texts. If writing is an internal monologue, then the social context doesn't have to be taken into account in the composing process. Furthermore, in considering those whose strategies are different as unskilled or "egocentric" (a term borrowed from Piagetian developmental psychology), this approach labels such students as cognitively deficient or, at least, infantile. Thus cultural differences can get diagnosed as a kind of deficiency. (We must note in this context that there are alternative perspectives on thinking, as for instance the "social cognition" school of Vygotsky, which would argue that the sociocultural context is not only a mediating factor but intrinsic to cognition.) In fact, that the process school acknowledges the agency of the writer in producing the text is a corrective to the form-focused approach, which treats writers as passive. But in perceiving writing as simply an interaction between the mind and the text (or the mind and the language, in some versions), the approach reduces the complexity of the writer. Therefore in some versions of this approach (called the "expressive process" approach) "writing with power" means negotiating the mind-text interaction with fidelity to one's own intentions and aspirations, ignoring external "distractions" like the audience and the context (see Elbow 1981). However, sociopolitical and institutional pressures cannot be wished away; power in writing derives from negotiating these tensions effectively. The perspective is further limited by its focus on the *how* at the cost of the *what* of writing. Cognitive strategies are emphasized at the cost of rhetorical structures, discourse conventions, and knowledge content that inform the product. In ignoring features of the product, this approach treats the rhetorical structures of the mainstream social groups as the norm (by default). Thus, students are taught to accept the discourse conventions, rhetorical features, and thought patterns of the dominant groups as the universal, skilled means of communication.

To consider the content-focused approach next, it provides one important source of context for the writing—the knowledge of the audience—different from the previous two orientations, which lack an explicit focus on context. However, the understanding of academic knowledge is unproblematized. What is established/legitimate knowledge is always open to contestation. Knowledge from many other paradigms, schools, and communities has to be suppressed in order to legitimize certain constructs. The ones that are legitimized serve the needs and purposes of the dominant community. This means that knowledge is interested. The need for writers to critique dominant knowledge and create new knowledge that serves more ethical and democratic interests is not appreciated in this movement. Furthermore, knowledge is always changing through processes of debate and consensus. This understanding would enable us to consider how students can engage in new knowledge construction, rather than merely reproducing the preconstructed knowledge of the respective disciplines. Furthermore, the relationship between knowledge and texts is mainly conceived according to the now-infamous *conduit model*—that is, that knowledge flows into the text. But it is important to realize that this connection is more multidirectional—that is, that texts create knowledge. The genre conventions and discourses play no small role in shaping the knowledge presented. In short, the content-focused approach adopts a static and conservative perspective on knowledge. Furthermore, the knowledge traditions belonging to the minority communities of multilingual students are provided little or no place in writing. While students from the dominant communities have a head start in knowing the legitimized forms of knowledge, minority students are forced to master them at a second remove or reproduce constructs that lead to their inequality and disempowerment. Multilingual students need to engage the established paradigms of knowledge critically, in terms of their own knowledge traditions, treating academic knowledge as still open to questioning and change.

Finally, the reader-focused approach avoids some of the limitations of the other approaches and comes close to understanding the discursive differences of ESOL writers. It eschews the prescriptivism and normative tendency of the form-focused approach and acknowledges the different shapes texts take according to the contexts and communities of writing. It goes beyond the finished product to consider the cognitive strategies, knowledge content, and audience expectations that shape the text. Furthermore, in contrast to the writer-focused approach, which reduces the writing process to individualistic and mentalistic terms, this orientation takes into account influences from the external social context. Also, it goes beyond the normative perspective of the content-focused approach to give dignity and validity to the knowledge traditions belonging to the students' communities. Thus the orientation is able to accommodate greater pluralism in form, knowledge, and composing strategies. However, the power of discourses in constructing texts and writers needs to be understood at greater depth in order to address some of the more complicated issues in switching discourse communities. The notion of writing to different communities means more than just shaping a preconstructed text to suit different audience expectations. The constitution of the text itself will change depending on whom one is addressing. Similarly, the writer's identity and values will also be represented differently. Writing to a particular readership involves more than "knowing about" their expectations; it involves sharing their values, interests, and knowledge so that we may relate better to those expectations. This is achieved not by a static stocking of information but by an ongoing participation in the community's changing patterns of social relations and cultural practices. One must become a relative insider to the discourse community in order to write effectively to that circle. A source of tension here is that the ESOL student is often marginalized in these disciplinary groups, whose power is associated with the English language and Western communities.[5] In fact, the academic community might not accept each new entrant willingly, as it prefers to remain closed and preserve its vested interests. Also, communities have hierarchies and relegate some members to the lower rungs or fringes so that a few can monopolize power. Therefore, there is conflict both *within* and *between* discourse communities. The limitation of the content- and reader-focused approaches is that they impute egalitarian and democratic motivations to disciplinary communities. Although they accept that the discourse conventions are different in different communities, they consider them equally accessible to all writers. Therefore they assume that writers can switch from one community to the other at will. They fail to take into consideration the power conflicts among communities, ignoring the threat multilingual students may face in being repressed or alienated by the academic discourse. These approaches fail to interrogate how knowledge and discourse conventions can themselves be ideological and foster inequality and domination.

The preceding discussion on the underlying assumptions and preferred practices of ESOL writing approaches enables us to identify their dominant ideological tendencies. Since composition scholars have not performed this ideology critique well, we have to borrow for our purposes constructs formulated by Henry Giroux (1983, 205–31) to classify literacy models. The form-focused approach is informed by what Giroux labels *instrumental ideology.* This perspective on human activities as pragmatic/utilitarian, as activities that subjects can be conditioned to accomplish without consideration of their ethical or emotional life, is associated with the "culture of positivism," the technocratic social orientation, and behaviorist psychological practices. Writing is similarly treated as a mechanical "skill" for expressing predefined, value-free knowledge through abstract structures of language by passive subjects. By considering issues of power and difference irrelevant to the writing activity, it could influence writers to serve predetermined social ends and institutions and maintain the status quo. The writer-focused approach, in considering literacy as a goal-oriented, cognitive activity of negotiating knowledge through language, preserves the agency of the writer. It displays *interaction ideology,* which envisions power as being achieved out of an interaction of the subject with the structures around him or her. However, it simplifies power inequality by personalizing it and blaming the individual for powerlessness. At its best, this ideology encourages an attitude of happy idiocy—you can achieve power and success by acting on your environment with personal creativity, skill, and intelligence. But this attitude encourages turning a blind eye to the "external" material and social constraints that often limit (and sometimes defeat) human agency. Furthermore, in considering cognitive processes and strategies to be universal and differing only according to each individual's psychological development and cognitive maturity, it explains away cultural differences. Although content-focused and reader-focused approaches accommodate a consideration of the contexts and discourses of disciplinary circles, they orientate to them in a pragmatic and utilitarian manner. Students can employ these discourses with adequate acquaintance and practice, they seem to say, without ideological implications or harm. It is true that the reader-focused approach displays a more relativistic ideology in being sensitive to the different ways in which knowledge is defined in different communities and the different conventions used to talk about this knowledge. However, on the basis of inculcating communicative competence in talk to the chosen academic community, this approach too can influence multilingual students to accept uncritically the values behind academic discourses. This happens because the rules of use and forms of knowledge are not problematized adequately to realize their ideological nature. In general, though content-focused and reader-focused approaches perceive difference, they do not relate it to power. They fail to pose a deeper level

	Form-focused	Writer-focused	Content-focused	Reader-focused
L1 basis	current-traditional paradigm	cognitive process theory	WAC	social process
Pedagogy	sentence combining, paragraph formation, cloze writing	brainstorming, planning, revising, etc.	linked/sheltered teaching, genre analysis	discourse analysis
Linguistic connection	structuralist	transformational generative	communicative competence	sociolinguistic
Philosophical basis	behaviorist, structuralist, Skinnerian, normative, deductive	rationalist, nativist, Cartesian, empirical, inductive	social cognitivist, Vygotskyan, normative, situational/naturalistic	social constructionist, Wittgensteinian, relativistic, ethnographic
Ideological basis	instrumental	interactional	reproductive	reproductive

Fig. 1. Distinguishing writing approaches

of questions that would reveal the unequal status and ideological nature of discourses: Why do such textual/academic norms exist? Whose interests do such norms serve? Have these norms been contested? Do these norms limit possibilities for our students? Are there other sets of norms that can expand possibilities? Hence these approaches display a deterministic brand of *reproductive ideology* that, at best, considers an internalization of the values, culture, and knowledge of the respective disciplines as a necessary condition in order to communicate successfully with scholars.

We can chart the differences between the dominant writing approaches as shown in figure 1.[6]

My intention here is not to brush aside the significant advances each of these movements has made in our understanding of ESOL writing. The four components discussed here are quite fundamental to writing, and we cannot ignore any one dimension in our pedagogy. At the same time, the answer to their limitations is not an eclectic pedagogy that would put together all these approaches in order to modify the relative shortcomings of each. A critical writing approach requires a fundamental shift of emphasis. These four dimensions of the text have to be situated in a clearly defined sociopolitical context. We will find that the structure of the text, the thought processes of the writer, the knowledge assumed, and the character of the reader will take different shape and implications in different social settings. The text begins to show the tensions of negotiating the various options and constraints presented by society. My argument for a *focus on social context* should not be construed as a case for one more dimension of textuality that is added on to the other four foci presented by the writing approaches discussed earlier. The social dimension is more fundamental to the other four. It shapes the very constitution and ramifications of the other textual components. In considering specific research findings and classroom practices generated by these composition approaches in the following chapters, I will show the difference made when we locate writing in actual social contexts of conflict and struggle.

Conclusion

To teach critical writing, then, we need to adopt a new orientation to our professional activity. We have to consider teaching as an ideological and interested enterprise. The question for us is not *whether* teaching is political but *what* politics should motivate our classroom practice. We can choose to adopt egalitarian, empowering, and ethical interests or, by default, to be agents of other people's narrower interests. Furthermore, in engaging in critical teaching we should adopt an independent, reflective, socially aware, and multidisciplinary orientation to our day-to-day classroom activities. In using writing approaches, we have to similarly search for pedagogies that favor emancipatory interests and values. Though we will benefit from the tradition of knowledge and practices developed in the history of our profession, it may not be possible to recycle existing approaches for our purposes. However, the teaching of critical writing cannot be reduced to a set of axioms, methods, and procedures guaranteed to succeed universally in all classrooms. Pedagogy is an ongoing, situated, engaged practice in response to the conditions encountered in everyday classroom experience and the unique challenges faced by our students as we help develop a literacy that is socially responsible.

Application

A. The Teacher's Writing Education
It is important to reflect on our own experience of learning writing. Our feelings, attitudes, and motivations as learners are a good indication of the strengths and limitations of the specific literacy pedagogies we have encountered in the past. If you have learned writing in a second language you can use the following questions to reflect on that experience. If not, you can consider your experience learning college-level writing in your first language. You may write a literacy biography using the

following questions as prompts. After you write this, you can share it with your colleagues in your course to see how they would assess the strengths and limitations of your learning experience.

1. What aspects of text construction created the most discomfort for you? What were the different stages of your development as a writer? What was your motivation for learning writing—to earn a grade, to fulfill a degree requirement, to express your inner feelings/thoughts, for professional advancement, to become socially functional? How did your motivation influence your development as a writer?
2. What were your impressions of the assignments your teachers gave you? Which approach (as outlined earlier) did their pedagogical practice resemble? Did you ever feel that the classroom activities bored you? Why or why not? Did you ever feel that their grading was unfair? Why? Did you ever feel that you were being forced to adopt an identity or an image of yourself in your writing that you were not comfortable with?
3. What are the implications of the literacy skills you have acquired for your professional and social life now? Would you have preferred the learning experience to have been different—that is, to have suited your "real-world" needs? How?

B. Analyzing our Teaching Philosophy
It is also important to understand your values and ideologies as a teacher. Do you agree or disagree with the following statements?

1. Teaching is for the purpose of passing on certain universally valid skills, facts, and competencies to students.
2. The pursuit of knowledge is an end in itself—attaching other economic or social motivations to education is a corruption of the learning activity.

3. Teaching a new language is all about enabling students to master the basic grammatical system that makes communication possible.

4. Writing development is all about enabling students to string sentences together in a grammatical and elegant way to construct well-organized larger structures like paragraphs, sections, and chapters.

5. One can teach without letting one's own values and interests affect classroom activities and agendas.

6. The teaching techniques and methods handed down to us (from research institutions and professional circles) are bound to be successful in helping any student group achieve competency in literacy, as they derive from scientific research and scholarly expertise.

7. The curriculum and testing procedures established in my institution have been put together by knowledgeable scholars and experts, and they can be followed closely to achieve what is best for our students.

Consider why someone would disagree with these statements as a step toward understanding the rationale for critical pedagogy.

C. Analysis of Textbooks

Choose an ESL composition textbook that you have found useful for your classroom purposes. This can also be your personal favorite in your teaching experience. Try to characterize the philosophy of the textbook according to the classifications offered in this chapter. It is quite possible that some textbooks are eclectic in nature, putting together different foci of writing. But they may still place a heavy emphasis on one or the other of the approaches. Discover the strengths and limitations of this textbook by considering the following questions.

1. Consider the main activities offered in the textbook to discover which component of writing the authors

consider to be crucial in writing (i.e., form, writer, content, or audience).

2. How do the authors relate to the cultural and linguistic difference of multilingual students? (Which of the three attitudes described in chap. 1 do they display—deficit, estrangement, or resource?)

3. Is there any consideration given in the book for the life outside the classroom of these students and their writing (i.e., their native communities, social context, or economic status)?

4. How would you characterize the definition of writing these authors may provide (from your impressions of the textbook)?

5. To what extent does the textbook offer you, the teacher, any creativity to devise activities and methods of your own choosing in response to your ongoing classroom experience? Or does it offer a completely "prepackaged" course that leaves little room for your contribution or initiative?

6. Where would you place this textbook in terms of figure 1, which describes the different orientations to writing? To what extent does the text share the philosophical and ideological characteristics of the respective approaches?

Chapter 3
Issues of Form

From being the sole pedagogical activity undertaken in writing classrooms, grammar instruction has become a neglected area of writing development. Many instructors would now frankly acknowledge that they don't have any place in their classrooms for explicit instruction or discussion of such matters as syntax, paragraph organization, or text structure. According to current pedagogical wisdom, form will take care of itself when students undertake the process of writing appropriately. Many instructors accept that their feedback on student writing features only matters related to idea development. It is true to some extent that the appropriate grammatical and textual structures are *discovered* in terms of the message and purposes motivating the writer. Form is shaped by content—to evoke a now well-known slogan. But there are several important reasons why we should give more explicit attention to form than we currently do.

To begin with, we should realize that form shapes content as well. And if we understand that grammar and form are ideological, we realize that they have to be negotiated appropriately to express critical perspectives in writing. Not to develop a sensitivity among students to the ideologies represented by particular grammatical and textual structures is to nurture an innocence toward language that can be detrimental to independent expression. Students may be surprised to find that their language or form militates against, and sometimes compromises, the messages they are interested in conveying in their essays.

Furthermore, professional and academic institutions outside the composition classroom give a lot of importance to form. There is research evidence that faculty members in the various disciplines take grammar into account when they assess student submissions—ironically giving form more importance than writing instructors do (see Faigley and Hansen 1985). We hear of complaints from the wider professional world that present-day college students are grammatically incompetent. It is perhaps a reflection of these concerns that we now have increasing evidence that students—especially those from ESOL and language-minority backgrounds—demand grammar instruction from their writing teachers (see Delpit 1995). Their motivation and morale are affected when teachers show disinterest in these aspects of writing. It is quite possible that such desires of students reflect the traditional bias that writing is all about "correct spelling" and "good grammar"—a bias they may have inherited from old-fashioned textbooks or teachers. But there are other important reasons why we should respect student preferences. Lisa Delpit (1995), an African American educator, argues that minority students who don't have access to the dominant codes (i.e., standard English, institutionally valued registers, and established genre conventions) are being told to sink or swim by well-intentioned teachers who ignore form. There is some truth to the claim that getting students to focus only on ideas and neglecting the place of established codes and conventions may lead to their further marginalization. In the academy and the social mainstream any hint of nonstandard codes is stigmatized. Even in a pedagogy that aims to critically negotiate grammar and not just use form prescriptively, it makes a difference to have an awareness of the established codes. As an ESL student, I was confused about both what was expected and what I should achieve as a critical writer before developing a good understanding of the established conventions. When I became more acquainted with what was considered "correct," I felt more confident to resist these structures and reconstruct them to suit my purposes.

In the discussion that follows, I will demonstrate how we can help students negotiate the structures of writing in terms of the ideological, cultural, and social concerns that matter to them. First I will critique current research on grammar treatment in the writing process. Then I will reconsider the place of functional grammar in text structure. Ways in which some of the valid insights from these approaches can be used for critical writing will be articulated. Next I will discuss the influential research by the school of contrastive rhetoric (CR), one of the earliest approaches to the understanding of cultural differences in the form of essays. Among the research orientations it has inspired is the work of genre analysis (GA), especially from scholars in ESP/EAP. GA brings to the study of linguistic/cultural differences a sophisticated research orientation by explicating the genres of writing in a variety of academic and professional contexts. I will show how the insights of CR and GA can be tapped to help students appropriate structural patterns and achieve their critical purposes.

Negotiating Grammar

Error Correction

Perhaps the most meaningful way for teachers to orientate to grammar in composition courses is in relation to the writing activity of their students. Teachers typically edit the essays of their students, highlight grammar errors to let students discover the problems and revise correctly, provide overt instruction on grammatical features that characterize specific genres of writing (i.e., adjectives in descriptive writing, adverbs in narrative writing, subordinate clauses in argumentative writing, etc.), or provide exercises for individual students on syntactic features that have been inappropriately internalized. In this manner, grammar instruction is tied closely to the writing purpose, contextualized by the expanded discourse of the complete text, and personalized according to the varying needs of each student.

Still, not all researchers are convinced that grammar correction helps students. Truscott (1996) reviews a large body of research to argue that "grammar correction is not effective" (340). He backs this up with the practical experience of many teachers who find that their students make the same errors over and over again and that there is little connection between correction and learning. Claims of this nature may only serve to convince those of the "process writing" persuasion that there is little point served by attending to the grammar concerns in student writing. But Ferris and Hedgcock (1998) fault Truscott's conclusion because the research goals, methods, and contexts of the studies reviewed are so diverse that it is unwise to make strong generalizations from them.

There are other reasons why grammar instruction may not work. A lot depends on when and how grammar feedback is provided by the teacher. Many teachers are not comfortable providing explicit grammar explanations. This is especially a problem for many "native English" teachers who may not have consciously studied grammar as a system. (Many nonnative teachers like me, on the other hand, have at least gone through the traditional grammar-translation method of instruction so that we can explain grammar points formally to our students!) This disparity means that many teachers are not in a position to address grammar concerns in classrooms or understand the multifaceted reasons for "error." We must also remember the pressure under which teachers work in classrooms, which may motivate them to prescriptively enforce correct usage (from their intuitive knowledge) rather than spend time on discovering and explaining the rationale behind students' choices.

Ferris and Hedgcock (1998) summarize the available research on effective practices of grammar feedback in the following manner.

1. Most sentence-level mechanical correction is best left to the latter stages of the editing process. However, generalized feedback about students' major error patterns in early drafts may be helpful to them.
2. It is important for teachers to be *selective* in addressing students' written errors. Errors that should receive the

greatest attention should include **serious** ("global") errors that interfere with the comprehensibility of the text, **stigmatizing** errors that most disturb NES [native English speaking] audiences, and the students' most **frequent** errors.

3. Except for students at very beginning levels of language proficiency, **direct** correction techniques (in which the teacher corrects writers' errors) are not effective or appropriate. **Indirect** techniques, such as noting the location and/or type of error and asking students to find and correct their own errors, are most effective for intermediate to advanced students. (202; emphasis in original)

It is important to prioritize and pace the focus on grammar appropriately. Getting students obsessed with grammar problems at early stages of the draft is to distract them from developing their ideas in relation to their purpose and audience. Taking into account the proficiency level of the student is also important in choosing what kinds of grammar structures we should help them acquire. Although there are inconsistencies in the professional literature in defining such matters as serious and less serious errors, or global and local errors, it is important to distinguish between different types of grammar problems. Certainly, orientating to errors that create problems in communicating ideas (e.g., those that relate to syntax) is more important than focusing on ungrammaticality in such matters as articles, determiners, or prepositions that don't usually interfere much with textual comprehension.

In terms of the types of pedagogical activities that would serve students best in developing their grammatical competence, Brown (1994) has identified successive stages of grammatical proficiency that will warrant different tasks. His stages are as follows.

1. The random error stage: The learner hasn't acquired the rules behind the target language features. Therefore, he/she uses specific items in various ways.

2. The emergent stage: This is the stage of the interlanguage when certain structures are used with greater consistency—although the rules displayed do not reflect the system of the native speakers.
3. The systematic stage: The learner is approximating the system of the language with greater systematicity. An indication of this proficiency is that the learner can correct his/her error when pointed out by others.
4. The stabilization stage: The learner has fewer errors at this stage. He/she can also self-correct. (211–12)

In the first stage, controlled writing exercises (e.g., rewriting a given paragraph in a different tense or person), guided writing (e.g., composing a paragraph based on given prompts/questions, copying of model essays), and dictocomps (i.e., rewriting an essay after listening to a passage and recollecting the content through key words) are appropriate.[1] Intermediate-level students can be led through a structured approach to editing: they can be given a chart with grammar symbols and pointed to locations in their essays where they have grammar problems. More mature students should be encouraged to become independent in their editing. Ferris (1995) suggests activities such as peer editing to help students identify their own errors and develop a way of explaining and keeping track of them. Eventually they should be encouraged to chart their progress in error reduction in their own essays by maintaining a log.

Although the current state of studies on grammar correction has generated many sensible suggestions, from the perspective of critical writing these pedagogical activities should be practiced with a fundamentally different orientation. The obsession with errors in the field of ESOL writing leads to the danger of conveying a sense of failure and handicap to our students. The rigid adherence to correctness and standardized norms can stifle creativity and contextual variation in grammar usage. A healthier approach would require changes of the following nature:

from	*to*
error	choice
linguistic homogeneity	linguistic diversity
knowledge of grammar rules	metalinguistic awareness
linguistic competence	communicative competence
correction	negotiation

Teachers of critical writing should consider grammar usage as an activity not of reproducing the rule-governed system but of negotiating from a range of available options to represent the writers' identities, values, and interests in the most satisfactory manner possible. What we may reject as an error may be motivated by serious concerns of values and identity for the student. Rather than imposing uniform usage unilaterally, and thus suppressing the creativity of the student in representing his or her interest in the writing activity, it is important to negotiate the best way in which his or her purposes may be achieved through the range of grammatical resources available. In engaging with individual students with a sensitivity to their unique rhetorical intentions and purposes, teachers may in fact facilitate something more significant than simply developing proficiency in correct grammatical usage. We may enable writers to move toward a reflexive, critical, and metacognitive awareness of the language system. Such an approach may develop the independence of writers for marshaling the resources of the language according to their needs and values. After all, the important point behind linguistic proficiency is developing the communicative competence of writers—that is, the ability to creatively tap the potential of the grammar to represent their values, interests, and purposes in the social activity of communication. It is in this manner that we can guard against the danger of giving the impression that the English language is uniform or static. ESOL students, who come from a variety of "nonnative" English-speaking communities, know that the English language is plural in the way its system has evolved globally. They face the need to use grammar variably in different contexts of communication. What we teach as correct grammar (whether the standardized

American or British variant) is relevant for only certain specific contexts and communities of communication. What we define as "incorrect" grammar may be appropriate in other contexts of writing, not least in informal genres of narrative, satire, and parody where the writer has to codeswitch or style shift. Note also that language is still changing, and it is the ability of students to push against the grammatical system for expression that makes a language accommodate the values of other communities.

Min-Zhan Lu (1994) narrates an example of how students may be encouraged to negotiate usage, developing in them the awareness that even grammar is not free of ideological interests and values. Lu explores the peculiar usage "can able to" in the essays of a Chinese student from Malaysia (e.g., "As a Hawaiian native historian, Trask can able to argue for her people"; "If a student can able to approach each situation with different perspectives than the one he brought from high school, I may conclude that this student has climbed his first step to become a 'critical thinker'"). Since the modals "can" and "may" are used according to their conventional meanings in other places in the student's writing, it appears that "can able to" is used with a unique meaning of its own. In fact, Lu realizes later that in the student's native language "can" and "be able to" have an interchangeable meaning. The student points out to the teacher (with the help of her English dictionary!) that "be able to" has an additional meaning of "have permission to" that is not connoted by "can" in English. Therefore she puts together both structures to coin "can able to." (I will go on to demonstrate below how this coinage is motivated by ideological and cultural considerations.)

An important lesson here, to begin with, is the limitation of contrastive linguistics (see Lado 1957). It was assumed by this popular pedagogical approach in the 1950s that a structural comparison of the nonnative student's first and second languages would help *predict* (in the strong version of this model) or at least *explain* (in the weak version) the structures the student is bound to use incorrectly. But to assume that students are bound to err in L2 grammar is to adopt a deterministic perspective. It is also untrue in the present case. The Malaysian student is not blind to the differences in Chinese and English. She insists on using the peculiar structure because she is struggling to bring out certain ideas that are important to her. This example shows us the dangers of jumping to the conclusion that any peculiarity in L2 writing is to be explained by influences from the student's first language. In being thus judgmental, teachers sometimes ignore the creativity of students who negotiate unique meanings. Teachers may also suppress other explanations for why a structure may sound peculiar—that is, explanations that testify to students' rhetorical independence and critical thinking.

Why then does this student use this structure? Since the student has personally gone through a lot of pressure from her family against following higher education (partly because of her status as a woman and partly because of her community's traditions), she is cognizant of the struggles one has to go through to think critically and act independently. To express this need to achieve independence despite community constraints, she uses "can able to"—a structure that connotes for her "ability from the perspective of the external circumstances" (Lu 1994, 452). She is also inspired by her understanding of Trask's ability to still speak for her people despite the external constraints of being a minority historian. The student therefore tries to communicate the possibility of an individual's potential to act through a struggle against external limiting constraints. In fact, the instructor makes this grammatical usage a point of discussion for the whole class. The other students agree that it is the dominant American ideology of individual transcendence and personal power that makes them treat "can" and "be able to" with similar connotations. The Malaysian student wants to convey a different orientation to ability and is thus forced to fashion a new usage for her purposes.

There are many pedagogical benefits that derive from discussing this grammar "error" without prejudices or preconceptions. The writer and the rest of the class now understand grammar as ideological. The choices we make hide or em-

phasize the values we want to convey to our readers. In trying to find out from our students the reasons why they use a
peculiar structure, we help them acknowledge the serious
considerations motivating their language usage. Such discussions enable students to use grammar meaningfully, rather
than opting for certain choices mechanically. In the process,
students also develop a metalinguistic awareness of the values and interests motivating grammar. These skills are of far
more significance for developing writing competence compared to simply enforcing grammatical correctness in the
dominant dialects.

Understanding student motivations for using unusual
grammar structures doesn't exhaust our responsibilities in
writing instruction. Can "incorrect" usage be permitted in the
essay? How far should students go in reworking the dominant
dialects? Lu provides a multifaceted answer, opening up different possibilities. She states that at a later point of the course
she got the whole class to explore alternative grammatical resources to embody the Malaysian student's meaning while being mindful of the rules accepted by the native speech community. The writer resorted to using "may be able to" in
deference to standard grammar. This ensured that she was
within the bounds of rule-governed usage, while also conveying her unique perspective. Some of the other students
considered possibilities such as adding an "if" clause to "be
able to" or even using "can able to" with a parenthetical explanation of this unusual usage. The latter is a form of com-
promise, as it acknowledges that the writer is aware of using
the structure in a peculiar way for a unique rhetorical purpose. On the other hand, another ESL writer, a student from
Vietnam, argued that he would use "can" and "be able to" in-
terchangeably because their connotations of agency inspired
modes of resistance and individual empowerment against the
fatalism of his own community. The "standard" grammar
structure thus became an ideologically favored option for a
minority student—a structure he used not mechanically but
with critical thinking. Lu concludes this narrative of grammar
instruction by noting that the structure "can able to" took on

a life of its own in her class. After being playfully used in a class discussion, "it became a newly coined phrase we shared throughout the term" (1994, 454). The pedagogy thus simulates the process by which dialects develop: peculiar usages become "standardized" once their meanings and purposes are socially shared.

What all this demonstrates is the benefit of negotiating grammar for one's purposes. Students are being trained to make grammatical choices based on many discursive concerns—that is, their intentions, the context, and the assumptions of readers and writers. Students also learn that in certain special cases they may try out a peculiar structure for unique purposes. But they should indicate to the audience that they are using this with full awareness of the established grammar system. Thus, rather than being treated as a sign of immaturity, this usage may be treated as a mark of independent and critical writing. Furthermore, demonstrating the heterogeneous and changing nature of the grammar system is very important for ESOL students, as they come from communities where different dialects of English are well established. This doesn't mean students are free to use their vernacular versions for all contexts of communication. Negotiating grammar means being sensitive to the relativity of style and usage in different communicative situations. Overzealous teachers who impose correctness may stifle the development of a repertoire that will help students style shift or codeswitch according to their differing communicative contexts. Lu's exercise conveys the valuable lesson that we don't have to be at the mercy of our grammar system. When the established system is inadequate or inappropriate for our purposes—which is not surprising, as the language is considerably influenced by the dominant group's ideologies and interests—we may negotiate appropriate usage and in the process reshape the system. This is certainly not an instantaneous or individual process. It is important to engage with the linguistic system with the understanding that there is always tension between stability and change, dominant usage and emergent usage, sociolect and idiolect, in any language.

There is no formula available for teachers on how this pedagogy of negotiating grammar can be practiced on a regular
basis in classrooms. It is clear that this is a time-consuming
and painstaking activity. We cannot develop a pedagogy
around any and every mistake a student makes in writing. We
simply don't have the time and resources to do so. We should
identify the frequent errors a student makes, exploring the
possibility that the writer is using a particular structure with
certain important assumptions and a systematicity of his or
her own. We should then spend time with students individually to explicate their assumptions and work out ways of expressing those interests in terms of the dominant system. On
certain occasions it is also necessary to make such peculiar
structures a matter of class discussion. What's important is to
inculcate an attitude toward grammar—of grammar as contextual, ideological, and negotiable. A few significant occasions of classroom discussion may serve to convey to students
the importance of developing this metalinguistic awareness.

Text Linguistics

While the pedagogy of error correction typically focuses on
sentence-level grammar from a structuralist tradition, there
are other schools that approach grammar according to intersentential relationships. These schools may also look at traditional grammar features for the way they function in ex-
panded/connected threads of discourse, in addition to
studying the grammar of text structure. Though there are different orientations to this descriptive activity, we may use the
umbrella term *text linguistics* for these schools. This approach has become a popular research tool in composition,
enabling scholars to explain the linguistic bases for skilled
and unskilled writing.

Hunt's (1965) T-unit analysis was among the earliest models to be developed for this purpose. The T-unit, or minimal
terminable unit, is defined as "one main clause plus any subordinate clause or non-clausal structure that is attached to or
embedded in it" (Hunt 1965, 4). To demonstrate writing de-

velopment and textual complexity, Hunt developed measures such as the number of words per T-unit, the number of T-units per sentence, the number of clauses per T-unit, and the number of words per clause. The model has been used in many research activities in L1 (see Hillocks 1986) and L2 (see Gaies 1980) to explain how essays having less of these features show less skilled writing. In effect, the ability to compose longer and more complex sentences is taken to indicate writing proficiency. Spurred on by this research, teachers adopted the pedagogical practice of sentence combining to develop writing fluency in their students. Clauses and phrases are provided to students to combine in complex relations, sometimes with the help of grammatical clues such as connectives and adverbs. Reviewing the pedagogical history of this approach, Grabe and Kaplan (1996) say that "there is evidence that sentence combining does lead to writing improvement to some extent; the instructional approach has achieved some measure of success and cannot be labeled a failure" (43–44). To some degree, this approach makes students conscious of syntactic patterns, promotes sentence variety, improves syntactic fluency, allows for a denser informational load in sentences, and builds writing confidence.

However, teachers who use sentence combining have to be mindful of its limitations. This pedagogy sometimes encourages the misleading notion that the essay is generated by stringing one sentence with another to produce extended texts. The essay is not a collection of grammatically correct sentences. There are larger discoursal and rhetorical processes that account for its coherence. Students who have syntactic fluency don't necessarily display complexity or effectiveness in their writing. They could simply be verbose. It is not impossible to write long complicated sentences violating coherence or ignoring the rhetorical process of thinking, planning, and organizing the text.

A text-linguistic approach that takes into consideration the role of cohesion and coherence is the now well-known work of Halliday and Hasan (1976). Theirs may be treated as a functional orientation to grammar—that is, one based on what roles grammatical structures play in tying the text together and facilitating comprehension. Halliday and Hassan have come up with new classifications and patterns to explain text organization. Cohesive devices, for example, are words or phrases that signal to the reader a relationship with previously stated or soon-to-follow information in the text. Halliday and Hassan (1976) chart the major grammatical relations that build cohesion in the text as follows:

1. Reference: "Siva is a good writer. *He* writes on global warming very persuasively."
2. Substitution: "Siva's essay on global warming was very persuasive. Have you read *it?*"
3. Ellipsis: "Siva's essay appears in the *New York Times.* It was written [*by?*] last year."
4. Lexical cohesion: "The *person* who wrote this article teaches in. . . . The *writer* argues that. . . . The evidence provided by this *scholar* is. . . ."
5. Conjunction: "He has done extensive research on the subject. *Also,* he draws from personal experience."

If cohesion relates largely to the grammatical and lexical relations of the surface-level text, coherence is about the deeper-level semantic relations. The way in which the ideational content of the text is developed may be discussed either in terms of how the *reader* processes this information or how the *writer* chunks it. Halliday's (1985) notion of theme/rheme structure, based on the way the topic and the comment are organized in the sentence, is an example of the writer's perspective. Other schools have used distinctions like topic/comment, given/new, and focus/presupposition to orientate to the organization of ideas from the reader's perspective. Extending this further to understand the progression of the text in even longer syntactic sequences, Lauttimatti (1978) comes up with the model of "topical structure analysis." According to her orientation, the coherence of texts can be analyzed according to any of the following patterns:

parallel progression (where the topics/themes of the successive sentences are the same);

sequential progression (where the comment/rheme of one sentence becomes the topic of the next);

extended parallel progression (where some forms of sequential progression are embedded within parallel progression).

The ways in which these text-linguistic models lent themselves to quantitative research made them popular among composition researchers who were under pressure to prove the scientific nature of their studies during the 1980s. There have been some interesting avenues of research in both L1 and L2 circles that have found patterns of cohesion/coherence correlating with differences between skilled and unskilled writers. Witte and Faigley (1981) find that cohesion is a good predictor of writing quality across different grade levels. They also claim that cohesion functions as a good indicator of differences in students' invention skills. The implication is that skilled writers employ cohesion devices effectively. In the L2 context, Schneider and Connor (1991) found that topical structure analysis correlated well with readers' judgments of writing quality in a sample of essays from TOEFL's Test of Written English. Connor (1996) draws from many other studies she has conducted on coherence to argue that the model "works best if it is applied after an early draft, when students are still prepared to make substantive changes. . . . Student response has been positive and writing has improved, specifically with regard to clearer focus . . . and better development. . . . [S]tudents become careful and critical readers of their own texts" (87).

It is important to realize, however, that the relationship between cohesion and coherence may be complicated by semantic and ideological considerations. Despite the argument of Halliday and Hasan (1976) that the surface structure of the text must make a substantial contribution to the coherence of the text, it is easy to imagine counterexamples. Texts that have the appropriate devices to build cohesion may yet fail to generate meaning. Similarly, coherence itself is a domain that depends on deeper layers of semantic potential. What makes a text coherent depends on other ideological and cultural assumptions that often shape the import of cohesive devices and coherence structures. Consider an example like the following.

> Terrorists, of whichever ideological background, should be universally condemned. The marauding government soldiers behaved in an inhuman way in the village. The UN should inquire into their activities for possible war crimes.

This is an example of parallel progression only for those who are not confused by the treatment of "terrorists" and "government soldiers" as synonyms. In the mainstream media, these terms are often used as antonyms. But if we can treat this text as coming from an alternate media source (e.g., published by activist circles), and if we are familiar with notions like "state terrorism" or "institutionalized terrorism," we may understand that government soldiers can behave like "terrorists" in certain contexts. Of course, this interpretation is finally motivated by ideological considerations. It is hard to imagine the American mainstream media calling GIs "terrorists" even in reports of civilian killings in the My Lai massacre (in Vietnam) or the No Gun Ri massacre (in Korea). It is important therefore to help students go beyond the surface-level syntactic and grammatical structures to negotiate how these interpretive cues may be defined in terms of the differing cultural and ideological assumptions they and their readers hold. Simply alerting students to the role played by these background assumptions in the encoding and decoding of text will go a long way toward making students critical writers.

Some teachers in ESOL have found models of *critical linguistics* useful for teaching grammar in an ideologically sensitive manner. In some of the early versions of this model, critical linguists adopted Halliday's functional grammar to interpret the ideological meanings behind syntax (see Fowler and Kress 1979). They interpreted examples like the following for their hidden meanings.

1. The president fired the worker for insubordination.
2. The worker was fired for insubordination.
3. For insubordination, the worker was fired.

What is involved here is more than a matter of building co-herence by shifting phrases to create new foci in the theme/rheme relationship. The transposition of the object in 1 ("the worker") as the new subject in 2, and the eventual dele-tion of the "by" phrase, reduce the focus on the person who did the firing, thus mitigating the power relationship. The sentence also conveys an impersonal tone, creating the impression of an abstract institutional process, encouraging us to ignore the hu-man relationships involved. The third sentence, by moving the adverbial phrase to the position of the new theme, somewhat bluntly reminds the reader of the reason for firing. The syntax effectively conveys the indignation or sarcasm of the writer. Recent versions of critical discourse analysis, especially those spearheaded by Kress (1985) and Fairclough (2000), are in-formed by poststructuralist and semiotic traditions to provide a more complex reading of ideologies in expanded texts. These scholars assume that there is no one-to-one correlation be-tween specific syntactic patterns and ideologies. They are open to the possibility that there may be multiple ideologies in a sin-gle text—sometimes in tension with each other.

There is no easy discovery procedure that can be given for teachers and students to decode ideology from syntax. This is a very interpretive exercise. We can only create a sensitivity to ideological issues by encouraging students to read and write texts in the light of social context, shared knowledge, and cultural attitudes. While being sensitive to the dominant assumptions of their audience, students will work toward questioning and changing these assumptions where impor-tant ethical concerns are at stake. Thus coherence in writing is creatively achieved.

Negotiating Form

Let's now proceed to consider how ideologies shape textual patterns larger than grammar and syntax. Approaches such as contrastive rhetoric and genre analysis have explored the rhetorical challenges for multilingual students in academic text construction.

Contrastive Rhetoric

It used to be the case that when native English teachers discovered modes of paragraph and essay organization that they were unfamiliar with, they resorted to blaming the students for the confusion. So the unfamiliar textual patterns were explained away as reflecting the illogical thinking and ineffective communicative traditions of ESOL students. Robert Kaplan did a great service to the profession by developing a healthy relativism and openness in teacher attitudes. He borrowed from the Sapir-Whorf hypothesis, popular in the 1960s, to argue that different languages constituted different cultures and thought patterns; these in turn accounted for the different paragraph organization in student essays. The lines he drew to illustrate the circularity of oriental writing; the different types of parallelism in the Semitic, Russian, and Romance languages; and the arrow-straight linearity of English have become legendary in the field. Kaplan's (1966) initial essay teaches us that if the structure of the essay fails to make sense, teachers have to understand the logic students themselves employ in their writing, instead of applying their own preconstructed schemas.

However, we have now begun to use more complex orientations to culture and ideology—thanks to theoretical developments in the social sciences. In the light of these developments, Kaplan himself has been revising the model of CR to make it less deterministic and rigid. We have to reexamine CR's theoretical premises to evaluate its relevance to critical writing. At least in its early versions, when it was influenced by a strong interpretation of the Sapir-Whorf hypothesis, CR treated students as *conditioned* by their linguistic and cultural background. CR generated sympathy for ESOL students by arguing that they were hindered from seeing the logic behind other thought patterns or adopting it themselves.

Kaplan's later theoretical revisions, clarifying that these styles are students' own preferences rather than those abstractly imposed by culture (1976) and that these styles are developed from social and communicative practices rather than cognitively imposed on them (1986), have helped reduce the imputation of mental deficiency and cognitive determinism to students. But even these changes haven't done enough to alleviate the notion that ESOL students are fated to use their "native" patterns. As late as 1996, Kaplan still seemed to hold that "different cultures have different rhetorical preferences for the organization of written text. . . . Contrastive rhetoric preferences not only shape written text in distinct languages and cultures, but tend to manifest themselves consistently, if subtly, in the writing of students learning a second language" (Grabe and Kaplan 1996, 197).

Apart from the passive role given to students in negotiating culture, what makes CR simplistic is the monolithic and discrete way in which cultures and texts are defined (as evidenced by the statement quoted earlier). We now know that there is considerable interaction, borrowing, and fusion between cultures and communicative genres. The hybrid nature of cultures in the postmodern world creates considerable problems in defining which constructs of a particular culture are unique and "native" to one community and which are borrowed (or interactively shaped in contact with another culture). If the monolithic definition of cultures and genres is rejected, it becomes easy to see how students may move across cultures and texts in their communicative practice. Though students may come with certain preferred traditions and practices of text construction of their own, they can still creatively negotiate alternate structures they are introduced to.

Recent poststructuralist perspectives further complicate cultural definitions. We learn that defining, classifying, and labeling cultures is often a politically motivated activity. The interests of the classifier play a significant role in the way the culture is defined. Ryuko Kubota (1999b) thus reveals how the dominant definitions of Japanese culture have the consequence of propping up the more powerful Western (Anglo-

American) cultures as more logical and sensible. This is a colonizing enterprise, bent on developing a universal appreciation of Western cultures and of dependence on them by other communities. The activity of the subordinate groups in providing alternate definitions of their culture has to also be situated in sociohistorical context. Kubota shows that the nationalists in postwar Japan have had to emphasize the purity and uniqueness of Japanese culture by resorting to stereotypical and essentialized constructs.[2] Both attempts (of Western and local scholars) tend to simplify the plural, hybrid, and complex nature of Japanese culture. Culture then emerges as a contested construct. How it is defined is tied to the interests of the community concerned.

There are many implications here for compositionists. In drawing from essentialist culturalist definitions to explain the writing of students, we are reducing the complexity of Japanese communicative traditions. In using these constructs in an abstract way without going into the contexts, interests, and ideologies that motivate these definitions, we are adopting a simplistic attitude to culture. Finally, we ourselves may contribute to this cultural stereotyping by generating similar essentializing constructs to explain the patterns of thinking/behaving/communicating of ESOL students. We have to interrogate the interests and ideologies that influence our own definitions of our students' cultures. Neither cultures nor our exercises in defining them are neutral or disinterested.

Just as cultures are plural or hybrid complexes, sometimes displaying many conflicting strands and traditions jostling together, texts too are multivocal. CR works by treating textual structures as having discrete forms—as having a normative (or at least a uniformly defined) character in each culture. Postmodern discourse analysts are now prepared to see how the same text could accommodate multiple rhetorical traditions and discourses. In a fluid/changing social context, such texts are now becoming quite common, and they still remain meaningful and coherent (see Fairclough 2000; Kress 2000). Furthermore, texts are not only cultural but are also ideological. We have to be sensitive to the ways in which the values informing a specific genre or text may have implications for shaping/representing the identities and thinking of the students. These textual identities have implications for the social status of the writer. While CR posits that texts may create cultural dissonance for students, it overlooks the implications of writing for issues of power. This is partly because CR defines culture as an autonomous social domain, without relation to power. In building bridges for multilingual students to move from C1 to C2 (or from a "native" culture to a secondary culture) in their writing, we have to be sensitive to the subject positions provided for them in the new textual tradition. Differences in culture may be transcended, but impositions of ideology have to be resisted. In such cases, we have to be prepared to accept a differently realized text from our students.

We must understand that Kaplan couldn't have adopted these sophisticated definitions of culture, as his earliest paper preceded the advent of movements like postcolonialism, postmodernism, and cultural politics. Furthermore, considerable advances have been made in research methodology and data collection relating to the empirical study of text construction. In his seminal 1966 paper, Kaplan largely studied paragraph organization. He made his characterization of "cultural thought patterns" by reading the texts not in the original languages but in English. The assumption was that the L2 writing of the students was sufficiently culturally transparent to manifest the patterns of L1 and native culture even in a different language. Later scholars have made it a point to study the texts written in L1 in order to make generalizations about that culture.[3] Still it is wrong to compare the writings of professional writers in many non-school-related genres and claim that these texts show a generalizable pattern of writing that is distinctive to a culture. There is a linguistic and cultural determinism here that influences researchers to think that whatever the writing context or product there will be a uniform rhetoric displayed. Fortunately, recent scholars have become more sensitive to the different genres of writing and the different levels of expertise of writers as they make cultural comparisons.[4] It is important to relate comparable genres and writings in characterizing rhetorical differences. Furthermore, CR researchers have to keep in mind different factors that may mediate culture in the construction of texts. Before we identify culture as the cause of textual differences, we must also consider how the schooling and previous writing background of the writer may influence him or her to write differently. In a comparison of Chinese students from Canada and Hong Kong it was found that each group wrote differently because each had been given different writing instruction in their respective schools (see Mohan and Lo 1985).

While Kaplan studied only paragraph structure, the domain of analysis has become more complex now. There are other areas of surface structure that have been studied—development of the thesis, cohesion and coherence, and topic development. Furthermore, whole genres like narrative, persuasion, and argumentation have been compared. Going beyond the surface structure, other deep structural aspects such as contrasting attitudes, reader/writer relationships, and background knowledge have been studied.[5] There has also developed a body of research on the composing processes of writers. Different styles of planning, revising, peer reviewing, and drafting the essay are now being described.[6]

Despite these laudable developments there is still the limiting procedure that different student populations are compared in making such cultural descriptions (e.g., one set of students writing in L1 vs. another set writing in L2—albeit from the same language group). It is assumed that the rhetorical pattern of the whole linguistic/cultural community will display itself without complications from personal differences of the individual students. This assumption denies agency to the subjects to have their own ways of negotiating different rhetorics. There are only a few rare studies that compare the writing in different languages of the *same* student (see Kubota 1999a).[7] How does a bilingual writer switch between English and vernacular academic writing? Why do individual writers adopt different rhetorical patterns in texts as they move from one language to the other? What features of their rhetoric remain the same, which change, and why? To exemplify the complexity of the negotiation process that takes place in bilingual writing, I will provide in the next section samples of writing from a scholar writing in English and Tamil in three different rhetorical contexts (a local English-speaking audience, a local Tamil audience, and a Western English-speaking audience).

Though CR is a rare research and pedagogical tradition indigenous to ESL with considerable value for teachers, it must develop more complex types of explanation for textual difference if the school is to enjoy continued usefulness. Though difference is always going to be there in writing, and though much of it may derive from culture, the ways in which this influence takes place can be positive or negative, enabling as well as limiting, and teachers have to be aware of all these possibilities when they teach student writing. More importantly, teachers must keep in mind that no one needs to be held hostage by language or culture; students can be taught to negotiate conflicting rhetorical structures to their advantage.

Genre Analysis

Much of the early CR research on writing took place on a generic version of the "academic essay," usually understood as a five-paragraph piece of expository writing on a specific "theme." It is now widely felt that this genre may not have much functionality beyond the classroom and pedagogical contexts. The WAC movement has spearheaded a more focused writing instruction that develops the skills and competencies required for specific disciplines in the academy. This movement is aligned to the EAP school in the L2 field, where researchers and teachers are interested in developing the communicative competence needed for students to succeed in their particular fields of study. EAP is part of the larger umbrella movement of ESP—where the registers, genres, and discourses of a wider range of nonacademic domains are being studied.[8] A subgrouping in EAP is EST—English for science and technology—which orientates to the communicative styles in the technical fields. All these movements are interested not only in issues of form but also in register, knowledge constructs, background assumptions, cultural values, and styles of social relationship. Though we will discuss the contributions of these schools regarding their other concerns in the appropriate chapters to follow, here we will consider their contributions to the understanding and teaching of form.

In an important sense, these schools have approached their study of form with assumptions different from those of CR. While CR adopts the relativistic orientation that writers from different cultures relate to form variously and/or that form in the same genres is realized differently in different cultures, EAP holds that there are common genre rules for specific fields of writing that students have to conform to if they are to communicate effectively to a particular disciplinary audience. The EAP-related schools are therefore more objective, descriptive, and empirical, as they study texts closely to characterize the genre conventions that emerge with some regularity. It might in fact be said that CR needs precisely this knowledge before it can proceed to compare texts from different cultures. Without a clear understanding of what the different genre conventions are in specific disciplines, it is difficult to make comparative statements. These movements are similar to CR, however, in that they too are normative. Both assume that there are clearly defined, rule-governed, discrete conventions for specific genres in particular contexts of writing. When the text deviates from the predefined conventions, it is treated as a failure. (This attitude differs from current movements that treat texts as hybrid, mixing different rhetorics in a strategic way.) Furthermore, it has been assumed that scholars from any cultural background have to adopt these value-free, neutral rules if they are to communicate in a particular discipline (see Mohan and Lo 1985). Other scholars in EAP arrive at the same normative position about academic genres through a more pragmatic attitude. They assume that though these genre conventions may be culturally and politically partisan to certain circles, others have to adopt them for the utilitarian function of getting their communicative objectives accomplished (Swales 1990).

What Swales (1990) calls genre analysis in L2 circles is exemplary of the studies developing in this movement. While the writing conventions in many different academic disciplines are still being studied for descriptive purposes, Swales's description of the research article (RA) has reached a sophisticated level of model building. Others who have studied specific disciplines—like Geisler (1994), who describes philosophy essays, and Paul (1996), who analyzes writing on chaos theory in physics—still find Swales's model useful as a heuristic device to consider how these more specific genres diverge from Swales's description. At any rate, the RA is the quintessential academic form of communication. The end product of all intellectual inquiry and empirical research in any field is an RA. It is through the RA that new knowledge is legitimized. I have found it useful to introduce Swales's rules of the RA form to my undergraduate students in order to acquaint them with the basic academic genre of communication.[9] It can be argued that the RA is mainly a postgraduate and professional level of writing. But that objection concerns all pedagogies related to the EAP and WAC movements. In what sense can we expect undergraduate students to practice the conventions of a specific discipline when they are not insiders to those scholarly circles? Can they do authentic writing for those disciplines when they are not full-fledged scholars? But in another sense, college students are prospective members of the scholarly community, with one foot already in the academy by virtue of their student status in a higher-educational institution. It is good for them to know the conventions that matter to the professional discourse of their teachers and mentors as they attempt to approximate that discourse.

I will first introduce Swales's description of the RA structure and then consider the concerns critical pedagogues may have against it. The form and flow of the RA have been likened to the hourglass. The introduction (I) section is broad in the generality of concerns it deals with. Here, authors situate their study in the overall research tradition and disciplinary discourse. The methods (M) and results (R) sections then narrow down in the next stages of the text to deal specifically with the author's study. The article broadens again in the discussion (D) section as the implications and significance of the findings are situated in the widest possible context. The first two sections (introduction and method) are thus mirror-imaged by the other two sections. Swales tabulates his research findings on the linguistic and rhetorical differences between the sections as shown in figure 2.

Feature	*I*	*M*	*R*	*D*
Movement	outside-in	narrow	narrow	inside-out
Reporting statements	high	very low	low	high
Present tense	high	low	low	high
Past tense	fairly low	very high	very high	fairly low
Passive voice	low	high	variable	variable
Authorial comment	high	very low	very low	high

Fig. 2. Features across the IMRD sections. (Adapted from Swales 1990, 137.) Reprinted with the permission of Cambridge University Press.

Such observations have influenced many scholars to posit that I and D are complex, while M and R are simple. This is of course corroborated by ethnographers of writing, who have observed that I and D take more rhetorical effort and composing time, while M and R are rarely redrafted (see Knorr-Cetina 1981).

Of the four sections of the RA, the most amount of research has taken place on the opening of articles. Swales labels the *moves* characterizing this structure the Create a Research Space (CARS) model. The components of the introduction are as shown in figure 3 on the next page.

Swales (1990) goes on to make the strong claim that "the three moves occur at a high frequency in their assigned order" (145). When such a fixed definition is given for the structure of the introductory moves, any variation by multilingual scholars will raise problematic questions. In fact, when Swales analyzes an article written by an ESL graduate student who fails to adopt move 2 before move 3, he considers this as

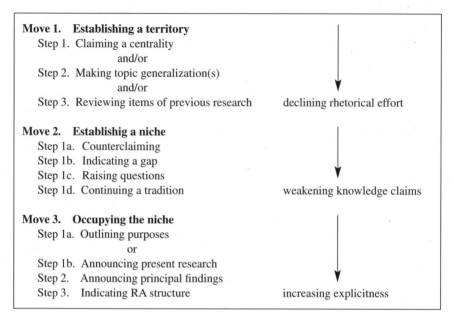

Move 1.   Establishing a territory
  Step 1. Claiming a centrality
            and/or
  Step 2. Making topic generalization(s)
            and/or
  Step 3. Reviewing items of previous research   declining rhetorical effort

Move 2.   Establishig a niche
  Step 1a. Counterclaiming
  Step 1b. Indicating a gap
  Step 1c. Raising questions
  Step 1d. Continuing a tradition   weakening knowledge claims

Move 3.   Occupying the niche
  Step 1a. Outlining purposes
            or
  Step 1b. Announcing present research
  Step 2.   Announcing principal findings
  Step 3.   Indicating RA structure   increasing explicitness

Fig. 3. A CARS model for article introductions. (Adapted from Swales 1990, 141.) Reprinted with the permission of Cambridge University Press.

deriving from the ineptitude of the writer and sees no reason to modify his model (158).

Recent studies on the structural divergences of RAs of multilingual scholars bring into focus the underlying logic of both center and periphery academic communities. Apart from the cultural differences, these structural divergences also point to material inequalities and ideological conflicts. The structure of the RA, as described by Swales, is motivated by values and interests peculiar to the West. For example, Anna Mauranen (1993b) makes the interesting point that the aggressive manner in which the argument of the scholar is presented—distinguishing one's research from that of other scholars, with its originality clearly conveyed, and prominently highlighting the thesis at the beginning of the paper—is informed by a "marketing discourse." These conventions are influenced by the competition among Western scholars for publication and knowledge production. Apart from the recognition the research may bring to the scholar, such publications define his or her very professional survival (in the form of tenure, grants, promotion, and patents). Therefore these scholars have to "market" their ideas/findings to the community of scholars (after first convincing the editors of a particular journal) with skills of salesmanship. On the other hand, many non-Western scholars don't adopt such a "front-weighted" presentation or set out their thesis with an aggressive claim of originality. Rather than establishing an agonistic relationship with rival scholars, they may in fact adopt a more collaborative tone in showing how their study confirms/enhances/develops established knowledge. For many of these scholars, knowledge production doesn't imply the same amount of competition or socioeconomic consequences. As Hess (1995) argues, many non-Western academic communities don't place such heavy emphasis on research and publication (or even tie them rigidly to the evaluation and promotion of the scholar) in professional life. It is also the case that in many communities, one's study is not necessarily valued for its uniqueness. Though one may do original research, one may win respect for the work by showing how it fits into the community's valued traditions of knowledge.

Such sociocultural factors may also explain the use of metacomments in the RA. Mauranen (1993a) shows how Finnish scholars employ less explicit cohesion devices to signpost the stages of their argument. On the other hand, North American scholars employ devices that border on redundancy. The text anticipates the coming argument, reminds readers of each step of the argument that has been covered, summarizes important points made, and cross-references different sections. For nonnative scholars like me, who prefer a less explicit development, it appears as if the reader is being insulted and treated in a condescending way. We expect readers to do more interpretive work. Besides, the American style appears to control the reader's understanding of the argument, leaving nothing to chance or misinterpretation. But this also appears to be biased. For non-Western scholars it gives the impression of imposing the writer's view excessively on the reader, preventing him or her from coming to his or her own conclusions. But it is possible that this is more than a cultural difference. Since Americans come from a heterogeneous community and are often thinking of communicating to a diverse international readership in the global language of English, they cannot take things for granted. Scandinavian and Asian scholars can assume a more homogeneous readership, especially when they write in the vernacular, and thus require less explicit metacomment devices to guide the interpretation of their papers.

Access to material resources may also explain why non-Western writers do not adopt the Swalesian RA structure completely (see Muchiri et al. 1995; Canagarajah 1996). It has been noted that articles from periphery scholars lack move 1/step 3—reviewing current literature. This also means that they downplay the related move 2—establishing a niche for their work in relation to dominant scholarship in the field. This is not just a cultural disposition of developing one's ideas without deferring to others' work. There is also the problem that many periphery communities are off-networked from center-based disciplinary communities and publishing circles. The price of journals, the limited facilities in the local libraries, the slow mail system, and the lack of access to current publications all mean that periphery scholars don't enjoy the facilities for a thorough and informed literature review (see Muchiri et al. 1995; Canagarajah 1996). We have to consider, similarly, how aspects like the amount of time minority students have for composing at leisure (free from other commitments), their access to library or computer facilities, and their ability to participate in important circles of scholarly discourse may have an impact on their writing.

A historical perspective on the development of academic genres of writing shows that these conventions took shape in response to the material and social constraints existing at different times. Robert Boyle, an influential scientist belonging to the Royal Scientific Society during the seventeenth century, promoted the experimental approach in his circles through the development of a suitable mode of written report. Boyle's writing conventions enabled him to cope with the material and social constraints he faced in legitimizing his approach to knowledge (see Shapin 1984). The methodology section of research papers first gained considerable significance as Boyle had to enact the practice of *communal witnessing* of research. According to this practice, gentlemen of high standing signed their names attesting to the results observed at the end of the experiment. Boyle had to textually construct the experimental context by describing in detail the expensive and delicate air pump that he had put together painstakingly for his research purposes. Since others couldn't be expected to construct the same mechanism, the writer had to give detailed information on the way that instrument was put together and the ways in which it functioned in the experiment. Through the methodology section, Boyle attempted to simulate the research process and facilitate a "virtual witnessing" for others in the scientific community. In later times, when experimental instruments began to be mass produced and became standardized, a mere mention of the procedure was enough to satisfy other scholars. Correspondingly, the role of the methodology section has been reduced in the RA structure, as we can see from Swales's current description.[10] This historical orientation shows that the RA is an evolving genre shaped by changing contextual forces. Normative attitudes to form ignore the place of social influences on writing.

The purpose of demonstrating these challenges is not to argue that marginalized scholars are passive in the face of their material limitations; nor are they conditioned by their ideological preferences to be uncommunicative in the Western academic genres. These scholars attempt to negotiate the conventions in their favor. This negotiation may take different forms. They may appropriate the established conventions in their own terms. They may fuse their own preferences into the dominant genres to construct a multivocal or hybrid text. Or they may resist certain conventions effectively to create alternate styles of communication. This orientation is a corrective to the CR perspective, which doesn't provide much scope for writers to negotiate cultural differences with a display of their own agency.

Recent studies show how novice/student writers construct such multivocal texts through their own initiative (without expert advice) when they wrestle honestly with the discursive challenges they face in their academic tasks. In an illuminating case study of a Chinese and a Japanese female graduate student, Belcher (1997) shows how they produce embedded forms of argumentation in otherwise narrative texts to gently and tactfully challenge the biases of their faculty advisors (and, in effect, critique the dominant discourses in their fields). This writing strategy derives from a community-based and gender-influenced desire to show respect, understanding, and cooperative engagement in knowledge construction. Despite the risks involved in antagonizing their thesis committees and failing to obtain their degrees, the students manage to evoke respect for their projects. Belcher goes on to make a case for such nonadversarial forms of argumentation and dialogue, in terms of the styles preferred by certain feminist and minority scholars. After all, well-meaning faculty members (and journal referees) should look for creative, original, and challenging modes of textuality that *add* something to the discourse, rather than demanding texts that slavishly mimic the existing style in a formulaic manner. Center scholars who believe in creative, personalized, "original" realizations of texts (admittedly a somewhat romantic notion of writing) should make a space for divergent modes of writing from minority scholars. Belcher in fact goes a step further to argue that these alternate modes of argumentation and reasoning are a healthy corrective to the established academic discourses. Indeed, center-based scholars are themselves reconsidering the place of adversarial modes of argumentation that are not conducive to meaningful dialogue and ethical relations in intellectual engagement.

A case study I conducted on the writing of a scholar in Sri Lanka shows an even more complex negotiation of discourses in the RA genre (see Canagarajah 2000). The textual analysis following also exemplifies how we can conduct more complex studies in contrastive rhetoric, in light of the methodological and theoretical limitations identified in the previous section. I append to this chapter three texts on a similar subject by a single writer in the same genre (the RA). But they are written in two different languages (English and Tamil) and for three different audiences (in a local Tamil academic journal, in a local English academic journal, and in a Western English journal). I compare here only the introductions and the conclusions of the texts to analyze how the thesis is foregrounded. What is interesting to observe is the transformations in the three texts as the writer shuttles between discourses and contexts (see the appendix to chap. 3).

There are certain aspects of the form that are common to all three texts. In terms of Swales's moves, there is no niche created for the writer's thesis (move 2), no findings are announced (move 3/step 2), and the development of the argument is not delineated (move 3/step 3). But the structure of text 3 is relatively different from that of texts 1 and 2. There is a new component (not listed in Swales) that I call "mention of methodology." (Rather than reserving a separate section for the method, the writer makes a brief reference in the introduction itself.) There is also a tighter formulation of the "problem" in the announcement of the research (move 3/step 1b). The outline of the purpose of the paper is also more formal (move 3/step 1a). The writer is thus making a significant switch to the academically valued discourse (at least according to Swales's definition of it), as he is writing this paper for a mainstream Western publication. In writing to a local audience in texts 1 and 2, on the other hand, he sticks more closely to a more narrative, informal, indirect style of writing. What is more interesting behind this pattern is that texts 1 and 2 are in Tamil and English, respectively. Despite the linguistic difference, they are rhetorically similar. On the other hand, even though texts 2 and 3 are both in English, they are rhetorically dissimilar. This implies that language is not the important variable in this comparison. We cannot assume that each language has a distinct rhetorical pattern (as is done in some versions of CR). The equation $L1 = C1 = R1$; $L2 = C2 = R2$ doesn't seem to be valid. Moreover, this writer has two distinct rhetorics for the same language (his L2, English). He uses English in one way for the local readership and in another way for a Western readership. The latter two texts make us acknowledge the possibility that there may be plural forms/discourses for the same genre in the same language.

The tighter formulation of the problem in text 3 is important for another reason. From a chronological point of view, this paper was composed earlier than text 1. If the writer had clearly worked out the paradox behind his thesis in such a well-formulated way two years earlier, why did he fail to use this formulation in text 1, which was written later? It is certainly not because he cannot think in a context-free and abstract way or because his native language doesn't encourage this form of thinking (as some proponents of CR would put it). The more probable reason is that he doesn't wish to write this paper that way. It is the audience and the rhetorical context that motivate his choice, not inability (i.e., cognitive deficiency, cultural deficit, or linguistic handicap). In fact, text 2, which was written much earlier than the other texts, also suggests a relatively tighter formulation of the thesis as compared to text 1. Furthermore, in text 3 the concluding paragraph shows a better sense of closure to the argument than the more open-ended conclusions of texts 1 and 2. (In fact, the conclusion of text 1 in Tamil is a very personal statement to the readers, apologizing for any positions taken by the writer that may have hurt their feelings.) Moreover, text 3 presents a logically inferred conclusion—that is, that while the Saiva Tamil thinking has not lost its power in its interaction with the parallel strand of liberal Christian culture, the tension could considerably modify the nationalist ideology of the Tamil regime. This statement, clearly derived from the preceding analysis, suggests a linear organization for the essay. Why didn't the writer present a version of this statement in move 3/step 2, where the thesis typically occurs in English RAs? It is not because the writer didn't know this rule but because he didn't like the effect of a "front-weighted" thesis (see Mauranen 1993a). He prefers to let the readers form their own inferences and come to their conclusions with less control from the writer (following an end-weighted thesis).

All this shows the writer negotiating the form of text 3 in

his own way. He adopts some of the features of Swales's moves and ignores others. Certain other moves are realized differently at other places in the article (e.g., the announcement of findings may appear at the end of the article rather than at the beginning). In effect, this is a hybrid text that accommodates the values of divergent discourses and communities. Note also the influence of material constraints, which make the writer adopt unusual measures in certain cases. Although he mentions a few publications in text 1, he doesn't discuss them in text 3 to fulfill Swales's obligatory literature review. Sri Lankan scholars have told me that since they don't have complete access to publications, they choose not to discuss them at length. Because they cannot do a thorough literature review from their limited library resources, they sometimes consider it prudent not to talk about other studies at all. This is an avoidance strategy. The writer may still feel confident that this gap won't affect the value of the paper because publications on such remote communities are nonexistent in the research literature. The fact that this negotiated/hybrid text is not perceived as lacking coherence or focus is proven by the fact that it got published in a Western journal after the usual refereeing process.

The way in which this writer shuttles between different texts, languages, and cultures shows that multilingualism is a resource, not a handicap. As we begin to grant agency to multilingual writers, we must become sensitive to the different *strategies* used by students to negotiate the essay form in terms of their values and interests. We will take up this matter in the next chapter.

Conclusion

The preceding comparison is important for the many correctives it spells out to current pedagogical practices pertaining to form in ESOL writing. These are in fact the themes developed in the preceding sections as we orientated to both grammar and rhetorical structure.

Not all differences in L2 texts result from inability to meet the established rules of academic writing; in some, the writers may negotiate the conventions in their favor to construct creative new forms that suit their interests and preferences.

Not all differences occur because writers are blinded by their cultural peculiarity; in some cases the writers don't desire the dominant conventions because of other social and ideological considerations.

Not all differences in L2 texts can be explained purely according to a discursive or intratextual orientation; some of them need to be explained in terms of the writers' social and material life.

Writers are not trapped within their linguistic and cultural systems; they can shuttle confidently between different discursive and rhetorical contexts and construct multivocal texts that benefit from their multiple discursive backgrounds.

The linguistic/cultural differences of multilingual writers are a resource, not a handicap.

Grammar and textual form shouldn't then be treated as immutable structures that should be adopted slavishly. These are resources that need to be exploited to achieve one's rhetorical intentions and purposes. We should develop pedagogies that help students to critique and reconstruct these rules creatively.

Application

A. Analyzing Models from Creative Bilingual Writers

It is good to expose students to creative periphery writers who experiment with grammar and form in English writing to represent their own values and interests. It is good for ESOL students to know that there are celebrated "nonnative" writers who have not been stigmatized for their deviations from "standard" grammar. I have introduced Okara (Nigeria), Raja Rao and Rushdie (India), and Adisa, Bennet, and Walcott (the Caribbean islands) to show their divergent uses of the language. Following are questions on a poem by Walcott that offer suggestions to help develop a critical orientation to grammar. The poem *Saddhu of Couva* (see Walcott 1986, 372) is a remarkable cross-cultural experiment. Expressing the alienation of an Indian subject in the Caribbean, Walcott—a Black person—uses a dialect that reflects the thought patterns and idiom of an Indian.

Some questions for students
1. How many violations of standard English grammar do you observe in this poem?
2. Given that Walcott has many other poems in standard English, why would he do this in this poem?
3. Imagine this poem being written without these grammatical "errors." What would the poem have lost in its effect? What are the implications for the identity of the character and consciousness evoked in this poem?
4. Many readers become conscious of these grammatical eccentricities only when they are pointed out. To what extent does Walcott manage to fuse features of nonstandard items with conventional English syntax?
5. Many postcolonial writers simply implant a few lexical items from nonnative languages into standard English syntax to evoke the culture of their persona (e.g., Narayan, Achebe). We see in this poem that the "nonnativeness" is largely syntactical. How does Walcott's experimentation with language signify an advance from the practice of other writers?
6. There are many postcolonial writers who use nonstandard grammar for comical effect. When we realize that Walcott is using this dialect for a character he sympathizes with, and in a poem that gains a tragic dignity (as the character willingly goes to his death at the end of the poem, realizing his alienation from his

own people and their new habitation), what does this
show about Walcott's attitude to nonnative dialects?
7. Knowing that Walcott has won international respect
as a poet (including the Nobel Prize in 1996), how
does this example complicate our understanding of
social stigmas attached to the creative uses of grammar in one's writing?

B. Error Analysis and Discussion of Ideological Choices
To understand the "grammar" of the student essays we
get for grading, we can fill the following chart systemat-
ically throughout the semester so that we can understand
why students use certain peculiar structures. This activity will help us better explain the differences to our students. It will also help us understand the motivations for
these peculiarities. We may have to consult the student
in conferences or other scheduled interviews to fill the
fourth column—regarding their possible reasons for such
peculiar usages. While being open to ideological explanations, we must also identify structures that have been
inappropriately internalized. (Students can also be asked
to fill such a chart for the essays of a chosen peer.)

	"Error"	*Rule of the student*	*Rule of the system*	*Possible reasons for difference*
Student A				
Student B				
(And so on)				

C. Discerning Ideology in Form
It is easy to recognize ideological stances of writers from
the content of their writing (i.e., theme, views, opinions,
information, thesis). But it is harder to understand that
form or structure can also embody ideology. Although

this is somewhat abstract, form works in very subtle ways to reflect and represent ideological interests. We become sensitive to its ideologies only if we ask questions at a deeper level, beyond the surface structure. An interesting exercise is to read descriptions of available genres of disciplinary writing to explore what they include and what they leave out. After characterizing the main features of a specific genre, we should step back from the description to ask questions at a further level that explore the underlying assumptions of that form. Following, I suggest the type of questions that will lead us to discern ideological values in certain academic genres of writing.

Here is a summary of what Marcus and Fischer (1986) consider the valued genre features of a dominant version of ethnographic scholarly writing.

> Realist ethnographies are written to allude to a whole by means of parts or foci of analytical attention which constantly evoke a social and cultural totality. Close attention to detail and redundant demonstrations that the writer shared and experienced this whole other world are further aspects of realist writing. In fact, what gives the ethnographer authority and the text a pervasive sense of concrete reality is the writer's claim to represent a world as only one who has known it firsthand can, which thus forges an intimate link between ethnographic writing and fieldwork. (23)

Questions
1. What scope does the form have for the expression/exploration of the identity of the writer/scholar?
2. From what textual and genre features does the writer gain authority as a researcher/scholar? To what extent is scholarly authority rhetorically constructed? To what extent is it intrinsic to the scholar?

3. To what extent does the text encourage readers to adopt alternate interpretive positions?
4. What is the attitude to the real world? That is, is it independent of us? Is it easily knowable? Is it open to interpretation?
5. What attitude to knowledge is encouraged? Does the writer possess it? What gives authority to one's knowledge? What is acceptable evidence for one's conclusions?
6. To what extent does the *process* of research and knowledge production find expression in this genre of writing? Why are these aspects hidden?

Chapter 4

Issues of Self

Matters of grammar, structure, and form are usually addressed in relation to the end product of writing. But practicing and teaching writing with an eye on the final product is an incomplete, if not misdirected, activity. It is important to understand the processes that lead to the final shape of the written product. In some of the earliest research and theoretical endeavors heralding this shift of perspective, scholars considered the activity of the writer. Proceeding along this line, they narrowed down their perspective further to the operations of the mind of the writer. Now we know that there is much more to process than what goes on in the mind. The writer has to negotiate many social conflicts and material concerns while producing the text he or she desires. Still, the move made in our discipline to orientate to the cognitive, psychological, and affective dimensions of the writing self is very important. Therefore, we will consider some of the important insights generated from this line of inquiry before we critique and complicate this orientation with a critical pedagogical perspective. Even the orientation to the mind of the writer can be made more complex if we take into account material and social influences in the thinking process.

Cognitive and Expressive Process

Reacting rightly against a formulaic and detached production of the text, proponents of the "expressive process" approach emphasized the representation of one's "self" in writing. These scholars were influenced by Romantic notions of expression that valued spontaneity, originality, and authenticity.[1] Writers were urged to look for their "authentic voices" (as distinct from views and language demanded by society, tradition, or convention) and embody them in texts that were creative, personal, and sincere. The very process of writing could be a way of discovering one's "true" self. Some even went to the extent of saying that ignoring the audience and listening to the inner voice produced powerful writing (Elbow 1981). The perception of the differences between good and bad writers was that the former write with greater independence and originality, while the latter are complacent, uninvolved, and perhaps disingenuous.

This perspective on writing has commonsense appeal to all of us. This school didn't have to be developed through a research tradition or even complex theoretical articulations. It was developed from insights of practicing writers and teachers on what worked for them. The current arts section series of the *New York Times,* titled "Writers on Writing," presents many contemporary artists saying that they write because it has a cathartic, therapeutic, or spiritually liberating effect.[2] For some time, ESOL compositionists too found a personalized writing practice a useful corrective to the formulaic writing that often takes place in classrooms for the sole purpose of getting a grade. Writing as a "discovery of meaning" and "writing as thinking" became the catchy slogans of this period (see Spack 1984; Zamel 1982, 1983). Free writing, invention heuristics, and peer reviews were the valued pedagogical strategies to develop the creative set of behaviors that would lead to self-expression and self-realization in writing.

But a more scientific and research-based approach to the question of effective mental strategies is what came to be known as the "cognitive process" approach. Rather than insisting on how people *should* write (in the normative and prescriptive attitude that characterizes form-focused and expressive approaches), cognitive process scholars consider it more empirically and pedagogically useful to study how they *do* write. Description rather than prescription was the primary objective. Based on case studies using the think-aloud methodology, or other studies on pauses, revision strategies,

and protocol analysis in clinically controlled research settings, scholars attempted to find out how exactly the composing process took place. Early research in this tradition was
conducted by Emig (1971, 1983), Perl (1979), and Sommer
(1980) in the L1 pedagogical scene. Through these methods
they could arrive at the difference in the practice of skilled
and unskilled writers. They provided the profile of skilled
writers as moving to reader-focused writing, away from egocentric and text-based writings. They treated writing as a recursive, generative, goal-directed, interactive process.

Developing these research insights, Linda Flower and John
Hayes (1981) went on to formalize the composing process in
a disciplined way. Their model divides composing into three
major components: the writer's long-term memory, the composing processor, and the task environment. While the first
component provides the knowledge and information that go
into the text, the third deals with the surface-level manifesta-
tion of the thoughts in the text. Making the ideas coherent,
clear, and relevant takes place at this final stage. The middle
component—the composing processor—acts like the CPU of
a computer and reflects the deep structural activity that takes
place in the mind. This component is the site of three opera-
tional processes that generate the written text: planning,
translating, and reviewing. The model of Flower and Hayes,
with dynamic flowcharts and complexly integrated components, encapsulates the new realization that composing is a
nonlinear, recursive, generative activity.

Borrowing this paradigm from L1 writing research, and using a similar methodology, scholars in ESOL have studied the
writing strategies of students from other cultures. Ann
Raimes's (1985) study showed that the problems facing writers and the strategies they use to overcome them are very similar for both L1 and L2 unskilled writers. Unskilled students
of both groups focused on local problems such as correctness
of spelling, vocabulary, or sentence structure and lost sight of
the larger rhetorical purpose; they were "egocentric," writing
for their own understanding rather than for the reader; they
had a limited conception of the role of revision. Vivian Za-

mel's (1983) study on the strategies used by *skilled* L1 and L2 writers complements the finding of Raimes. She found that the reason they were skilled was simply because they had a more complex perspective on writing: they understood writing as a recursive, generative, exploratory activity.

Since this early research work, other studies have followed in the same tradition in ESOL circles. Tony Silva (1993) provides a useful review of this research knowledge. Though his objective is to show the differences in the composing process of ESL students, he states that the empirical studies confirm that the composing process is basically the same in both L1 and L2 writing.[3] The divergences are mostly found, according to Silva, in the "subprocesses of planning, transcribing, and reviewing" (Silva 1993, 661). The differences are summarized as follows.

> Though general composing process patterns are similar in L1 and L2, it is clear that L2 composing is more constrained, more difficult, and less effective. L2 writers did less planning (global and local) and had more difficulty with setting goals and generating and organizing material. Their transcribing was more laborious, less fluent, and less productive—perhaps reflecting a lack of lexical resources. They reviewed, reread, and reflected on their written texts less, revised more—but with more difficulty and were less able to revise intuitively (i.e., "by ear"). (Silva 1993, 668)

Though Silva is only reviewing other people's research, and refrains from making value judgements, it is important to question the framework of this comparison. It is clear that L2 writers are being measured against L1 writing—with the latter functioning as the implicit norm. The oft-used adverb "less" shows that the L2 writing practice is perceived as falling short in certain ways. When Silva goes on to discuss the instructional strategies suggested by this research, he argues that L2 students need more of everything: "it is likely that L2 writing teachers will need to devote more time and attention across the board to strategic, rhetorical, and linguistic concerns" (Silva 1993, 670). The instruction envisioned sounds remedial—making up for things ESOL students lack. It is interesting to consider how our attitudes toward multilingual writers would differ if we characterized ESOL writing as an activity of its own. In second language acquisition (SLA) circles, scholars have started criticizing what they call *the comparative fallacy*—the notion that L2 competence can be described only in relation to L1 or "native speakers" (see V. Cook 1999).[4]

Practitioners who study the L1/L2 comparative-research tradition on writing cannot be blamed if they derive the following generalizations from the literature:

> that there are universal cognitive strategies underlying the writing activity;
>
> that L2 writers who produce texts that are realized differently from the academic norms are unskilled;
>
> that L2 writers compose differently because they use wrong or limited strategies;
>
> that unskilled writers, to the extent that they use egocentric strategies, are immature and perhaps cognitively deficient;
>
> that if and when L2 writers fail to display the established composing strategies or products, this is due to deficiencies of their linguistic or cultural background.

In the sections to follow, we will complicate these widely held assumptions by situating the writing self in context.

Contextualizing Cognition

While the findings about basic cognitive strategies in the composing process and the desirable values in expressive process are valuable for pedagogical purposes, we must modify these constructs with an awareness of the social and material influences on writing. The problem with the orientation described earlier is that the interaction between the mind and language (or the mind and the text) in the composing process is perceived as an isolated activity. We adopt a more complex

perspective on the challenges facing the writer when we con-
textualize cognition. It is not hard to find psychological models, like Vygotsky's, that theorize a social cognition, constituting thinking strategies that intrinsically accommodate
social context into their workings. Compositionist Pat Bizzell
(1982) shows the influence of these models in her effort to
reinterpret the cognitive process in terms of the sociolinguistic challenges and community membership of nonmain-
stream students. Flower (Flower et al. 1990) too has made
some later attempts to accommodate context into her model.
Interestingly, the composing model is unaltered in its essen-
tials in these revisions. The strategies simply become more
difficult and complicated as they are made to process constraints from a context that is largely rhetorical in nature. The
skilled writers are able to employ a richer array of strategies
to constantly evaluate their goals in relation to the contextual
constraints, revise their goals and strategies, and shape the
composing process effectively to achieve their objectives. In
a sense, it is the same model that is reinterpreted now in terms
of constraints represented by the rhetorical context. But we
have to be open to the possibility that the writing process may
be radically altered in the face of the divergent contexts and
conditions confronting multilingual students.

Let's begin with the cultural context of multilingual writers. We must recognize that notions like personal expression,
originality, and authenticity (popularized by the expressive
school) assume a particular cultural orientation to the self. In
the more individualistic Western culture, the self is defined
as an autonomous entity. The "I" is distinct and separate from
the collective. Scollon (1991) states, however, that the "I" of
the Chinese students he taught in Taiwan included the "we."
Writers compose to affirm, consolidate, and enhance the
thinking and values of the community: "One is writing to pass
on what one has received" (Scollon 1991, 7). Similarly, a
scholar from mainland China who struggled with composing
in the United States talks of the new sense of self she had to
develop in order to write effectively here (see Shen 1989).
Flaunting the "I" in one's writing was dangerous in the con-

text of the Cultural Revolution, as authorities could take this as a subversive act of resisting the established ways of thinking. To celebrate the "I," or to develop thoughts and views in divergence from the community and its history, went against the preferred mode of writing. Therefore this scholar had to modulate the "I" in deference to the "we." Finnish scholars in the ESL profession have conveyed that writing that foregrounds the self too openly and directly is construed as tasteless in their culture (see Connor 1999; Mauranen 1993b). Though we have to be careful not to generalize these traits as true for all students from a particular culture, we should understand the challenges some from such cultures may face in negotiating the values of the expressive school.

Based on findings like those described earlier, Ulla Connor (1996) goes on to argue that in the context of academic writing "the expressionist approach to writing about oneself is not fruitful by itself" (74). Since advanced college-level writing requires exploration of academic subjects and not writing about oneself, she feels that this school doesn't have much relevance to ESOL writing. But I would argue that even in academic subjects, the expressive process has implications for developing a distinctive perspective and voice. I will demonstrate later that it is not always desirable to let the dominance of the "we" hold sway over writers. This sometimes turns out to be a manipulative claim made by undemocratic forces to suppress critical perspectives in the name of upholding community interests and cultural traditions. (On the other hand, we shouldn't go to the other extreme of endorsing the claim of Western compositionists who equate the realization of the American sense of "I" in their ESOL students to developing a radical/enlightened self that will resist the totalitarian cultures of their native communities.) What students should be encouraged to do is learn to negotiate the "I" and the "we" in their writing in a culturally sensitive way. How can students express their own perspectives in a style they feel comfortable with, challenging the received wisdom and unexamined assumptions of their community, while also displaying sufficient respect for their cultural values and norms? This is the project critical pedagogues have to consider. I will provide examples later.

Let's move on to consider how cultural differences may complicate the composing process. Scholars in CR point out that students from certain cultures relate differently to peer feedback on written drafts. Allaei and Connor (1990) find that East Asian students find it difficult to make negative comments on the drafts of their peers. Women, especially, have been claimed to be more affirmative and supportive in their comments rather than adopting an agonistic stance (Belcher 1997). Middle Eastern students are said to find it difficult to share their writing publicly, particularly if it is of a personal nature (Allaei and Connor 1990, 24). Such an attitude would prevent them from participating freely in peer-review activities. Moreover, divergent patterns of behavior in group activity will also have implications for composing. Carson and Nelson (1994) point out that Chinese students saw their roles as nurturers in collaborative interaction, whereas Spanish-speaking students perceived their stance as a critical one. This difference in attitudes will create conflicts in the ways in which both groups engage in peer reviewing and revising.

Furthermore, cultural factors may modify the extent to which writers personally engage in the writing process. There is evidence that students from certain cultures expect greater intervention from the teacher in the writing process and that they in fact profit from teacherly authority (see Radecki and Swales 1988). In such cases, the composing process of ESOL students may not be inner-directed. It thrives from external intervention. Leki (1991a) finds in her case study of ESOL students in EAP programs how some find it productive to follow certain formulaic methods of writing. Such generic forms provide a convenient heuristic to get their writing and cognitive tasks simplified. Students eventually find that they succeed in their academic tasks when they begin with such writing templates.

Whether a student would adopt the recursive/generative composing process would depend a lot also on the educational context in which writing takes place and the types of instruction the student has received. For example, in some in-stitutions teachers may teach process writing but have a prod-uct-oriented testing system. In my institution (CUNY) there has been a standardized test for basic writing for a long time. In what is known as the Writing Assessment Test (WAT), stu-dents have to write an in-class argumentative essay in fifty minutes on a previously unseen prompt. After failing two such tests, a student is dropped from college. In my ethno-graphic studies I find that this testing system creates a lot of conflicts for students (see Canagarajah 1999a). Though stu-dents are interested in adopting a generative writing process in the classroom, they lose motivation when they realize that they won't have the time to engage in elaborate brainstorm-ing, planning, drafting, and serial revision in the duration of the writing test. The pragmatic wisdom circulating among students is that those who can quickly draft five paragraphs on the prompt, with the expected thesis statement and topic sentences, with a minimum of grammatical and spelling prob-lems, pass the test. Those who attempt to be complex and orig-inal fail, as they don't have sufficient time to achieve their ob-jectives. Students therefore resist a recursive/exploratory writing process and adopt a formulaic approach. They also pressure teachers to adopt a form-based writing pedagogy in the classroom. In such cases, rather than stigmatizing ESOL students as adopting limited strategies, we should analyze the "wash-back effect" from testing policies and institutional re-quirements.[5]

We have to also consider the implications of the writing as-signments given in a class to inquire whether or not students would use a process approach. Consider the uninspiring con-ventions in the staple genre of essay writing in many class-room contexts: the teacher is the sole audience for the writ-ing; the topics are largely knowledge displaying rather than knowledge producing; the sole purpose of these essays is the earning of a grade; the grade is usually based more on form than content. Classroom essays are thus a genre of their own—different from the more communicative and functional genres of academic and/or nonacademic writing in the "real-world."

context. Classroom writing can militate against the practice of process strategies, as students don't feel encouraged to discover meaning, develop original ideas, or express themselves in a noncommunicative genre of writing.

Furthermore, we have to take into account the previous writing instruction students bring with them when we analyze their divergent writing practices. In some educational institutions these students have been taught a product-oriented writing approach for culturally sensible reasons. Comparing the writing of Chinese students in British Columbia and that of those from mainland China, Mohan and Lo (1985) find that the latter adopt a product-oriented approach because they have received that instruction in their country. Despite their ethnic similarity, their educational background accounted for their divergent writing practices. It is easy to guess the reasons for the differences in the writing pedagogies in these countries. Leki (1995) reports a bizarre turn of events for a graduate student from China. Yang adopted process writing under an American professor teaching in China. But when he went to a university in Zimbabwe for two years after that, he was expected to write in a product-oriented fashion "because they said you put in too much of your own ideas. We're not interested in your ideas. Your ideas are not authoritative. That's what they said to me. So they said, you must quote, basically, you quote and you cite the author. So I thought I learned that lesson" (quoted in Leki 1995, 246). Later, when Yang moved to the United States, he found that he was again a failure: "I quoted a lot and I mentioned a lot of authors' ideas and their points and I didn't put in much of my own. I wasn't critical, not much criticism, not much comments. So that wasn't a good paper here. They have very different requirements" (quoted in Leki 1995, 247). Yang had to switch between product and process writing in deference to the changing pedagogical cultures of the different countries he visited.

The least conspicuous of the contextual influences on the cognitive process is also the most recalcitrant in the writing activity—material context. The ways in which economic resources, technological facilities, and geographical background shape writing are clear from research in less developed communities. Since the basic material resources that facilitate writing (i.e., pen, paper, word processor, printer, etc.) are taken for granted in the West, mainstream composition scholars bracket them off in their theorization of writing. In my ethnographic observation of how Sri Lankan scholars write, however, I found many striking differences in the composing process caused by economic and technological deprivation (see Canagarajah in press). In a context of prolonged civil war, these writers don't have the free space or time to engage intensely in the composing process. Their rhetorical plans—global and local—have to be constantly revised as they have to temporarily halt their writing, forced to struggle with the problems of finding cash and food for their families. They have to start afresh each time there is some respite from the fighting in the region. Sometimes they forget their earlier train of thought or develop new perspectives that make them revise their plans. It is also difficult for them to generate and organize reference material because they don't have complete access to the books they need for their projects. Furthermore, their transcribing process is more laborious, time consuming, and intermittent. They simply don't get the free stretch of time to sustain their writing activity or to approach their task with a calm and collected mind. Since the unsettled political context requires people to be constantly alert to dangers from the fighting, to flee from the advancing battle zones, and to work in more than one job in order to survive the economic hardships, the first draft is often the final product for local scholars (assuming that they can fully complete even this). Writers also inevitably suppress the desire to revise and produce multiple drafts. The difficulties in obtaining writing paper force them to make grammatical or typographical corrections in the copy text of the first draft itself. It is possible that these writing practices, developed under pressure from everyday living conditions, then become habitual. Both readers and writers in the periphery develop literacy practices shaped by the conditions existing in their communities. Though literate communication may take place smoothly between them as they become attuned to these exigencies, these practices will confuse outsiders and result in periphery scholars' denigration.

Of course, contextual influences don't always have to be limiting. Sometimes they can be enabling for the composing process. Prior (1998) talks of how the composing process is significantly influenced by everyday happenings—that is, casual conversations, social activities, and other communicative events. He narrates how Lilah, a graduate student in sociology, finds new impetus and critical directions for her research from attending international festivals, eating in restaurants, and watching television documentaries. Similarly, Prior himself finds that a game played by his wife and daughter generated models for his own research and writing. These examples suggest that ideas don't arise by themselves in the mind of the writer or from memory (as posited in the Flower-Hayes [1981] composing model). Everyday experiences and material conditions shape the composing process in dynamic ways in diverse stages of the writing. My intention here is not to reject the contributions of the cognitive and expressive process schools; I find it necessary to consider how contextual forces may complicate the writing process in both beneficial and limiting ways.

Critical Thinking in Academic Writing

While it is important to characterize the thinking process in more complex terms, teachers have to also explore how they can encourage students to think critically as they write. Before I discuss how critical thinking is defined by a liberatory pedagogy, it is important to realize that there are different schools that undertake to inculcate such thinking processes in the educational context. Since many divergent approaches to critical thinking are usually lumped under the critical pedagogy umbrella, this has recently resulted in needless debate in TESOL circles.

Among some scholars, critical thinking has become a cliché for simply independent thinking. Consider this quotation from an altogether unexpected compositionist to be using this notion—Linda Flower.

> But what is important in college is not the apparent genre or conventions, but the goals. The goals of self-directed critical inquiry, of using writing to think though genuine problems and issues, and of writing to an imagined community of peers with a personal rhetorical purpose—these distinguish academic writing from a more limited comprehension and response. (Flower et al. 1990, 251)

What does Flower mean by critical inquiry? Her statement suggests that it comprises self-directed inquiry, problem-solving strategies, and personal argumentative stances—all of which add up to what is usually promoted as independent, original, authentic writing in the process model. Many composition teachers in ESOL do understand critical thinking this way.

Another tradition of critical thinking encourages processes of rational thinking and everyday argumentation under this label. The scholars Dwight Atkinson, Bob Kaplan, and Vai Ramanathan have published a series of articles critiquing this tradition of critical thinking. After examining fifteen textbooks that implement thinking approaches in freshman composition courses, Ramanathan and Kaplan (1996) outline the channels through which ESOL student writers are inducted into critical thinking. The channels are: "1) developing students' sense of informal logic toward strengthening their reasoning strategies; 2) developing and refining problem-solving skills; 3) developing the ability to look for hidden assumptions and fallacies in arguments" (226). They rightly point out that the reasoning strategies, problem-solving skills, and argumentation processes are largely male, Eurocentric, middle-class-oriented "social practice" (Atkinson 1997, 73). This perspective is theoretically well motivated. The scholars clarify that thinking skills are not mentally isolated or culturally neutral. Thinking skills are socially shaped and, therefore, community specific. But then they adopt two problematic moves in their argumentation that are more controversial: (1) they associate this orientation of critical thinking with practitioners of critical pedagogy; (2) assuming that this form of critical thinking is culturally alien (and therefore difficult) for multilingual students, they recommend that this type of pedagogy is uncongenial for ESOL composition pedagogy.[6]

A closer look at critical practitioners such as Freire (1985), Giroux (1992), and others shows us that what they assume to be critical thinking is different from the practices described by Atkinson, Kaplan, and Ramanathan. (I am referring here to the school described by the latter scholars and not to their own position.) Compare the orientation of adherents of critical practice (CP) with that of ESOL scholars and textbook publishers of critical thinking (CT).

CT version	CP version
monological thinking	dialogical thinking
asocial/mentalistic	socially grounded
objective/instrumental	self-reflexive
dispassionate	ethical
neutral	politically engaged
rationalistic	multimodal
universal/transcendental	context bound
leads to understanding	leads to social change

In CP, thinking is shaped by the historical experiences and social positioning of the subject. In fact, the life experience of the student may generate critical insights into issues without someone else having to teach critical thinking. Such thinking continues dialectically, by being corrected and consolidated by the student's everyday life. In CT, the thinking is divorced from social positioning, as teachers introduce reasoning strategies and skills seemingly in an armchair approach to thinking. Furthermore, the orientation of CP demands that the subject be always reflexive about the ways his or her thinking is shaped by values, open to the possible biases in his or her approach, and ready to conduct a self-criticism. CT, however, encourages an objective and detached approach where self-consciousness may only distort the clarity demanded for thinking. Moreover, CP is dialogical in that it encourages students to interrogate thinking in relation to material life, engage with their own biases, and negotiate alternate perspectives on the subject. In CT this sense of multidirectionality is missing, as students apply straightforward linear lines of reasoning to the problem. In the same vein, for CP, thinking cannot be divorced from ethical considerations of justice, fair play, egalitarianism, and inclusiveness. Thinking is also married to practical struggles for social change and political reform. This engagement considerably shapes the tenor of thinking and provides deeper insights into experience. CT may see such social activism as extraneous to (or even distorting) the thinking process. Finally, just as action interacts with thinking, there are other channels of critical thinking that CP acknowledges. Passion, imagination, art, fantasy, and even popular culture mesh in complex ways to enhance critical thinking (see Giroux 1992; Grossberg 1994). CP theorists resist the glorification of detached rational thinking.

Let's consider a simple example of how critical thinking may be taught according to the CP version in classrooms. We must note first that CP scholars would go a step beyond the typical questions posed in the CT pedagogy. CT may ask: "What reasons/arguments are offered by the writer to present his or her position? What problems do you see in this line of reasoning? Would you adopt a different position based on your own evidence/reasoning?" CP will proceed to another level of inquiry (to a higher order or secondary plane of questions): "What makes this writer adopt this line of thinking? What are the interests served for the writer in making these claims? What in his or her social positioning explains the way this argument is made? What in your social status and experience makes you relate to this subject differently? What are the other perspectives/angles on this subject? Which position provides greater scope for furthering the interests of the widest group of people? How may your spontaneous/immediate response to this argument display biases that favor your personal interests (or the interests of the dominant groups)?"

We have to ask if modes of critical thinking are partisan to a specific social group. This is not necessarily the case. This is not to deny that the detached rationalist thinking of CT is valorized and nurtured by particular social groups. Atkinson (1997) argues that this mode of thinking is predicated on notions of individuals as primary and autonomous units, self-expression as a celebration of the ego, and language as the primary medium for the thinking process. Sociolinguistic studies have demonstrated that middle-class (Bernstein 1971), Anglo-American (Heath 1983), and male (Tannen 1986) subjects practice this form of thinking more typically. But, even here, we mustn't deny the agency of subjects to cross discourse boundaries and engage in alternate ways of thinking, though this may not be the preferred or socially practiced form of thinking for them.

However, in the CP tradition, as I have defined it earlier, scholars acknowledge diverse channels for critical thinking. Some critical insights may not find verbalization at all. Schenke (1991) brings out the most paradoxical possibility when she illustrates how even silence can embody oppositional thinking. With ESOL students who have gone through traumatic experiences, she employs channels of empathy and affect to tap their memories for the development of critical insights. In fact, everyone has critical and oppositional insights into social reality—even without the prompting of teachers. The very contradictions in social reality are sufficient to introduce critical reflection based on everyday experience. The least-educated peasants in remote rural communities display critical perspectives on their context, even though they don't verbalize them openly for fear of retribution (see Scott 1990). There are of course differences in the extent to which subjects may make their critical insights more or less explicit, more or less ideologically sophisticated, more or less collectively sustained for social change. Often the articulation of critical thinking is prevented by the status quo, which has vested interests in enforcing the existing version of reality and using institutions like schools and the media to present a partisan worldview. Culture, in general, can sometimes be a repressive

force to distort critical insights that expose issues of inequality and injustice (Williams 1977). This is where the role of
teachers and socially conscious intellectuals begins. They tap
the intuitive oppositional thinking of ordinary people to build
a critical awareness. Even here, critical practitioners are quick
to insist that this teaching activity has to be reciprocal. Intellectuals should continue to critically examine their own biases in relation to the experiences of students, prepared to revise their assumptions and values based on this encounter.
Critical thinking is thus an ongoing activity; no one achieves
a culminating stage of perfection. In this manner, CP also
takes care of another criticism—that teaching critical thinking is an imperialistic endeavor. Critical practice is a hum-
bling educational process for the teacher and learner, or the
enlightened and the dominated, as they negotiate their differences and learn from each other, based on their differing
social experiences.

To argue, therefore, that it is difficult for certain communities to think critically is to stereotype them and belittle their
complex humanity. This is additionally a deterministic orientation, as everyone has agency to rise above their culture and
social conditions to attain critical insights into their human
condition. In fact, it is precisely because critical thinking is social practice that we cannot elevate it as the special preserve of
one cultural group or the other. If it is a special intellectual
property that one is born with, or if it is a mode of thinking endowed by one's language or culture, then critical thinking is an
exclusive activity. Since critical thinking arises through one's
engagement in the conflicts and contradictions in social life,
there is the possibility of achieving a reflexive understanding
of one's positioning (albeit sometimes only intuitively).

All this is not to deny that there are special questions relating to the expression of critical thinking in educational
contexts. There has been some debate among Australian critical pedagogues about whether critical literacy instruction
should begin before or after the introduction of the target language and dominant genres. In arguing that this should pre-
cede critical literacy instruction, Hammond and Macket-

Horarick (1999) memorably state that ESOL students cannot be expected to run before they can walk (531). But we should note that since critical thinking is not always implicated in language, students may already come with critical insights before learning the L2. To give an example of how such thinking may take place through other means (i.e., without the means of a language and even without instruction from the teacher), let me give an example from an ethnography I have reported elsewhere (Canagarajah 1993). In an English for general purposes (EGP) course in a Sri Lankan classroom, I discovered some graffiti in the American textbooks used in the course. The scribbles, etchings, and other marginalia showed satire, parody, criticism, and wit. Through these, the students were adopting a critical stance on the discourses and narratives of the textbook. For example, when Bruce moves into a higher-paying job in his quick rise up the social ladder, purchasing also a new car and a new house and then marrying again (in unit 4a), a student has written the vernacular proverb "New footwear hurts" in the margin. The comment implies that novelty, success, and material gain are not always pleasant. In a sense, the student is sarcastically detaching him- or herself from the typical American success story. In other textbooks, Bruce and his wife have been altered to wear horns or appear like animals. The paintings are supposed to ridicule their life of material and sensual pleasures. There are many other similar symbols and motifs that comment sarcastically on the characters and events represented in the textbook. Students already come with these oppositional perspectives; in teaching new languages and literacies to students we are only providing new frames/contexts where their critical thinking can find expression. Of course, these additional discourses will help develop their thinking in new directions as well. But one doesn't wait to acquire a genre of language and discourse to begin thinking critically.

It has also been proposed by the critics of CT that cognitive apprenticeship is the most effective way of teaching critical thinking (see Atkinson 1997). They argue that situated learning in high-context, high-interest texts, characterized by an expert-novice relationship, assures a culture-neutral model of cognitive development. However, discipline-specific writing instruction is by no means pan-cultural or culture-universal. The academy in general, and disciplinary groups in particular, have their own cultural biases. They are also aligned with dominant social groupings and implicated in power. There are studies that describe how academic communities (see Hess 1995) and academic knowledge (see Canagarajah 1996) are constituted in partisan ways. This mode of instruction therefore doesn't offer an "easier" induction into critical thinking. Students will still face the need to interrogate knowledge, as they will do in other domains of life, in order to attain a critical perspective. I will offer in the next chapter some ways in which students may interrogate academic knowledge.

Toward a More Complex Writing Self

To discuss cognitive strategies and critical thinking in the way defined by the dominant composition models is to treat thinking as a disembodied activity. To orientate to these activities as socially situated (as I have argued in the previous section) is to frame issues of the writer in terms of "self" or "subjectivity" (which I will define quickly). But first note that even the dominant schools come with an implicit notion of the selfhood of the writer. The cognitive process model assumes a transcendental consciousness that stands outside and above material constructs like language, culture, society, and texts to generate discourse according to the self-defined rhetorical goals of the writer. We are also presented a coherent and unified self that is in control of the writing activity. The emphasis on rhetorical goals and problem-solving strategies also posits a rational self that can achieve its objectives with proper planning, calculation, and discipline. Moreover, the self in cognitive models is largely abstract and idealized. It doesn't reflect the particularity, uniqueness, and diversity deriving from the social identities or institutional roles that one takes up.

If cognitive process assumes a transcendental/universal writing self, the expressive school imposes on the writer values and identities belonging to a specific cultural tradition. It is influenced by such Romantic and humanistic ideals as integrity, sincerity, and originality in its orientation to the self. Consider how Rohman's (1965) definition of "good writing" assumes a specific persona.

> That discovered combination of words . . . allows a person the integrity to dominate his subject with a pattern both fresh and original. "Bad writing," then, is an echo of someone else's combination which we have merely taken over for the occasion of our writing. . . . "Good writing" must be the discovery by a responsible person of his uniqueness within his subject. (107–8)

There is an indifference here to the relativistic nature of such criteria as "integrity," "fresh," "original," and "uniqueness." These constructs have to be realized in relation to diverse social conditions. Also, these notions mean different things in different institutions and discourses. Each community has its own conventions of what it means to be original or unique. These notions also change historically. Moreover, notions such as "originality" are intertextual; they can be defined only in relation to the other texts in a particular community. So what is original, fresh, and unique are texts that provide an individual realization of the existing conventions of the community. Furthermore, this school assumes that there is an authentic identity established for each of us, probably innately. This is why bad writing means taking on an identity that doesn't belong to oneself. The theory is also informed by an image of people as "individuals" separated from community and possessing their own "voices." There is the assumption of a self that can shape language and texts in the manner it pleases without being constrained by the codes the individual is allowed to acquire according to his or her position in society.

In order to represent themselves effectively in writing, mul-

tilingual students may not only lack an adequate understanding of the existing texts and conventions of the Anglo-
American academic community but also bring an ethos constituted by the texts and conventions of other communities. It
is not sufficiently appreciated by the process models that multilingual students have to negotiate with competing discourses and communities to define a favorable self in their
writing.

Negotiating Selves

Contemporary social philosophies have helped develop a
more complex understanding of the self. The following assumptions—deriving from schools like poststructuralism,
postcolonialism, social constructionism, and feminism—are
now widely shared in scholarly circles.[7]

The self is shaped considerably by language and discourses.

The self is composed of multiple subjectivities, deriving
from the heterogeneous codes, registers, and discourses
that are found in society.

These subjectivities enjoy unequal status and power, deriving from differential positioning in socioeconomic
terms.

Because of these inequalities, there is conflict within and
between subjects.

In order to find coherence and empowerment, the subject
has to negotiate these competing identities and subject
positions.

Therefore selves are not immutable or innate—they are reconstructed and reconstituted in relation to changing
discursive and material contexts.

With this more dynamic and complex understanding of the
self, we have also inherited a profusion of terms to describe
selfhood. This derives partly from the different schools theorizing the human subject and partly from the different psy-

chological dimensions and social domains that shape self-hood. I provide the framework in figure 4 to clarify the constructs that constitute the self.[8]

Identity	*Role*	*Subjectivity*	*Voice*
historical continuity	social variability	ideological positioning	rhetorical construction
principal	animator	imitator	author
racial/ethnic/national	institutional	discoursal	linguistic

Fig. 4. Distinguishing the constructs of the self

Though the linguistically based nature of the latter two constructs (subjectivity and voice) is fairly clear, it may appear that the other two constructs (identity and role) are extralinguistic. But even our historically defined identities (e.g., race, ethnicity, and nationality) and institutional roles (e.g., student, teacher, and administrator in the educational institution) are represented and constructed through language. I leave open the possibility that these social and historical domains may have an extradiscursive life as well. The third construct, subjectivity, refers to the constitution of our self according to discourses such as "responsible citizen/lazy immigrant/dependent foreigner" or "authoritative native speaker/fumbling nonnative speaker," which embody values according to the prevailing ideologies in the society. These three constructs (identity, role, and subjectivity) can be imposed on us or ascribed to us. But things don't have to be that deterministic. It is at the level of voice that we gain agency to negotiate these categories of the self, adopt a reflexive awareness of them, and find forms of coherence and power that suit our interests. The progression in these constructs from more macrosocial categories to microsocial dimensions of the representation of the self is significant. It is at the microsocial level of everyday consciousness and interactions through language that one is able to resist, modify, or negotiate the larger social structures. Language is especially suited for this function as its heterogeneity, hybridity, and polyvalence provide the resources for subjects to resist impositions of any kind.

This interplay between different dimensions of the self has considerable implications for writing. We mustn't fail to note that writing itself is a linguistic activity that shapes the self in complicated ways. We textually construct images of the self that appeal to us. Consider the following essay by Irina—an ESOL student from Ukraine—to appreciate the conflicts and negotiations taking place in the writing self. This is an end-of-term reflective essay titled by her as "My Experience with ESL at X College" (mistakes are as in the original).

When I first faced the WAT in August I spoke English good enough to communicate in. But I did not know how to write a good essay. That is not that I could not write or I did not know the letters, that is just I did not know much about the structure and developing of the American essay. So, I decided: "I should take the ESL class." Obviously, I did not pass my first WAT.

On the first day in my ESL class I understood that I was in a right place. In a first time I got to know that each essay is suppose to have thesis statement, which consist the main idea of the essay. To my surprise, I've got to know that thesis statement is not the last thing that we have in the essay. Also, there are a few paragraphs accompanied by topic sentences. And I have to tell those knowledge were amazing and useful to achieve. It may sound silly that someone who is an adult doesn't know simple things about writing. But I really did not know, just because in Ukraine we do not write in same way as we do here.

After I started write essays as I was taught in America I found that writing was not simple. I had to keep things relevant to each other, prove my thesis statement and given reasons. Thus, the second thing what I understood that I had to read a lot in order to gain a lot of information, examples, ideas (about different topics) which would help me to write my essays. I started paying more attention to what I was listening in the news, reading in newspapers and watching in T.V. In a few weeks later I knew pretty much about private life of selebraties, ruling of American governmen, rate of abortions in U.S., percentage of divorces in NY, level of medical treatment of eldery people and a lot more.

My next and important step was to utilize gathered information in my essays. Successfully or not, it is up to the teacher to grade my work, but I really tryed to do my best.

Moreover, a group work, which was provided by the teacher, helped me to understand meaning of the given passages, which sometimes were very confusing. Also, from group work I obtained a lot of different ideas and opinions.

Besides, I've made so many friends in my ESL class that I do not have in any other classes. I care about everybody in my ESL group as they are my own sisters and brothers.

I would say that everybody who feels like to get some knowledge in writing should attend ESL classes. This is the only class where you can get an answer on any questions that you have about writing, also, individual help from a teacher, which you can hardly expect in regular English classes. I was fully satisfied with my ESL class.

At the level of **identity,** we see in the writer a conflict between the Ukrainian and the American. Irina evokes her Ukrainian identity to explain why she didn't know the American conventions of essay writing. From that past identity, there is a progression in acquiring a new identity as a person who is knowledgeable about American culture and lifestyle. It is interesting that Irina doesn't present the Ukrainian style of writing as valid in its own right. The assumption is that the American style of writing should be known by everyone—hence her apology for not knowing these constructs even though she's an adult.

In representing this progression, Irina adopts the "good student" **role.** She represents herself as a student who is highly motivated for learning English and writing—someone who is prepared to do hard work, appreciates the course, and benefits from the instructor and her fellow students. In a course that is graded, where the teacher is the primary audience for one's writing, it is to be expected that Irina will find this role advantageous to her. In deploying these roles and identities somewhat consciously, Irina unwittingly takes on other **subjectivities** valued in this community. For example, she takes on the ethos of a person who succeeds through hard work. Of course, this is the dominant liberal democratic ideology of individualism—so different from the traditional Marxist ideology of collective empowerment that has been stereotypically associated with the former Soviet Russia (where Irina comes from). She also seems to invoke the "multiculturalist discourse" that is popular in American academia. She is happy to have interacted with culturally diverse students—whom she considers "my own sisters and brothers."

What is more important is the way Irina negotiates these roles, identities, and subjectivities to construct a **voice** for herself in the essay. Irina chooses to accommodate the dominant discourses and institutions in order to get approval and respect from the instructor. It is understandable that since this course is graded, Irina is under compulsion to satisfy the dominant discourses and institutions. In the process, she fails to resolve some of the tensions in her text. Though she adopts the multiculturalism discourse in showing respect for students from other cultures, she doesn't seem to develop a respect for her native Ukrainian discourses and styles. She is also diffident about claiming success in her education, as she hedges tentatively: "Successfully or not, it is up to the teacher to grade my work, but I really tried to do my best." Despite the grammar problems, she constructs a decent set of paragraphs to claim a voice for herself. One can only imagine how a more creative and independent voice could have been constructed if she had wrestled with the competing discourses more directly. It would have made a difference to the essay if she had attempted to incorporate more actively her Ukrainian identity and negotiated her English writing with her native discourses. After all, instructors are more impressed with writing that comes out of a more rigorous and frank engagement with one's conflicting selves. Though Irina knows this (having associated herself with this instructor for a whole semester), the product-oriented final-examination system in this institution (graded by unknown instructors) pressures her to adopt the safe approach of representing the dominant notions of the self in the academic context.

To illustrate more effective ways of negotiating such tensions, we have to go to the professional writing of multilingual scholars who are under less institutional pressure to conform than are students categorized as remedial. Xiao-Ming Li (1999) narrates how she has struggled with her outsider status in English all her educational life. Though she has reached the position of being published in academic and journalistic circles in English, she still considers herself "nonnative" in English literacy. But she has now matured to the position of looking at this tension as an advantage. She considers her nonnativeness as providing her a critical vantage position, just as her English educational background provides her unique insights into her native Chinese language and culture. She states: "To honor one's own voice is both liberating and challenging. Each writing becomes an exploration of the world and self, and a constant wrestling with words to go beyond the ready and given. Yet the process is complicated by the fact that I am still a language learner and imitation is part of learning a new language. . . . But being a non-native speaker, I have learned, does give me the license to march to a different drum, to some extent" (Li 1999, 50). One might interpret the negotiation of her selves in the following way: though she has conflicting **identities** (Chinese and English), the **role** she has had to play in American educational institutions as a successful and persevering student has motivated her to develop an alternate **voice.** In the process, she has also developed a critically informed **subjectivity**—one that is mutually detached from both Chinese ideologies and American discourses. Unlike Irina, who suppresses these tensions, Li confronts them frankly and constructs a voice that benefits from her disadvantage, lack of proficiency, and alienation in the English-speaking academic context.

In a sense, the position articulated by Li is what is theorized by Kramsch and Lam (1999) as the "third position" of textual identities: "the potential of written text to help non-native speakers define their relation toward the native speakers whose language they are using and to offer them what we [call] 'textual identities of the third kind'" (70–71). Considering the writing of advanced/professional writers in other languages, Kramsch and Lam discern the power they experience in creating alternate textual identities to resolve the conflicts they face in the native and foreign languages: "Written texts offer non-native speakers opportunities for finding textual homes outside the boundaries of local or national communities. . . . Indeed they make non-nativeness in the sense of 'outsideness' one of the most important criteria for creativity and innovation" (71). It is easy to understand how writing can create a safe haven from the identity conflicts experienced in society in everyday life. Not engaged in face-to-face communication, writers have the detachment and relative freedom to construct (sometimes playfully) alternate identities to transcend the conflicts they experience in social life. Asking my ESOL students in a study on writing about their attitudes to writing compared to speaking in English, they said that they all preferred writing (see Canagarajah 1999a). Among the reasons they gave were the following.

> Their speech accent (which drew attention to their nonnativeness) was not foregrounded in their writing.
> Lacking the need to be spontaneous, they had the freedom to plan and craft the text in the ways they desired.
> Writing gave more scope for control in communication (i.e., they could choose to submit or destroy the text they had produced).
> As the agent was somewhat detached from the text (unlike in face-to-face oral communication), they could try out alternate identities playfully without the need to tie themselves rigidly to ascribed ethnic/racial/national identities.
> Writing gave more scope for collaboration and help in text construction, unlike speech, which was more individual.

Multilingual students thus recognize that writing provides some interesting avenues and resources for the construction of a more empowering sense of self.

We mustn't forget that the outcome of discursive negotiation depends on the motivations and interests of each writer. Therefore not everyone resolves the conflict in the way Li does—even if they have the linguistic competence to do so. Ulla Connor (1999), reflecting on her bilingual writing experience, finds that she has quite deliberately moved from her Finnish identity to a distinctly American identity. Finnish identity is associated with restraint and reserve, while she experiences American writing as more aggressive and individualistic. After struggling to gain such a voice, aided by editorial help from her American husband, she discovers during a furlough in her native Finland that she has indeed become very Americanized. Her Finnish colleagues discern the distance she has traveled during her writing experience away from home. Connor concludes her article by saying that she decided soon after that experience to get American citizenship. What her experience shows is the reverse situation of the examples discussed earlier. Rather than national identity shaping voice, the newly acquired voice imputes a nationality. This is a testament to the power of discourses in shaping social identities. Connor's experience is important for another reason. We see an ESOL scholar accommodating the "nonnative" identity quite willingly, without displaying much tension or conflict.

What makes Connor different from Li has to be explained in terms of motivations and interests. Being married to an American and having a son born here in the United States, Connor has greater motivation in adapting to life in the United States. Coming from a European nation that shares other cultural/historical connections with the United States, and sharing the skin color of the country's dominant group, her transition is relatively smooth. But Li is physiognomically different, and she cannot escape her ethnic/race identity easily. The far greater cultural differences between Chinese and American communities would also create deeper conflicts for shifting to an American identity or voice. Therefore, Li negotiates a voice and subjectivity that strategically resolve these conflicts in a way that is advantageous to her.

In order to develop a taxonomy of strategies multilingual writers may employ to negotiate the subjective conflicts they face in writing, we may label the strategies discussed earlier as follows:

1. Avoidance. This strategy is adopted by Irina as she chooses not to engage with the conflicting identities from her Ukrainian and American communities or to foreground them in her writing.
2. Accommodation. This strategy is exemplified by Connor as she resolves her conflicts in favor of adopting a voice and identity influenced by American discourses and re-strains her native Finnish.
3. Transposition. This strategy is articulated by Li, and Kramsch and Lam, as adopting a voice that defines it-self dialectically by working against the conflicting dis-courses.

We must add to this list a few other ways of negotiating identity conflicts in writing. Some students may directly re-sist the established discourses in order to adopt a clearly ver-nacular-based voice. In a case study on theses written for postgraduate degrees by Sri Lankan teachers, I found Sri's writing exemplifying this strategy (see Canagarajah 1999c). Sri shared the Hindu religious background of a traditionally monolingual family. In a community that was going through a nationalistic struggle for self-determination, Sri valued the Tamil ethnic identity. Ideologically, he was at home in a sub-jectivity influenced by discourses of linguistic and cultural purism. Sri therefore adopted the role of "radical student"— a person who questions the institution and defines himself as different. A voice shaped by the vernacular discourses was appropriate for this purpose. In a case study on the writing pedagogy in his school, Sri writes:

Whenever I ask to write a composition on one of the given topics, only the very same students write, but even then, they too never speak or utter sentences in English. From my observations they feel shy, hesitation in pronouncing words in English. [They feel] others might laugh at me, etc. This creates problem in the language classrooms. Only some students volunteer to read a passage or answers written by them. There are some students who perform well, who have a good family background. . . . Making meaning in the actual context is also a problem to many students. At least I could conclude, from the interviews, questionnaires, and observations most of the students (I am not ashamed to say even the teachers, including myself) need much attention not only in the field of writing English but also in the fields of listening, speaking and reading, in order to acquire or learn and master the language. (38–39)

There is a relaxed conversational tone as Sri narrates his classroom experience. There is little attempt to document his observations or to authenticate their veracity. In the final sentence there is a surprising personal interjection that is honest in its appraisal. Also, the reference to other skills in a study dedicated to writing seems to be a deviation. But such is his discursive background that the writer feels comfortable about commenting on many things in his teaching experience as he goes along with his narration. These rhetorical features are acceptable in the vernacular academic discourse. Sri is also frank in using a creolized form of local English with its own grammar rules. To sum up, though there is some negotiation in textualizing the strengths of vernacular discourses in an alien language, and claiming an identity that goes against the dominant discourses in this genre of academic writing, the voice lacks complexity. Sri adopts the vernacular one-sidedly, without creatively making a place for this voice in this unusual genre. I label this strategy *opposition* and distinguish it from *appropriation* (a more synthetic and dialogical strategy of negotiating a space for one's vernacular-based voice in the established mainstream discourses).[9]

bell hooks (1989) demonstrates how a more dialogical voice of "talking back" would sound. Her book of that title uses street speech, vernacular idioms, narratives, anecdotes, and verbal play in an argumentation that is addressed to the mainstream scholarly community. Of course, she is informed by the constructs and discourses generated in academic contexts. But she pushes the conventions of citations and documentation to the endnote, so that the vernacular voice will receive greater prominence. What hooks does is to appropriate the academic discourses for her purposes. Motivated by the desire to present an African American ethnic identity and oppositional ideological subjectivity, inspired by the need to expand the academic discourse and ensure a democratic inclusion of other knowledge-making practices, she adopts a double voice. While being distinctively Black, the voice shows modifications deriving from a negotiation of the established discourses for this academic genre. hooks talks as a person knowledgeable about the academic discourses, but as one who strategically resists them and infuses them with her vernacular rhetorical values. We may call this strategy appropriation—the act of taking over dominant discourses and using them for one's own agendas. This is different from transposition in that the latter piggybacks on conflicting discourses to construct an alternate voice; appropriation takes over the dominant/alien discourse and shapes it for achieving one's own purposes. Though there is some extent of discursive mixing and textual hybridity going on in both practices, the strategy of appropriation is more resistant. For another example of appropriation, consider the bilingual writing of Sivatamby that we discussed in the previous chapter.

It is important to realize that each of these strategies may have different outcomes in terms of stylistic effectiveness and critical communication. It is clear that some strategies have possibilities of challenging the dominant discourses and textual conventions to democratize knowledge and communication. Others strengthen the established discourses. Among the strategies we have observed, accommodation confirms the established discourses. The voice may succeed in being coherent and homogeneous, while somewhat lacking in ideological complexity. Avoidance may have serious problems of incoherence, as conflicting discourses are left unresolved.

The writer adopting such a strategy may also face the danger of being ascribed negative roles—as illogical, sloppy, immature, or unproficient. The writer may unwittingly generate unfavorable identities and roles, ironically, while deferring to the dominant discourses. The other three strategies (transposition, opposition, and appropriation) construct independent voices by positing a discourse counter to that of the established writing practices. The strategy of opposition, however, is not sufficiently dialogical or negotiatory in promoting the vernacular discourses in the new communicative situation. Although this strategy has critical potential, there is the danger that the text may not communicate to the target audience that comes with different genre and discourse expectations. Seeing little connection to the present rhetorical situation, the audience may rule the text as irrelevant, ascribing pejorative roles and identities to the writer. The writer may be denied entry into that communicative circle, and the text may be silenced. The final two strategies—transposition and appropriation—have more liberatory and communicative potential. Although they establish a discourse counter to that of the dominant conventions, they still establish a point of connection with the established genre conventions. Therefore, the audience for that genre of writing may find some bridges in the effort to understand and appreciate the new oppositional discourse. Writers using these strategies are negotiating with the established rhetoric to construct a more positive voice for themselves. These strategies have greater chances of challenging the dominant discourses and inserting the alternate values and ideologies represented by the writers. The writers themselves are empowered as they work out an independent voice for themselves rather than being silenced, accommodated, or rejected by the dominant discourses.

Why do these multilingual writers adopt these different approaches? What motivates the different strategies they use to represent themselves in their writing? Recent developments in SLA enable us to conduct such discussions about motivation in a socially relevant manner. Traditionally, we have worked with constructs like integrative and instrumental motivation (Gardner and Lambert 1972) or (as a corrective to those) intrinsic and extrinsic motivation (Brown 1991). The first construct in each pair—that is, learning a language to join the target speech community (integrative communication) rather than learning for obtaining certain practical objectives, or learning a language for self-accomplishment and personal interests (intrinsic motivation) rather than learning under compulsion to attain institutional rewards—has emerged as accounting for success in teacher lore. But both sets of constructs fall short in many ways. Both fail to take account of issues of power in attaining one's communicative objectives. These constructs give the impression that one only needs the right motivation to succeed in language acquisition. There are serious socioeconomic constraints that shape one's motivations and the power to attain one's objectives. Furthermore, motivations can be contradictory, multiple, and changing—just as identities are. More importantly, one's motivations will have implications for one's identity and will in turn be shaped by concerns of selfhood. Influenced by similar lines of reasoning, Bonny Norton Peirce (1995) has come up with the construct *investment*—which is influenced by Bourdieu's economic metaphors for language learning and usage. Peirce demonstrates how the investment of some of her adult immigrant students in learning English to achieve important symbolic and material resources for their and their family's survival helps them develop counterdiscourses and oppositional identities to transcend silence and marginalization in the new language. One's social positioning and the alternate identities desired in the new community considerably influence the approaches and consequences in language learning.

How do we use investment to explain the different strategies adopted by the writers described earlier? Irina is a recent immigrant, married to an American citizen. She is looking forward to completing her graduate studies and beginning employment here. She has an investment in accommodating (rather than resisting) the dominant discourses for the new identity she desires. Her ethnic identity doesn't cause many problems in making this process of acculturation possible.

Since she doesn't have the linguistic resources to display her new voice, she prefers to avoid negotiating the discursive conflicts in her writing practice. Connor has a similar investment in accommodating the dominant discourses, given her professional and family life in the United States. Her ethnic identity also favors relatively easy assimilation. In the case of Li, Sri, and hooks, who present various forms of opposition, their social positions invite different forms of stigmatizing, stereotyping, and oppression. They face greater resistance from the target language community for acculturation and integration. They also face deeper claims of solidarity from their native discourses and communities, deriving from their long histories of struggle against domination. They therefore have an investment in seeking ways of developing a critical voice that is informed by the struggles they face. Again, their access to linguistic resources would permit them different levels of accomplishment. Sri, who lacks resources and is grounded firmly in his native community, negotiates discourses less critically compared to Li and hooks, who have an investment in developing hybrid discourses and voices.

In order to understand the bilingual literacy of our students, we should take into account their investment in developing positions of strength in the representation of their selves in the new language and community. Complexity in voice is achieved by working with and working against the competing discourses to achieve an empowered selfhood.

From Cognitive Strategies to Discourse Strategies

There is a difference between the strategies discussed earlier and those specified by the models of the composing process. The latter are more microdiscursive, while the ones I have outlined are macrodiscursive. Also, the models of cognitive process theory are not grounded in larger social and material contexts. After a review of L2 writing research, Tony Silva (1993) claims that studies on macrolevel writing processes are wanting. Based on the examples given earlier, it is possible now to come up with a taxonomy of strategies used by multilingual writers to negotiate their challenges in writing. We must also develop a critical perspective on the effects and consequences of these strategies. Such a framework would enable writers to evaluate the success of their writing, develop a reflexive awareness of their writing strategies, and explore a range of alternate strategies to cultivate a critical voice.

As we move toward building such models, we must examine other similar research on strategies adopted by multilingual students to negotiate discourses. Ilona Leki (1995) has come up with a taxonomy of strategies based on an ethnographically based case study of ESOL graduate students. The strategies she identifies are as follows.

1. Clarifying strategies (e.g., talking to teachers or colleagues to understand the nature of the assignment better)
2. Focusing strategies (e.g., rereading the assignment several times, or rereading books, to narrow down the scope of the assignment)
3. Relying on past writing experience (e.g., evaluating the strategies used in the past and making connections to the present assignment)
4. Taking advantage of first language/culture
5. Using current experience or feedback to adjust strategies
6. Looking for models (e.g., consulting books, research articles, and book reviews for examples of format and language suitable for the assignment)
7. Using current or past ESL writing training
8. Accommodating teacher demands (e.g., trying to satisfy the teacher by doing the project totally according to his or her interests and opinions)
9. Resisting teacher demands (e.g., completing a project in accordance with the interests of the student)
10. Managing competing demands—subdivided into managing course load, managing work load, managing the

demands of life, et cetera (e.g., making modifications in the project according to other commitments)

A related orientation to strategy is that developed by scholars belonging to the school of learner strategy training (see Oxford 1990). They have come up with a different set of constructs to describe the strategies learners use. Their constructs are: affective strategies (for anxiety reduction), social strategies (for becoming culturally aware), metacognitive strategies (for evaluating one's progress), memory-related strategies (such as grouping and rhyming), cognitive strategies (such as analyzing and summarizing), and compensatory strategies (such as guessing meanings from context). Though the constructs are theoretically attuned to perceiving learning as an individually driven, autonomous, context-neutral activity, there are some important lessons for the consideration of writing strategies. The model posits that these strategies will be differentially used, based on the learning styles of students (e.g., visual, auditory, or hands-on; reflective or impulsive; analytic or global; extroverted or introverted). Students will adopt the strategies that suit their preferred styles of learning and motivations. Success doesn't depend on using a specific set of strategies. Furthermore, the more successful students have a reflexive awareness of the strategies that work for them, and they build on them progressively (see Green and Oxford 1995).

The typologies of Leki and Oxford are useful for teachers to help writers choose their strategies wisely for empowerment. It is important to display to students the implications of using different writing strategies for issues of identity, discourse, voice, and fluency. Students should be encouraged to negotiate the discourses strategically for the construction of a critical voice in their writing. Though this is certainly an interesting beginning, the strategies identified by Leki and Oxford are focused on learning skills in general rather than on writing. They are more pedagogical than rhetorical in orientation (though Leki's model is occasioned by writing pedagogy and has greater relevance to it). Also, the list is more descriptive in

Strategy	Voice	Ideology	Textual realization
accommodation	monological	uncritical	coherent
avoidance	monological	uncritical	discordant
opposition	monological	critical potential	discordant
transposition	dialogical	critical	coherent
appropriation	dialogical	critical	coherent

Fig. 5. Strategies of textual negotiation

nature than evaluative. The types of strategies I propose (including some of the strategies identified by Leki) are focused on issues of text construction. Also, true to critical pedagogy, I am making some value judgements on the extent to which these strategies would help the writer represent his or her self in an advantageous manner. A socially engaged, ideologically informed orientation to writing strategies will go a long way toward coherent and critical text construction. I offer the strategies developed through my earlier examples as a suitable alternative. To summarize, they are as shown in figure 5. I will provide additional examples in the following chapters on how these strategies can help us understand ways of negotiating academic knowledge (chap. 5) and community membership (chap. 6) with relative levels of success.

Conclusion

The move to the focus on the thinking and expressive strategies of writers by the "process movement" is important. The move celebrates the agency of writers to negotiate textual and ideational structures of writing in the ways they desire. But the narrowly cognitive and individualistic way in which these processes are theorized reduces the value of this approach. Theoretical schools attuned to critical practice help develop a more socially grounded and psychologically complex orientation to the struggles for the representation of self through the conflicting discourses confronted.

A. Discovering One's Learning Strategies

An important contribution of learner strategy research is the realization that multilingual students already come with well-practiced strategies of negotiating discourses and literacy. In an increasingly multilingual and multi-cultural global context, everyone has worked out ways of coping with challenges in communication with "out-group" members. It is important therefore to discover (and help students discover) the strategies that work for them. An important pedagogical implication of this mode of research is that making students critically reflect on their learning strategies is a path toward effective teaching.

Outline a series of questions you will ask your students to find out the strategies they use to cope with challenges in writing and language acquisition. These questions can be posed in teacher conferences or classroom activities to generate student self-awareness and teacher knowledge. Some sample questions are:

- What do you usually do when you are stuck for a word as you converse with a native speaker or when you write an essay?
- What do you usually do when you are given an assignment on a subject about which you know absolutely nothing?
- What do you usually do when you are asked to write an essay when you are struggling with many other assignments from other courses (i.e., what strategies do you adopt to compose the essay)?
- To what extent do you try to satisfy the expectations of an instructor when you write for a grade?
- If you feel uncomfortable with the rules and conventions of writing (in a specific genre for an academic discipline), what do you do to resolve this conflict?

- What are some of the things you do to leave a personal stamp on your writing?
- What do you do if the position you adopt in an essay goes against the dominant opinion on the subject?

One can then interpret the answers of the students in relation to the typology developed by Leki, Oxford, or myself (in this chapter) to analyze the dominant strategies of the individual students.

B. Journal Writing for Literacy Awareness

Many scholars find personal writing, in the form of journals and biographies, useful for helping students understand their modes of negotiating discourses (see Leki 1995; Peirce 1995). Writing gives a sense of detachment from the stresses of face-to-face communication and enables students to critically reflect on their struggles. Kramsch (2000) interprets the biographical writing of nonnative scholars to discern the voices they construct as they negotiate their conflicts of identity. For Kramsch, the very activity of commenting on discursive struggles is a reflexive act that contributes to the construction of voice. It is useful therefore to incorporate the writing of journals or biographies as a requirement of one's course. Teachers may formulate some stimulating prompts that will enable students to develop a sensitivity to their competing discourses. Find out how they resolve these conflicts in favor of constructing a coherent voice. Some useful prompts are:

- Reflect on the reasons for the discomfort you feel in writing in English.
- What image would you like to project of yourself in your English writing—why are you successful (or not) in presenting this image?
- What do you think is the image "native English" speakers form of you from your writing?

- What do you usually do to shape this image in your favor?

C. Literacy Autobiography

This is increasingly being encouraged to develop a reflexive awareness of the teacher's own voice, negotiating strategies, and composing processes. Ulla Connor describes it as follows: "A literacy autobiography is an account of significant factors and events that have contributed to your development as a reader or writer. In writing this autobiography, you will explore in some depth the origins of some of your attitudes and theories about reading and writing as well as your reading and writing practices" (1999, 41). This writing activity helps teachers to relate their own development as writers to the composing theories they use in their classrooms. The results of this project can considerably modify their understanding of composing theory and perhaps help them understand the struggles of their students better. See Belcher and Connor (2001) for some biographies by multilingual professionals. See how they negotiate voice in their writing.

Chapter 5

Issues of Content

There are reasons why ideational content is often ignored in pedagogies of language and literacy. According to the structuralist orientation, ideas are too fuzzy, idiosyncratic, and variable for rule formulation. The more abstract rules of form are treated as the deep structure of communication. As in structuralist linguistics, composition scholars have been preoccupied with matters like paragraph structure, intersentential cohesion, suprasentential coherence, and rhetorical moves. Schools such as contrastive rhetoric, text linguistics, and even cognitive process have not been overly concerned about theorizing the formation or uses of knowledge in text construction. Knowledge is taken for granted or simply ignored.

Though the cognitive process movement may be expected to say something about knowledge, it has been more interested in charting thinking processes and not thought content. While this movement provides a place for ideas in writing, content is treated as extraneous to the composing process. "Knowledge of topic" stands outside the monitor and the task environment, which constitute the main processing unit of writing (according to the Flower-Hayes model described in chap. 4). Although there is a recursive interaction between the different operations of the central composing processor (i.e., planning, translating, and reviewing), content doesn't participate in this dynamic relationship. Once knowledge is channeled into the writing task, it is then processed appropriately to meet the rhetorical objectives of the final product. It is significant that the box that represents knowledge precedes the other activities of composing. Though composing may be a recursive activity for this school, knowledge is treated as entering in a linear way into writing. It proceeds from the mind to the text. Furthermore, knowledge is largely a given; it is not treated as radically affected by the composing process or textual representation (although it can be pared down, reorganized, and reconsidered). Moreover, it is noteworthy that the component that represents knowledge in this model is labeled "the writer's long-term memory" and explained as "knowledge of topic, audience, and writing plans" (Flower and Hayes 1981). The implication is that knowledge is already inside the head of the writer. From whatever process it may have been produced, it is now stored in his or her memory. Note also that the ideas that find expression in the text are treated as coming from the individual writer. These constitute traditional assumptions of knowledge that are now being questioned.

A powerful contemporary insight into knowledge is that it is socially and rhetorically constructed. Writing is closely implicated in the construction of knowledge. As we know, research findings disseminated through journal articles enjoy greater legitimacy compared to those presented orally in conferences and seminars. The textual representation of knowledge is what all scholars and intellectuals value and deal with. In the process of writing, however, the intended audience, context, genre, and communicative objectives play a significant role in shaping the knowledge that is textually represented—hence the notion of the social and rhetorical construction of knowledge. Though it is easy to understand that knowledge is important for writing, it is not well appreciated that writing is important for knowledge. If writing and knowledge are so closely intertwined, it is important to take content more seriously in teaching composition.

Redefining Knowledge

Schools as diverse as postcolonialism, feminism, and postmodernism have theorized knowledge with greater complexity. Research on the ethnography of writing, the sociology of science, and academic literacy has brought out fascinating observations to confirm the social and rhetorical character of knowledge. We may outline the emerging perspectives on knowledge in the following manner.[1]

- *Knowledge as contingent.* What is accepted as legitimate knowledge changes according to the dominant discourses and social conditions of the time. Foucault (1972) observes how the views of Mendel in botany were rejected as eccentric when he first put them out. But at a later time, when the assumptions and framework of the field had changed, there was a readiness to accept similar positions put forward by other botanists. Kuhn (1962) uses "paradigms" as his metaphor to demonstrate how the grids we place on reality change over time. Paradigms make a space for what is treated as appropriate evidence. In turn, evidence that fails to fit may force a revision/reconstruction of the paradigm. There are also external social motivations for the change of a paradigm. Knowledge thus gets redefined as the discursive paradigm changes. This view goes against the traditional notion that knowledge is absolute, unchanging, and universal.
- *Knowledge as personal.* According to the empirical tradition of science, we are expected to be detached and dispassionate as we engage in intellectual activities. Now we acknowledge that our feelings, imagination, biases, values, interests, and predispositions play a role in the constructs we form to explain reality. In addition to these subjective factors, our social position, location in space and time, and experiences shape our sense of reality and truth. Rather than distorting or polluting knowledge, our subjectivity *enables* knowledge construction. It provides us the tools to interpret reality. There is also now a greater respect for the role of interpretation in knowledge. Knowledge is not self-evident or transparent. It has to be interpreted through the adoption of a perspective, location, and set of values.
- *Knowledge as rhetorical.* Though we are used to making a rigid distinction between knowledge and language, or

knowledge and rhetoric, or medium and message, we are now prepared to acknowledge the extent to which these dichotomies are interconnected. First of all, if knowledge is personal and changing, it is through the rhetorical arts of persuasion that one's version of truth is legitimized as the collectively accepted truth. Ethnographers of scientific communication have found that there is a big gap between the conduct of research and the reporting of it (see Myers 1990; Latour and Woolgar 1979). When one reports research, the knowledge gets reconstructed according to such factors as the audience, current knowledge, the context of communication, language, and genre rules. We also now appreciate more how language records our current assumptions and how changes in language reflect/shape revisions in knowledge.

- *Knowledge as social.* In traditional understanding, knowledge is perceived to be individually discovered through the power of one's mind. Now we acknowledge that we construct knowledge by interacting with each other socially and engaging with our differing experiences in the light of the available frameworks to make sense of things. In the process, the community that interacts—it may be of differing magnitudes, such as a nation, an ethnic group, a subcultural group, a disciplinary group, or a school of thought—agrees on the things that make sense to the members in a manner that suits their interests and concerns. Through the process of debate and consensus building, they construct the frameworks, terms, values, and norms that constitute the accepted body of knowledge. As noted earlier, these knowledge paradigms are progressively reconstructed as the interests and experiences of the group change.
- *Knowledge as constructed.* Traditionally, knowledge has been treated as an impersonal stock of information and facts that wait to be discovered. Knowledge is out there. It is a product. It is preconstructed and predefined. But in the emerging understanding, knowledge is put together—*by* people, *through* rhetoric, *in* texts, *as* dis-

courses. This perspective challenges the normative and positivistic understanding that knowledge is free of human mediation or involvement, that knowledge is universal and absolute, or that there is a correct and incorrect knowledge that can be objectively verified.

- *Knowledge as contested.* The earlier orientations lead to the realization that knowledge is—and always has been—contested. It is through contestation that communities and groups struggle for the legitimacy of their own knowledge constructs. Similarly, individuals struggle for the validity of their own perspectives *within* their group. However, the parties that benefit from the dominant knowledge constructs hide the traces of all the contestation that has taken place and give the impression of immutability of knowledge, as it is in their interest to prevent others from questioning these paradigms. While the dominant groups always contest any challenges to their discourses and establish their knowledge in opposition to rival claims, marginalized groups are discouraged from adopting similar strategies to make a space for their discourses and interests.

Using English for Academic Purposes

It is significant that in recent times the English for Specific Purposes movement, and its branches like EAP and EST, are making it a point to orientate students to issues of content. These movements have been studying the knowledge constructs, discourse conventions, and registers of the specific disciplines in order to help students write in a meaningful and relevant way in their academic assignments. They rightly take pride in being pragmatic and facilitating "real" writing, oriented toward the serious tasks of academic and professional objectives. Apart from teachers themselves studying the knowledge constructs of the disciplines, steps are taken to engage students with the activities of these discourse communities. Pedagogies such as linked courses (where teachers of English collaborate with faculty from other disciplines as they tie their writing to the discipline-based assignments/curriculum), sheltered courses (where instruction is oriented toward the discourse of the student's specialty), reading/writing courses, and content-based instruction encourage students to engage directly with the knowledge of other disciplines.

While these pedagogical developments are salutary, the attitudes adopted toward the knowledge and discourses of academic communities have to be carefully examined. First of all, these pedagogical movements generally adopt a normative attitude to the knowledge of the academic disciplines.[2] The objective is to understand and use the content of the disciplines in order to satisfy the expectations of the faculty. The purpose of the teachers (and EAP researchers) is to describe academic discourses objectively, not to develop a critical perspective toward them. The attitude encouraged among students is to treat established academic knowledge as a given and then explore how this can be incorporated in their writing. Students are not encouraged to interrogate academic knowledge from the perspective of their own community interests and experiences. It is important to realize that such questioning is eventually complementary to the academy, as it is through such interrogation and contestation that new knowledge is always produced.

Second, these movements consider their philosophy to be pragmatic. Critiquing the constitution of knowledge is considered an idealistic enterprise that distracts students from the practical objective of using that knowledge in their writing. Also, understanding and adopting the academic knowledge is considered more important to ESOL students, as they need quick help to cope with the needs and requirements of the academy. Though some scholars in this tradition consider how knowledge is socially constructed (see Swales 1990; Myers 1990; Bazerman 1988), they may not recognize ideological interests and consequences as motivating knowledge. John Swales (1990), one of the leading practitioners of the ESP/EAP movement, explains that his reason for leaving out ideological considerations about academic discourse in his research "rests on a pragmatic concern to help people, both non-native and native speakers, to develop their academic communicative competence" (9). Interrogating academic knowledge is therefore considered unhelpful—that is, perhaps of secondary interest, irrelevant to the survival needs and sometimes plainly beyond the linguistic and intellectual abilities of ESOL students (see Benesch 1993 for a critique of this assumption). The attitude encouraged is to orientate more toward achieving academic success and communicative fluency, rather than developing a critical awareness of the underlying knowledge-making processes (see Johns 1990; Reid 1989).

Third, the pedagogical orientation is narrowed down to such an extent that, in the name of specificity, students are not encouraged to go beyond the immediate context and discourses of the disciplines. Broader contextual aspects like the material and historical bases of knowledge construction are treated as irrelevant. Similarly, the alternate discourses and communities that contest the established knowledge paradigms are not given adequate consideration. This pedagogy then encourages students to adopt a passive and dependent relationship toward the activities of the academic communities.

Fourth, even socially informed and epistemologically sophisticated orientations (such as those of Bazerman, Myers, and Swales) can get reduced in significance if they frame knowledge as skills to be mastered by students. Students are taught the rules and conventions of dominant disciplinary discourses but not taught to ask an additional level of questions related to the rationale and practices accounting for these rules. Joy Reid (1989) exemplifies this attitude when she exhorts ESOL teachers to "discover what will be expected in the academic contexts their students will encounter, and . . . provide their students with the writing skills and the cultural information that will allow . . . [them] to perform successfully" (232). When discourses are treated as skills and "information" leading to successful performance in the academy, students won't have a space for asking larger questions of power and difference. They will simply receive practice on using the established knowledge and conventions in the expected way.

The orientation to academic knowledge described earlier is adopted by some ESOL practitioners in conscious opposition to alternate ways of practicing EAP. The more challenging of the alternate approaches is that of Patricia Bizzell (1982, 1992) from the L1 writing scene, who has called on the academy to listen more seriously and intently for what students have to say. While expecting students to acculturate to academic ways, she urges the academy too to listen to students and make a space for their knowledge. ESOL teachers sometimes simplify this call to create a straw-man argument. Johns (1990) paraphrases Bizzell's position by saying that "it is the academy that must change to adapt to the many cultures that the students represent" (29). This notion is then dismissed by many ESOL practitioners as something that flies in the face of pragmatic and realistic approaches in ESOL pedagogy (see Johns 1990, 29). Often, as in the case of Ferris and Hedgcock (1998, 39), who dismiss Bizzell in a footnote, this argument is not given sufficient serious consideration. But we have to understand the assumptions and implications behind Bizzell's call.

If knowledge is constructed socially and relative to the experiences and discourses of different communities, multilingual students may bring with them knowledge traditions that are different from those of the academy. There is always a tension between the knowledge of the home and the knowledge of the school in any community (see Heath 1983; Bernstein 1971). We can understand the special problems for multilingual students if we can imagine the ways in which academic knowledge is largely Eurocentric (see Canagarajah 1996). Western academic institutions enjoy superior technological and economic resources to conduct research and to publish. The many research journals in the West enjoy elite status. These agencies play a gatekeeping function in knowledge production. These are but some of the factors that account for the hegemony of the West in intellectual pursuits, continuing from the legacy of the Enlightenment and the scientific revolution in Europe. ESOL students may therefore see their local knowledge traditions stigmatized as inferior, irrational, or superstitious in classrooms (whether at home or in the West!). Furthermore, some ESOL students will be confronted with an unfair disadvantage, as students from dominant social groups enjoy a head start in academic knowledge. Heath (1983) and Bernstein (1971) argue that dominant social groups both value academic discourses in their everyday life and see their own discourses valued by the academy. All of these differences may in fact cast multilingual students as outsiders in academia.

The threat here is not just alienation but reproduction. The knowledge paradigms of the academy have the power to shape the thinking and behavior of students as they exert their hegemony over other communities. There is a justifiable fear among minority students that if they indulge in learning and using academic knowledge they will gradually be won over by its values and modes of thinking. They fear that academic discourses will reconstruct their identity and community membership in ways they don't desire. For instance, a Sri Lankan student I will discuss later, Viji, resisted her teachers' advice that she should discuss her opposing position and make some concessions in order to sound more balanced and dispassionate. Coming from a discursive tradition that preferred frank and direct expression of opinions, she felt that the academic convention of objectivity was insincere. Our advice—that even though she may not believe in the rival positions, she should adopt such a neutral tone temporarily for the sake of the effectiveness of her paper—only made worse the impression of insincerity. It is understandable that minority students may not be satisfied with using dominant discourses in a detached and utilitarian manner simply for the sake of succeeding in the academy. In a context of competing knowledge traditions, they desire to demonstrate to academics the validity of their own ways of perceiving and interpreting the world and seek respect for their knowledge traditions.

All this doesn't mean that students in ESOL can refuse to take academic knowledge seriously or just voice their own community-based knowledge traditions without consideration for academic conventions. EAP practitioners misrepresent the argument of critical pedagogues when they accuse them of insisting that the academy has to adapt to the students' knowledge traditions rather than the other way about. There are constraints on what can be discoursed in specific contexts and communities. Previous knowledge constructs, interpretive traditions, and research practices in academic history exert a "passive pressure" on what can be spoken and written in the academy (see Bazerman 1988). Even if the "active pressure" of academic control and gatekeeping is not always felt, knowledge construction has to take place in the context of the existing and previous conversations. To express the student's own knowledge from his or her community, without consideration for the academy's conversations, is to blatantly violate the contextual norms and lose the target audience. Students with such an attitude may be further marginalized as ignorant and inept, as the academy would fail to make sense of their contribution. What critical practitioners recommend is to *negotiate* with the existing knowledge constructs and conventions to insert one's own perspectives relevantly. To expand the metaphor of conversation, though we may have a different point to make in a gathering of scholars, we have to find a strategic and relevant entry point into the ongoing discussion. This strategy is not unusual for the academy, as it is through such processes of questioning and reconsideration that new knowledge is always formed. If they perform their critical function relevantly, multilingual students may perform the academic function of knowledge production quite effectively, as they have oppositional experiences that can initiate questioning. They bring with them knowledge from alternate paradigms that can provide a critical detachment from the dominant discourses. Therefore ESOL teachers should introduce academic knowledge to their students—with the motive of helping them find their niche in it and reconstruct knowledge in terms of their own intellectual traditions, rather than adopting it wholesale as the normative discourse one should faithfully represent in one's writing.

To give an example of how such negotiation in writing may

take place, let me narrate the dilemma of Viji—a student/
teacher in a certification course in English language teaching
(ELT). Coming from a fundamentalist Christian background,
she was oriented toward interpreting the missionary enterprise of teaching English in Sri Lanka as a positive experience.
She therefore opted to write her final research project on the
topic "Approaches of the American Mission in Teaching the
English Language during the British Period in Jaffna." In her
initial drafts, she began her thesis by quoting Bible passages
that enjoin missionaries to evangelize the world and pro-
ceeded to show how the missionaries' spiritual commitment
led to effective educational strategies. But she was quickly
reminded by her faculty advisors that this approach clashed
against the postcolonial discourses popular in the academic
community (both at home and abroad). In the heightened nationalist context in Sri Lanka, the tendency was to interpret
the missionary English teaching experience as a colonizing
activity (as articulated in a paper presented at this same university just two years before Viji wrote her thesis—see
Suseendirarajah 1992). In subsequent drafts, therefore, Viji
began her report with a review of the current knowledge on
missionary education. She then gradually called for a need to
reconsider this period from a balanced perspective. Claiming
that much of the nationalistic scholarship on the pedagogies
of the missionaries was stereotypical and inadequately researched, Viji made a case for seeking more diverse sources.
Using her church contacts, she fished out documents on cur-
ricular proposals, minutes of statutory body meetings, teaching material, and policy documents relating to her subject.
Though she was initially inclined toward writing a straightforward narrative with considerable personal involvement in
her subject, her change to a more objective and critical stance
(prodded on by her advisors) enabled her to negotiate the
competing knowledge constructs effectively. The "passive
pressure" of the preceding conversation on the subject motivated her to do more careful research and modify her thesis
effectively. Her text goes on to develop a unique perspective
on missionary pedagogies. She argues that the missionaries

adopted a communicative pedagogy informed by whole-language principles that was ahead of its time. Through Sunday schools, sermons, Bible reading, and evening storytelling times on their verandahs, missionaries taught the language while accomplishing their spiritual and moral objectives. Viji was thus able to produce new knowledge and develop a more complex position by negotiating with competing discourses on the subject.

Consider the textual realization of her negotiation of knowledge in the following section.

> "Ye shall be witnesses unto me unto the utmost part of the earth" (Holy Bible, Acts 1:8)—the final command of the Master to the disciples of Jesus Christ has been fulfilled through the centuries ultimately paving the way for a band of missionaries from the American Board to reach the shores of Jaffna in 1813. Though the supreme goal of the missionaries was to evangelize, they found themselves being compelled "to seek the aids of learning" (Plan:1823) in order to prepare the ground for sowing the seed of the Gospel. (1)

It is interesting that the quotation from the Bible, which was cited in the author's initial drafts as a proud announcement of the educational endeavors of the missionaries, is subordinated here to convey the rationale for their educational activities. The tone also changes from laudatory to matter-of-fact. The citation that follows the Biblical quotation (Plan:1823) refers to the proposal by a school board for starting one of the first missionary educational institutions. This bureaucratic text is at tension with the Biblical verse, foregrounding dispassionately the pragmatic motivation of the missionaries in developing literacy in English. Viji is orientating to the academic audience effectively here, while not giving up her own interest in making a case for the value of missionary pedagogies. She achieves her own interests with sensitivity to the dominant views and discourses of the academic community.

This is another example of the strategy of *appropriation* we discussed in the last chapter.

Pedagogical Alternatives

What Viji's example suggests is that we must seek similar ways of enabling students to bring their knowledge effectively into the academic conversation and initiate changes in the established discourses. As we consider pedagogical alternatives for encouraging this negotiation, we need to first consider the approaches proposed by EAP pedagogues in the past. In the initial excitement of orientating to disciplinary content, teachers in both L1 and L2 writing endeavored to acculturate their students to specific academic disciplines. They did this in collaboration with subject-based faculty, often tailoring their separate writing classes to the work that was going on in the areas of students' specialization. Reflecting on this experience, teachers are debating two related issues: how specific the academic content should be in the writing courses; and whether writing teachers are equipped to teach discipline-specific content in their classrooms.

Many ESOL teachers still believe that discipline-specific writing is what is real, useful, and necessary for their students. There is a general animosity against the personal essay, which was the stock assignment of writing teachers in the past (Brinton, Snow, and Wesche 1989). EAP specialists point out that the types of writing students are expected to do in their other courses do not accommodate personal essays. EAP writing is more objective, analytical, and argumentative and works in relation to a specific body of knowledge. Therefore EAP practitioners consider the usual composition-class assignments as irrelevant to student needs. The other stock pedagogical genre—the expository five-paragraph essay on a general subject—too doesn't go far enough because it is not oriented toward a specific disciplinary audience. As an alternative to these classroom genres, EAP enthusiasts are proposing direct engagement with academic content. Such practices as adjunct courses and controlled composition are recommended as useful pedagogical options. Ann Johns (1993) proposes that ethnographic approaches can be used by both students and instructors to observe how academic discourses are conducted by scholars. Such projects will also help them understand and describe the discourses of specific disciplines. This way the learning of content will accompany the writing about it.

However, many teachers now feel that teaching writing for a specific discipline is too idealistic for college-level students. To begin with, this pedagogy narrows down the communicative competence of ESOL learners. College students don't encounter specific writing tasks so narrowly defined, as in the case of professional scholars. At the undergraduate level, they are taking classes in different subjects (although sometimes the courses may be focused around their fields of specialization). Furthermore, not all of them are going to engage in writing to the academic community in their professional life. Many will go on to write in other nonacademic professional settings, requiring broader skills of communication. Ruth Spack (1988) argues that discipline-specific writing cannot be taught by compositionists. There may be some justification to this argument if one considers the following: disciplinary knowledge has to evolve through close interaction with the scholarly community (something undergraduate students don't fully experience); there are ongoing changes in disciplinary constructs and content that cannot be held static for pedagogical purposes; there is considerable diversity in discourses *within* each discipline and, on the other hand, subtle similarities *between* related disciplines (e.g., sociology, anthropology, cultural studies) that even professionals haven't managed to delineate; disciplinary discourses have not been clearly described for pedagogical purposes by the scholars of those disciplines (who intuitively practice the discourses based on their personal history of engagement).

Taking such problems into consideration, some scholars now feel that teaching English for general academic purposes may be a more useful approach for students (Widdowson 1983). Though this doesn't mean going back to personal expressive writing or the vague expository essay (discussed earlier), it may include activities like the following, which have broader academic relevance:

working with data: writing from information gathered by students themselves through interview/observation or available from other studies;

writing from other texts: summarizing, responding to, and critiquing readings;

argumentation: moving from personal accounts to more objective treatment of students' views, especially in engagement with the writing of their classmates.

Endorsing such strategies, Spack (1988) argues: "These skills are transferable to many writing tasks that students will be required to perform in other courses when they write for academic audiences" (44). It is thus possible to some extent to teach rhetorical and communicative skills that enable students to participate "peripherally" in the knowledge-making practices of the academy. Paul Prior (1998) in fact argues that all scholars adopt such an indirect and peripheral relationship with their disciplines as they strive to mesh their personal and nonacademic interests with the ongoing work of the disciplines.

Many ESOL teachers adopt this generalist position partly because they doubt the proficiency of ESOL instructors to teach discipline-specific knowledge. They point out that writing teachers don't have the in-depth knowledge of other fields to instruct their students on the respective knowledge traditions (see Spack 1988). If this knowledge is difficult to develop for a single discipline, it is even more difficult to do so for the variety of disciplines from which our students come each semester. Spack (1988) therefore makes a forceful argument that "the teaching of writing in the disciplines should be left to the teachers of those disciplines" (29). The content that should be taught in composition classes, for Spack, is humanities related—something close to the disciplinary discourses composition teachers largely affiliate with. She states: "The English composition course is and should be a humanities course: a place where students are provided the enrichment of reading and writing that provoke thought and foster their intellectual and ethical development. . . . We can . . . draw on our own knowledge and abilities as we strengthen and expand the knowledge and abilities of our students" (46–47). It is possible to take this position further and argue that the humanities are central to all disciplines and that the skills of critical thinking, close interpretation, and rhetorical sensitivity fostered by the humanities are helpful to scholars in their own persuasions. (I read a news report recently that stated that medical students in the New York City area are taken to local museums to interpret paintings through "close reading" so that they will develop an eye to detect hidden symptoms in their patients!)

Some EAP practitioners still feel that there are ways in which we can initiate our students into the respective disciplinary discourses despite our limitations. They argue that ESOL teachers are in a better situation to undertake this enterprise, as academic writing cannot be left to the faculty in the disciplines, who are not clear about rhetorical processes and provide inadequate feedback to their students. Braine (1988) therefore proposes that what we do in the writing classroom "is a simulation of the real thing" (701). However, this admission undercuts the claim of many EAP practitioners that their pedagogy is based on "real writing." Braine also proposes that we can resolve the dilemma for the ESOL teacher by letting students be the authorities in the content knowledge, with teachers dealing only with rhetorical concerns in the writing classroom. This approach too is unsatisfactory, as it negates the very reason for teaching content in the first place—that is, because students are not proficient in it. Also, we may not be able to make the distinction between content and rhetoric easily enough to undertake this pedagogical division of labor.

Peshe Kuriloff (1996) provides a better way of moving beyond the skeptics and zealots in EAP. After directing a WAC program of considerable success, she reflects self-critically on its inadequacies. She finds that teaching the isolated disciplinary discourses is limiting because it encourages the artificial compartmentalization of disciplines and leads to the inability to communicate even within the same field. Kuriloff doesn't react against this splintering of academic discourses by desiring a utopian uniform discourse: "Instead of reacting to the lack of coherence as a negative, we should look for a theory or pedagogy that incorporates the contradictions. Instead of expecting everyone to conform to a single standard, we can enlarge our definition of standards" (486). The way she proposes to do this is to look at the typical relationship between readers and writers in the academy. Although discourses may be different, the processes and relationships that produce these discourses may be common. She therefore demonstrates that there are some common rhetorical practices governing literate relationships in the academy—that is, negotiating the authority of the writer, developing mutual trust and accountability, and making one's assumptions and reasoning clear. Although this catalogue is not exhaustive, Kuriloff initiates a useful line of inquiry.

In terms of composition pedagogy, Kuriloff (1996) argues that much of what happens in the typical writing class can be a useful starting point. The interaction with their peers can teach students the mutual expectations and responsibilities that govern academic discourse. Teachers should ensure that there is meaningful communication taking place in classroom writing. Students would gradually proceed to more complex and intimate levels of literate engagement: "Fellow students might make the best audience for novice discipline-based writers, and fellow majors or those with advanced knowledge or experience in the field the best insider audience" (500). Teachers themselves should serve as "good hosts and hostesses" by "introducing our young guests to the senior scholars who guard the gateways to their professional communities or by giving them permission to write to audiences with which they are or can easily become familiar" (500). To achieve the latter objective, writing teachers should facilitate a mentoring relationship with discipline-based faculty and encourage them to communicate well with students.

In proposing this alternative, Kuriloff (1996) is motivated by a gradation of specialization in academic writing. She feels that students may move developmentally in the following order, with one stage sometimes facilitating the other.

1. Nonacademic writing (where personal and expressive topics may find a place)
2. Generalized academic writing concerned with stating claims, offering evidence, respecting others' opinions, and learning how to write with authority
3. Novice approximations of particular disciplinary ways of making knowledge
4. Expert, insider prose (Kuriloff 1996, 498)

The rationale here is that graduate students may have greater need for discipline-specific insider knowledge, which undergraduates may not need or be expected to demonstrate by their professors.

This means that one may devise an effective pedagogy focusing on the rhetorical *processes* underlying knowledge construction, rather than searching for the *product* of knowledge (as the EAP practitioners discussed earlier are doing). Instead of asking what knowledge constructs we should teach students, we may spend our time usefully by showing them the processes underlying this knowledge creation and transmission. Although Kuriloff focuses largely on reader-writer interactional patterns, such processes may include the socialization practices of scholars, the conventions of academic communication, styles of interaction, and cultures of disciplinary communities. This approach is empowering in the long run, as it makes students participate independently in knowledge construction, rather than being dependent on the constructs periodically fashioned by authorities. In fact, we must expand our perspective further and ask what are the social conflicts and agonistic relationships that characterize scholarly interaction as knowledge is constructed. In being sensitive to the inequalities in knowledge construction, students will develop a critical orientation to academic writing. They will struggle to make a space for their own interests in disciplinary discourses as Viji did in her thesis on missionary education. We will develop this social perspective on disciplinary practices more fully in the next chapter. We will discuss there how inducting students into academic discourse involves a critical socialization into the academic community's ways with words.

Reading/Writing Connection

An important pedagogical strategy of content-based writing instruction is to integrate writing with reading. There is much wisdom in this approach. Through engagement with its written texts, one can get a better sense of how knowledge is constructed in the academy. Publications are the valued form of knowledge dissemination for scholars. In reading academic texts, students also get to form the schema (i.e., conceptual framework, theoretical assumptions, rhetorical conventions) necessary for understanding the ongoing work of scholars in a discipline. Rather than absorbing isolated facts and information (which only makes them passive and dependent), students need a schema that will enable them to integrate/interpret new information in the appropriate way. For this purpose, it is important for students to see the use of the register and specialized terminology typical of a discipline in its written texts. Publications will also enable students to understand what issues are central in the conversation of the discipline at a given time and which scholars and institutions matter. Reading should therefore be treated as a mode of socialization into the knowledge-making activities of a discipline.

In addition to these benefits specifically related to the acquisition of discourse, researchers suggest other general uses for the development of writing and literate skills. The nature of reading/writing influence on the development of literacy can be theorized according to at least three models (see Eisterhold 1990). The *directional model* reflects the traditional understanding that more reading makes better writers. In this model, reading provides the linguistic and ideational input for written products. The *nondirectional* model presupposes a set of common underlying processes that contribute to enhancing both reading and writing. Rather than interacting directly, reading and writing serve to construct schema, meaning-making skills, and background knowledge that then serve both literate activities. The *bidirectional model* posits that reading and writing mutually help each other through direct intervention. But unlike the directional approach, it also posits that there is a qualitative progression in literacy skills as reading and writing interact over time. Researchers have failed to find overwhelming evidence to prioritize one model above the others; they therefore recommend an eclectic approach in the use of these models for pedagogical purposes (see Eisterhold 1990; Ferris and Hedgcock 1998, 34).

Depending on their level of maturity, language proficiency, and educational level, learners may benefit from different directionalities of influence. For example, at early levels, beginning L2 students may find reading providing them models for their writing assignments. As they advance, the engagement with print develops a stock of information, strategies, and awareness that provides them confidence in reading and writing. Many will also find the reverse process true: that their writing enables them to read more critically and provides genre expectations for the easier processing of text. Bazerman (1988) points out that the more one writes, the more one develops the critical detachment to read texts analytically and independently. The motivation to write provides the mind frame to process the text according to theoretical positions, research paradigms, and ideological stances. The literacy influence thus becomes complex, reciprocal, and multidirectional after a point.

Ferris and Hedgcock (1998) provide a thorough review of the available research on the development of reading/writing proficiency. The main findings that emerge are as follows.

Proficient L1 and L2 writers are more likely to have read extensively for school and/or pleasure than their less proficient counterparts.

The development of L2 writing proficiency doesn't transfer directly from L1 literacy; it may depend on a constellation of interdependent factors such as L2 linguistic proficiency, L1 and L2 reading ability, L1 and L2 writing proficiency, and exposure to particular genres of writing.

There is support for Cummins's (1991) Cognitive Academic Language Proficiency (CALP) model. According to this model, speakers of all languages share a common cognitive/academic proficiency level that allows for the interlingual transfer of literate skills. This model lends strength to the possibility that, after a threshold level is reached, L1 literacy skills will help in the academic writing tasks of ESOL students.

This line of findings provides impetus to radical pedagogical activities orientated toward using reading and writing in L1 to help L2 writing, as well as using L2 reading to help L2 writing.

As we consider ways of developing critical reading/writing pedagogies for our students, we have to take note of Cheryl Geisler's (1994) provocative insight into the way literacy functions in maintaining the power of the academic community. Her argument can be simplified this way: schools and colleges wean students away from context-bound ways of reading and knowledge making that novices typically bring from lay literacy practices and oral communication contexts. Educational institutions teach students to treat texts as autonomous, to perform close objective reading within the bounds of the page, and to extricate abstract information for the display of knowledge. This she calls *autonomous textuality*. Those who can perform this reading efficiently are considered literate in academic ways and then labeled educationally successful. In doing this, the academy is really creating an audience for its work. The students are being provided with the tools and tastes to appreciate the knowledge constructed by the academy. However, academics graduate to another level of literacy that is not taught to novices. This is called *rhetorical process reading.* This is, ironically, a context-bound approach to reading—the very practice students were weaned away from. In placing the text and information in its context of production and sociality, the academics gain a critical knowledge into the relative, constructed, subjective, discursive nature of knowledge (as defined earlier). Through this reading, they are able to obtain a vantage point that enables them to interpret the text authoritatively and develop a qualified view of its status and significance. The resources to make this reading are obtained through face-to-face communication—once again, the very orality-based practices students are taught to treat as "lay" and inferior. It is through their personal interaction with other scholars in hallways, conventions, meetings, and correspondence that academics acquire the details about people and institutions that enable them to talk about the contextual features of a text. Lacking this information, novices can do nothing but perform an abstract (undigested) reading of the text for information. Geisler labels the knowledge of novices as *content knowledge* and that of academics as *domain-specific knowledge.* Though novices may know the theories and facts of a discipline, they lack the confidence and resources to apply the knowledge to new problems, to create new knowledge out of this, or to translate it with relevance to other fields and schools of thought. It is through such domain-specific knowledge and rhetorical process reading that new knowledge is created and academics exert their authority.

To add another twist to this hypothesis, Geisler says that academics practice two different forms of reading and writing. Though they practice rhetorical process reading, as described earlier, they *write* autonomous texts. In their scholarly publications, they suppress all the contingent and contextual information that will enable us to situate their knowledge critically. Such information pertains to their personal background, their biases and values, the history of their research activity, the institutions that funded or commissioned their work, and the processes by which their findings were reached. In fact, the IMRD (introduction/method/results/ discussion) genre conventions of research articles (discussed in chap. 3) lend themselves to this tendency. While using contextual information to critique other people's texts/ knowledge, academics want their own texts to be read un- critically for content value. Such are the practices by which their intellectual authority is maintained.

These divergent literacy practices spell out important strategies for critical pedagogies. First, it is important to break the faith of students in autonomous textuality. We have to encourage students to situate the text in context, to read be- tween and behind the lines, to develop a sensitivity to the rhetorical arts of the text, to translate it to their personal life conditions, and thus to adopt a critical angle on the text. Even- tually students should be able to identify and explore the ten- sions between the words of the author and other people's words (developing a sensitivity to intertextuality) in order to deconstruct the text. Students should also be encouraged to converse about the text in order to obtain additional contex- tual and background information regarding its construction. Such approaches would enable them to perform a rhetorical process reading—the type of critical reading that academics perform to construct new knowledge.

Bartholomae and Petrosky (1986) write about an interesting course they devised at the University of Pittsburgh for non- mainstream students that realizes critical possibilities in reading and writing. In reading academic texts, they encour- age students not just to bring out a fact with certitude (one that the author perhaps intended) but to take risks in developing a perspective that they themselves find interesting. The in- structors also encourage students to write about their reading. This need to compose a response motivates students to look at the text with some critical detachment. They could be mo- tivated to be active readers who situate the text in multiple contexts with reference to their personal life to generate a sig- nificant point of view. In this kind of assignment it is not enough to produce a fact, information, or a summary, as in other reading courses. Bartholomae and Petrosky hold that traditional pedagogy makes students treat the authors as authorities whose words they have to closely reproduce if they are to provide a safe interpretation. This pedagogy is laden with feelings of dispossession and confinement that are unhealthy for the literacy practices of the students. With a dramatic flourish, Bartholomae and Petrosky point out that all reading is a misreading. In order to produce an interpretation, readers have to bring their own agendas and perspectives into the text, casting aside fears about original authorial intentions.

This pedagogy also compels students to read each other's comments after they respond to the text. Reading their own writing gives further motivation to develop a meaningful perspective as students realize that their essays have communicative value. In texts read only by the teacher for the purpose of giving a grade, the students don't have enough motivation to develop a significant perspective. Bartholomae and Petrosky therefore see value in the paradox of reading one's writings and writing one's readings. In engaging in debate, discussion, and argument over each other's interpretations, and then revising their work with newly achieved awareness, students are collaborating in composing each other's writing. Thus they also simulate the academic processes of knowledge construction.

For the discipline-specific faculty who would argue that this approach may not be conducive to understanding the canonical knowledge in their fields, the authors respond: "But they will learn something about what it means to study a subject or carry out a project. They will begin to learn what a subject is—how it is constituted, how it is defended, how it finds its examples, ideas and champions, how it changes and preserves itself. And in learning this they will learn something about the work we do that will prepare them to read out texts as they could not were they to remain totally on the outside looking in" (Bartholomae and Petrosky 1986, 38). They are also not squeamish about the relative "outsider status" of their students in the margins of the academic community. They find this marginalization productive. It is from this position of tension that students gain the motivation and drive to critique academic texts, appropriate them for their purposes, create new knowledge, and thus write themselves into the academic community. In other words, the authors are not trying to induct students wholesale into the academic community. They want them to acknowledge their position on the margins of the academy and use this detachment to critique academic knowledge. Therefore, Bartholomae and Petrosky (1986) conclude:

> The course we've defined above demonstrates our belief that students can learn to transform materials, structures and situations that seem fixed or inevitable, and that in doing so they can move from the margins of the university to establish a place for themselves on the inside. At the end, however, these relationships may remain hesitant and tenuous—partly because our students will remain students . . . but also because they have learned (and perhaps in a way that their "mainstream" counterparts cannot) that successful readers and writers actively seek out the margins and aggressively poise themselves in a hesitant and tenuous relationship to the language and methods of the academy. (41)

This kind of pedagogy is congenial to the practice of multivocal literacies that I have exemplified through the texts of Li and Viji in previous pages.

Plagiarism

A particular concern teachers have about the use of academic knowledge by ESOL students is the possibility of plagiarism. There is the widely shared opinion that non-Western students tend to take information, facts, and views from academic texts and use them as their own without proper acknowledgment. It is important to understand the stereotypical explanations ascribed to this practice before we adopt a more complex attitude to ways of orientating to knowledge and texts. Pennycook (1996) documents colonial attitudes to local communities and their intellectual traditions in China and argues that these perceptions may still influence contemporary teachers in their attitudes to the writing of Chinese students. Local people were considered ignorant, lazy, lying, or lacking creativity, originality, and individuality. This amounts to a racist perspective on the capabilities of local people. Writers are also stereotyped as having fixed characteristics. These biases perhaps motivate teachers to apply punitive measures against ESOL students for what they consider "stealing other people's words." At their most charitable, teachers feel that the linguistic deficiencies of their students may force them to slavishly copy words and views from elsewhere.

As we adopt a nonethnocentric view of "plagiarism," we must consider a range of alternate angles to explain how non-Western students use texts in their writing.

1. Cultural practices
    Some communities treat knowledge and words as collectively owned. This is especially strong in orality-dominant communities. There is a weak ownership over spoken words in such communities, even though they may have a long literate tradition. Borrowing and sharing preexisting statements (with careful ascription) is therefore taken for granted in such communities. Such free borrowing of words is strong in the everyday life of my native Tamil community (see Canagarajah in press).
    Memorization of other people's words/texts is a valued practice in many communities. Previous texts and words are considered to have already stated well what we want to express. Keeping these words in mind is considered a good way of preserving useful information and ideas. Stored in deep memory, these texts can be ushered out for use in future occasions. Memorization is also considered to enable a reflective and gestated understanding of those words. When members of a community hold these words in common, they enable harmonious communication, as proverbs,

idioms, maxims, and motifs function as convenient frames of reference. These were some of the reasons given to me by my elders as I grew up in a community that valued memorization. Teachers and elders would often check our memory of sacred texts and classical literature during casual conversations. Those who could readily call to mind the requested texts were treated with admiration and respect.

In some cultures, the self is defined not in separation from the collective but in union with the community (as we discussed in chap. 4). From this perspective, writers in such communities express their identity through the words of others. To define oneself in opposition to the community or to strive for originality through new words is a violation of the local ethos. One's identity is constructed by weaving together the existing words from the community (see also Ramanathan and Atkinson 1999).

In communities where there is a totalitarian political culture, it is dangerous for students to use their own words. They have to defer to the positions and views of the leaders and show agreement with their words. Li (1999) discusses how this culture shaped her writing in China: "It was a time when 'doing' revolution was the only legitimate and noble ambition and other intellectual desires had to be pursued only in the sidelines, if not in secrecy. Most of our school time was devoted to reading and discussing Marx's and Mao's works, or criticizing revisionist and bourgeois ideologies around and inside us" (44). She goes on to demonstrate how developing individualistic stances was difficult when she moved to the United States for her graduate studies and wrote for teachers influenced by the process tradition. Another Chinese scholar, Fan Shen (1989) concurs: "In China, 'I' is always subordinated to 'We'—be it the working class, the Party, the country, or some other collective body. Both political pressure and literary tradition require that 'I' be somewhat hidden or buried in writings—and speeches; presenting the 'self' too obviously would give people the impression of being disrespectful of the Communist Party in political writings and boastful in scholarly writings" (460).

2. Educational practices

In some communities, students are taught to show respect to the original writers by quoting them without too much paraphrase or interpretation. The original thinkers are considered to have communicated wisdom with such beauty and grace that any attempt to paraphrase them is considered presumptuous. Similarly, differing from the views of those thinkers is considered arrogant. Using the words of these savants freely in one's own texts is not considered stealing because the whole community recognizes where these words come from. The readers actually focus on the fresh uses to which the writer is putting these words.

The role of education is treated in certain communities as integrating the student into the community's accumulated wisdom. Scollon (1991) summarizes his experience in the Taiwanese educational system as follows: "The Chinese student is not writing primarily to express himself or herself but for the purposes of becoming integrated into a scholarly community. The purpose of student writing is to learn to take on a scholarly voice in the role of commentator on the classics and on the scholarship of others. One is writing to pass on what one has received" (7).

3. Rhetorical tradition

In some cultures, good writing is defined as weaving your text with words from traditional religious/philosophical texts and classics. The originality lies in constructing your voice through the words of others. Xiaoming Li (1999), who has researched the differences in notions of good writing in China and the United States, defines the Chinese conception of the essay (known as the *zawen*) as follows: "The traditional zawen takes the stance of an objective observer dispensing nuggets of wisdom and commentary on topics of national interest, its style much more adorned with literary and historical allusions and direct quotations from Confucius and Mencius" (47). To some extent, this is true also of my Tamil community. In Tamil writing, quoting ancient classics is considered to make writing beautiful and powerful. Such display of knowledge doesn't necessarily *suppress* one's ethos. Through these quotations, moralisms, proverbs, and aphorisms the writer constructs an ethos that comes off as knowledgeable, cultured, well read, deferential, affirmative, and community centered. Also, the subtle variations in the use of the older texts, and the new contexts in which they are used, enable one to define one's identity. One's voice emerges through the cracks of the preceding texts.

It isn't necessary to explain here how these practices go against the traditional assumptions about good writing in the West. Values such as originality, independence, creativity, intelligence, and voice are defined according to the extent to which the writer deviates from preceding texts and thinkers. In effect, these values are equated with novelty in form and content.

We shouldn't, however, conclude that ESOL students are passive and helpless under the influence of their educational and cultural traditions. Sometimes their agency may get demonstrated through the conscious use of plagiarism for oppositional purposes. There is some research to show that plagiarism can at times be deliberately used in reaction against undesirable pedagogical and social practices. Pennycook's (1996) Chinese students say that they take the shortcut of speaking through other people's words and texts because they see little motivation for personal involvement in their ESOL courses. Seeing that English is a colonial language with alien values, envisioning limited prospects of using the language in their own everyday life, and bored with skills-oriented irrelevant pedagogies and curricula, Chinese students get along by reproducing existing texts. I found a similar oppositional act in the seemingly plagiaristic essays written by minority students in a course I taught in an American university (see Canagarajah 1997b). Asked how students responded to the ethnocentrism in curricula, they voiced views like the following.

(50) Sonny Tippens:
Our experience at the university is what we make it, to a certain extent. We don't have to take in everything, and believe it. Just remember it, put it down as the correct answer, and go on with the good grade. Not everything that is heard has to be believed, just recalled for a good grade. (INT 8/17)

Such attitudes may suggest possible motivations for their formulaic essays composed of excessive quotations from reference material.

The preceding argument should not to be taken as an advocacy of "plagiarism." The intention here is to reorientate to rhetorical practices from wider cultural and social contexts. However, even non-Western communities make distinctions between good borrowing and bad borrowing, good uses of memorization and bad uses. Pennycook (1996) argues that his Chinese students too noted that they could use these practices productively, meaningfully, and educationally or fail to do so (although he doesn't provide rhetorical examples of what good practices of plagiarism would look like in writing). Rebecca Howard (1995) describes in greater detail what is meant by "positive plagiarism." Those writers who take over other people's words and recast them in their own way, thus appropriating those alien texts according to their interests, are undertaking a sophisticated rhetorical act. But those who borrow other people's words and yet fail to rework or integrate them according to their own rhetorical purposes are displaying a less productive discourse. Martin Luther King Jr.'s speeches are a good example of this "positive plagiarism." They have been closely analyzed to show the extent to which King borrows from various texts, often without acknowledging the sources (see Miller 1992). Coming from an orality-dominant culture with a strong collective ownership of words, King feels free to borrow as he likes. But he recycles these words and texts from other places to suit his oppositional purposes. Not only do these texts serve to construct a unique voice for King, but they are placed in surprising new contexts and relationships to serve his radical ideology. King is thus *appropriating* other people's words for a totally different purpose (using a strategy similar to that of Li and Viji, discussed earlier). Keith Miller (1992) calls this kind of positive plagiarism "voice merging."

From this perspective, what is happening in the writing of ESOL students is not much different from the types of intertextuality we find in all writing—in fact, in all communication. In the context of postmodern thinking and digitized versions of literacy, we are now ready to acknowledge that knowledge is made up of borrowings from other texts. In our definition of knowledge earlier in this chapter, we orientated to knowledge as made up of discourse, rhetorically constituted in texts, and constructed in relation to other texts that have come before. Knowledge is intertextual, as it is constantly reconstructed in the light of ongoing scholarly conversations and publications. Behind knowledge lies not physical reality but other texts, followed by other texts (as even physical phenomena have to be interpreted in order to make sense—see Derrida 1972). In fact, all speech is made up of words infused with the meanings of other people of other times and places (as Bakhtin 1981 defines it). It is by taking over these words and texts that circulate in society through history, and reworking them in relation to our own purposes, that we make meaning. To give a more everyday example in contemporary life, everyone used to digital communication is now familiar with the ways we cut and paste texts—including our own—to form new texts. In a sense then, all of us are involved in forms of pastiche—differing not in the *quantity* but in the *quality* of the borrowings we do. This postmodern notion of intertextuality may help us understand the legitimate place borrowings and memorization have in writing.

Perhaps if we look at the essays of multilingual students carefully we may appreciate the creative and strategic ways in which they use their borrowings, as emerges through a close analysis I do of a student's essay elsewhere (see Canagarajah 1997b). The essay in question shows an excessive dependence on reference done in the library. Donnie writes a seemingly bland essay filled with quotations from academic sources in his effort to argue that the academy is a racist institution. When one reads the quotations closely, one finds that he has strategically picked these statements from respected educationists to make allegations against the academy in very direct and expressive terms. This is a safe way of representing Donnie's criticism, as he is making his point under the cover of the very academics he is interested in critiquing. Even the tone and style of communication that Donnie prefers—that is, passionate and uncompromising—are paradoxically represented through the voice of his academic sources.

We have to therefore consider how we can teach ESOL students to borrow other people's texts and words with critical thinking in order to accomplish their rhetorical and intellectual purposes. Looking at plagiarism from this wider perspective will prevent teachers from stereotyping multilingual students or rushing to punish them. We can in fact affirm some of the cultural and rhetorical traditions of our students in relation to the postmodernist notion of intertextuality and then go on to distinguish effective acts of borrowing from ineffective ones (or positive plagiarism from pastiche). Demanding the individual voice of the writer in a manner that denies or hides the place of intertextuality in all academic writing and knowledge construction is too simplistic a pedagogical practice.

Conclusion

One shouldn't be surprised if multilingual students sometimes fail to interrogate academic knowledge in their writing. The dominant pedagogies in ESOL reading and writing encourage a normative, objective, skills-based approach to knowledge. These pedagogies are based on the assumption that the purpose of reading or writing is to show mastery over the knowledge embodied in texts. They inculcate a respect for the established knowledge in the academic disciplines. What is emphasized in literacy proficiency is knowledge display and not knowledge creation or knowledge transformation. We cannot blame the pedagogies alone for this state of affairs. We have to take into account the temptation students may feel to hide within the safety of dominant knowledge paradigms rather than enter the uncharted territory of critique. Students also display a fear of the authority vested in academics and scholars. Some may even feel that it is by adopting the established positions that they can earn good grades and respect from their teachers. Teachers have to be sensitive to these concerns and shape a healthier attitude among students. Students have to realize that engaging with knowledge and creating a space for one's own perspectives cannot be separated from the rhetorical effectiveness of one's reading or writing. It is also through such processes of critique and reconstruction that knowledge is developed in the academic community. The examples of Viji and Donnie in this chapter show the attitudes that may motivate students to critically interrogate accepted knowledge and construct rhetorically effective texts. To invoke a notion introduced in the last chapter, Viji shows a clear *investment* in constructing an independent voice for herself, as she is cognizant of the unequal subject positions given to her as a woman, a nonnative speaker, and a Christian. She is therefore willing to *engage* with the competing discourses on the subject matter to make a space for herself by constructing a multivocal text.

Application

A. The Disciplinary Discourses of ESOL Composition
Describe the dominant discourses in your own field of ELT. The criticism has been frequently made that the dis-

courses of many academic disciplines have not been adequately described (see Spack 1988). Others consider the vague and nebulous status of ESOL composition in the context of the diverse fields that feed this discipline (see Matsuda 1998). To address these concerns, it is good for ESOL composition teachers to attempt to describe their own professional knowledge. This will also enable us to develop a clearer conception of our field. Answer the following questions.

1. Do ESOL composition teachers think of themselves as belonging mostly to the humanities, the social sciences, or education? (And more specifically, to English literature, composition, applied linguistics, linguistics, or rhetoric?)
2. What are the range of research techniques that are valued in our field? Which types of techniques are popular at present?
3. What are the theories that enjoy popularity in the field? Which theories are valued? Are these theories generated by ESOL scholars or those in other fields? Which fields have these theories been generated in?
4. Which books are being discussed widely by your colleagues? What does this show about the popular discourses in our circles at present?
5. Which scholars/researchers seem to be respected by your colleagues/mentors?
6. Do the answers to the preceding questions suggest any pronounced shifts in discourse from the way things were in the past?
7. In terms of the findings described earlier, does ESOL composition belong to the humanities, the social sciences, education, or psychology?

B. Understanding Student Attitudes on Academic Knowledge

Develop an interview module that would enable you to understand how your students orientate to academic discourses. How would they define what academics do in their work? What is their impression of academic knowledge? What do they value or abhor about this discourse? In which contexts do they choose between academic and community-based knowledge in their life? Which aspects of their community knowledge do they treat as superior to academic discourses? How do they manage the tension between academic and community-based discourses? Do they suppress, resist, ignore, or reject academic knowledge in such situations of conflict? What kind of students engage with these tensions honestly, and what motivates them to do so?

(You can focus your questions on a specific subject such as religion, progress, success, happiness, etc.)

After conducting these interviews, you can share your conclusions with your students to develop in them a self-awareness of their orientation to the academy.

C. Project-Based Pedagogy
Many teachers may think it idealistic to expect students to produce new knowledge in their writing. But by engaging in service-based research on community concerns students have produced useful knowledge. Such project-based pedagogies are useful for engaging multiple language skills (speaking, reading, writing) and learning skills (research in the library, use of the Internet, interviews, fieldwork) in a meaningful communicative and social context—see Warschauer 2000. Even high school students are increasingly engaging in these learning activities to develop knowledge that is acknowledged by city and school officers (see Cole and Zuengler 2000).

1. Choose a research-worthy topic for small groups of students in your class (e.g., drinking among college students, attitudes toward interracial dating in college, unsafe uses of the Internet by teenagers, etc.).

2. Get the group to define the project and segment the task.
3. Encourage them to do some preliminary research on the existing knowledge on the subject.
4. Facilitate meetings with other faculty, city officials, and interview subjects for the group to pursue the research.
5. Require a collaboratively written final report that spells out the new (perhaps challenging) knowledge deriving from the project.

Chapter 6
Issues of Community

Writing—in fact, any act of communication—is a social activity. We are addressing others when we speak or write. Even when we write for ourselves, we don't use a private symbol system, but language that is socially constructed. This assumption motivated my argument for a social orientation to matters of form, self, and content in the previous chapters. Let's address the challenges posed by community more explicitly here.

Traditionally, social concerns have been addressed under the notion of audience. Even pedagogies focused on form, content, or writer discuss the importance of audience awareness in writing. In some of these pedagogies, the text is tailored to the audience at a final stage of the writing process. This is usually an add-on, an afterthought, a cosmetic alteration before submitting the finished product. Audience awareness may include a range of concerns: simplifying the language to fit readers' proficiency, relating to their background knowledge, sustaining reader interest, or employing better cohesion devices and paragraph structuring to facilitate comprehension. Even in the more dynamic process models, which allow audience awareness to recursively shape the composing process and reconstruct other features of the text, audience is treated as one among many separate components.

What we are finding now is that audience is much more integral to the writing process. The consideration of audience influences all aspects of the text—from the very beginning of the writing process. We must take into consideration the fact that matters such as knowledge, conventions, genre, and register are defined and used differently by each community or audience. The very notion of the writer's self is social—the appropriate persona to adopt, the attitude/feelings/tone to be displayed, the footing and relationships to be maintained are defined variously by the different audiences. The writer has to take these expectations into account as he or she shapes the text accordingly. To go further, we are coming to the philosophical understanding that our very sense of reality is socially constructed. Each community develops its own ways of making sense of the world and of talking about it. In this sense, to begin to think is social—to use frameworks, words, symbols, interpretive orientations constructed by one social group or the other. Language is itself a quintessential social construct—the linguistic system embodies the values and experiences that matter to the speech community. To write, then, is to engage ways of thinking, knowledge, and language valued by one community or the other. At this point, the term *audience* is too inadequate and inaccurate for our purposes. It fails to go beyond the traditional image of the writer and the audience as separate and independent entities, standing on either end of an autonomous text as they interact in literate communication.

In the sections following, we will first orientate to the emerging understanding of discourse communities as holding the key to knowledge construction. From a critical perspective, we have to understand the conflicts involved in student access to, and acceptance into, the academic community. We will proceed thereafter to consider how the writing classroom can serve to initiate students into the ways and words of the academy by fashioning meaningful interactions for the writer with his or her peers and instructors.

Understanding Discourse Communities

To some extent discourse communities are analogous to speech communities, which ELT practitioners are familiar with from sociolinguistic scholarship. Like the other, discourse communities provide identity and group solidarity to their members, while socializing them into community-based values and norms. But the discourse community envisions language as a semiotic system, not just a value-free structure that serves as an instrument or medium for communicating a preexistent, transcendental reality that exists outside language. For the discourse community, the language and discourse of the group represent the sense of reality (and knowledge of reality) shared by that group. Language is not just an instrument to regulate and communicate social reality—it *constitutes* social reality. In this sense, all discourse communities—not just disciplinary ones—are knowledge-making communities. They are constantly reconstructing their understanding of the world through language and communication in the light of their changing experiences in social practice.

Of course, to appreciate the power and significance of discourse communities, we have to understand the *nonfoundationalist* philosophical assumptions that have permeated even popular culture these days. Contemporary society has given up the notion of a transcendental or preexisting reality that eludes human understanding. As we discussed in the last chapter, knowledge about reality, society, and selves is created socially. According to the social-constructionist orientation to knowledge, each community constructs its frameworks of reality according to its historical experience and interests. Knowledge is thus a social contract that members agree to uphold, even as they revise it according to their ongoing experiences and changing interests. Their discourse, communicative conventions, and social interactional patterns reflect and sustain their shared orientations to knowledge. In this sense, knowledge and "reality" are not universal constructs existing independently of subjects. Similarly, other distinctions we have made traditionally, such as objective/subjective, reason/belief, science/morality, truth/imagination, absolute/contingent (with the first construct in each pair always treated as conducive to valid knowledge), become obsolete. Knowledge making is frankly a relative, involved, ongoing, interested activity (as we discussed in chap. 5). It is difficult to come up with a foundational construct like "reality" or "fact" that can stand independent of language and evaluate each community's interpretation of life to decide whose is "correct."

Our orientation to life becomes complex when we realize that we are simultaneously members of multiple discourse communities. These communities are not exclusive. They overlap. Some communities subsume others. The larger academic community features disciplinary communities (linguistics, sociology, education, literature, etc.) that may contain specialized groups (sociolinguistics, applied linguistics, educational linguistics, and computational linguistics within linguistics), which may further be composed of diverse schools of orientation (ethnography of communication, conversation analysis, text linguistics, correlational linguistics, and critical linguistics within the sociolinguistics camp). Our membership becomes more complicated when we include nonacademic communities. While my ethnic background provides one kind of group identity, I may also be a member of a disciplinary group in the academy, a professional circle, and a special-interest group. This orientation assumes that it is not impossible to cross discourse communities, although we need to negotiate both the communicative differences (as in joining any new speech community) and the worldviews of the divergent communities. Our multiple memberships may create tensions within discourse communities. However, it is the infusion of new values and knowledge from the divergent members that is the motor for the knowledge-making activity of each community. Its discursive paradigms have to be revised according to the new perspectives periodically brought in by its members.

It becomes hard to define discourse communities when they display such dynamism in participation, changes in discourses, and complexity of intra- and intercommunity interactions. John Swales (1990) defines the constitution and character of discourse communities in the following manner.

1. A discourse community has a broadly agreed set of common public goals.
2. A discourse community has mechanisms of intercommunication among its members.

3. A discourse community uses its participatory mechanisms primarily to provide information and feedback.
4. A discourse community utilizes and hence possesses one or more genres in the communicative furtherance of its aims.
5. In addition to owning genres, a discourse community has acquired some specific lexis.
6. A discourse community has a threshold level of members with a suitable degree of content and discoursal expertise. (24–27)

We must recognize that this definition doesn't accommodate the ways in which the community is shaped by complicating relations with other communities. In this sense, the model defines the discourse community as a self-contained unit. The definition also doesn't explore the ways changes take place in membership and discourses. The model is thus static. Furthermore, the community is defined as homogeneous. As we saw earlier, there is a lot of diversity in the membership of the discourse community. Members come with other discoursal affiliations. They may hold positions and statuses within the community that are divergent and changing. Members may come and go as they accomplish many tentative and limited goals. The lexis, content, and discourse conventions themselves keep changing, apart from displaying considerable diversity. Simply consider the heterogeneity of members in the professional community of TESOL. There are those with doctorates in education, applied linguistics, linguistics, rhetoric/composition, and literature. We employ research methods borrowed from other disciplines—statistical methods, ethnography, linguistic description, psychological protocols, demographic surveys, sociolinguistic interviews, and textual interpretation. Our theoretical persuasions are also diverse, ranging from scientific positivism to postmodernism to informal theories of teacher lore. The discourses of each disciplinary community are multiple, overlapping, shared, and hybrid. How do we introduce a student to the TESOL discourse community in terms of its distinctive features?

Partly because of these problems, Paul Prior argues for turning these definitions on their head. People don't interact with each other because of shared content, language, and conventions; these shared features evolve as people interact with each other to achieve certain common interests. In this sense, Prior's definition is more practice oriented. He relates to the community in terms of its *activities,* not its *words.* Knowledge construction and communication are achieved by engagement, participation, and performance, not by detached learning of abstract rules. This perspective draws attention to knowledge creation as an interactive process that is constantly reshaped by the tensions between communities, institutions, and persons. Social and material changes in artifacts, relationships, and resources also influence knowledge creation. In this manner, Prior hopes to retain the diversity, flexibility, and mobility of the discourse community. He argues:

> Where the combined legacy of everyday tropes for, and structuralist theories of, discourse and society has encouraged us to imagine disciplines as autonomous objects existing in detemporalized space, as territories to be mapped or systems to be diagrammed, sociohistoric theories point toward an image of disciplines as open networks, forged through relational activity that intermingles personal, interpersonal, institutional, and sociocultural histories. (Prior 1998, 25)

Prior's articulation of a sociohistoric orientation is important for many reasons. The members cannot be expected to leave their own histories at the doorstep when they engage with others in a discourse community. The values, experiences, and interests they have acquired through their personal life histories will have a role to play in their knowledge-making activities and interactional styles in a specific community. Of course, the tensions created by the experiences of the members may be productive (not dysfunctional). They generate new discourses and contribute to the vitality and progress of the community. Additionally, the history of the community cannot be forgotten. Through time it acquires resources, statuses, and interests that also motivate its activity.

One feature that I would emphasize in the evolving definition of discourse communities is the place of conflict. Both Swales and Prior make it appear that anyone can join a discourse community at will. But we must think of discourse communities as power-ridden. Communities prefer to restrict membership to a closed circle that can preserve its vested interests. They colonize other communities and their own prospective members into thinking and behaving in supportive ways. Consider, for example, the relationship between novices and experts that Swales mentions. How are the "threshold level" of membership and hierarchical positions decided? The dominant members would work out mechanisms and conventions to keep others in the margins or would simply keep them outside the group. In fact, what constitutes "relevant" knowledge, register, genres, conventions, and terminology for the community may be periodically redefined to provide an advantage to the experts. The distinction between experts and novices, then, can give rise to conflict and struggle. It is not that the experts in the community don't like to include new members to boost the numbers in their group. But they would like to see that their vested interests and power are not challenged. Similarly, at the intergroup level, the community would like to spread its own discourses to other groups in order to legitimize its worldview and claim it as universally valid. Here again, the community will see that its power is not challenged by other groups.[1] Foucault's definition of what he calls "fraternities of discourse" captures the paradoxical generative and repressive functions of discourse communities. He says that their "function is to preserve or to reproduce discourse, but in order that it should circulate within a closed community, according to strict regulations, without those in possession being dispossessed by this distribution" (Foucault 1972, 225).

To illustrate the implications of this orientation to knowledge production, we can compare how scholars in the center and the periphery relate to each other. I have argued elsewhere that in academic circles there has developed over time a dependency of periphery communities on the center academy (see Canagarajah 1996). Through the hegemony of empirical scientific orientations in knowledge production, the enjoyment of technological and economic resources for further research, and the development of publishing networks that work as a clearinghouse for new knowledge, the disciplinary communities in the center have (perhaps unwittingly) made satellites of their periphery counterparts. In this academic superiority, the other histories of colonialism, the industrial revolution, the Enlightenment, and market forces have a role to play. Not least among the causes of the inequality are the mainly orality-based discourse conventions of the periphery circles. These differences place periphery scholars at a disadvantage when they attempt to publish articles in center academic journals. The knowledge of periphery communities is therefore treated as inferior, local, or nonstandard. All this sets up a conflictual relationship between scholars in the center and the periphery, although they belong to an academic community that broadly shares certain common objectives and values (that distinguish them from other nonacademic communities).

Socializing ESOL Students into Disciplinary Communities

This orientation to discourse communities generates important insights into the challenges in academic writing for students from bilingual and minority cultural backgrounds. If writing is not a detached mastery of the form and content of academic discourses but a socialization into the communicative values, norms, and processes of the academy, the challenge is complex for ESOL students.

> Though ESOL students are not total strangers to academic/English discourses (which enjoy global hegemony), they are not insiders to these communities. The fact that they have some awareness of these discourse rules doesn't mean that they can presume to be comembers of the target community. Moreover, (passive) com-

petence in academic discourses shouldn't be mistaken for mastery in performance. The latter comes through close association with the community and deep engagement in its communicative activities. Definitely, students from the dominant communities enjoy a head start in academic literacy, as the discourses of their family and social groups are closer to those of the academy.

Foreign and minority students may bring with them certain negative attitudes toward the academic community. The academic community has a history of denigrating the local knowledge and indigenous scholarship of some of these communities (see Hess 1995). In other communities, the Western academy has helped imperialistic forces further their interests (see Nandy 1990). It is not surprising that minority students are hostile toward the academy, as much as they want to join it in order to succeed in the contemporary world.

In order to facilitate a more direct engagement with the academic community and its discourses, we have to discover bridges or stepping stones. We can use for this purpose the commonalties in both communities or the discourse features of the academy that the students are already familiar with.

Students should be prepared for discursive struggle, with the realization that discourse communities are conflictual in their relationship. Insider status in the community is tied to status, prestige, material resources, and power. While the academic community does like to keep others in the fringes as a passive audience for its work, it doesn't like giving them insider status. So students have to treat writing and communication as struggle. They have to develop discourse strategies to achieve insider status through a process of conflict and negotiation.

Even as they gain relative insider status in the academic community, ESOL students may have conflicts regarding their identity and group allegiance. Their preferred identities may be different from those valued by the academy.

Furthermore, they may fear that academic success will involve ostracization or alienation from their native community members. Students need ways of resolving these conflicts as they continue to communicate to the academy. At the least they may require coping strategies to manage the (at times) conflicting identities and allegiances.

A related fear that students have in engaging with academic communities derives from their reproductive agendas. As students master academic discourses, they may become so fully influenced by their ideologies as to consider them superior to their native community's worldview. This could imply that they will become agents of academic discourses and spread those values in their own communities. It takes considerable independent thinking and critical skills to retain the hybrid identities and multiple subjectivities one comes with.

How do composition schools theorize ways in which students can cross discourse boundaries? The social process school in L1 composition circles has proposed what I call (in chap. 1) the *crossing model,* which has held considerable currency among ESOL writing teachers (see Bizzell 1982; Rose 1989). Scholars in this school propose that we demythologize academic discourses by showing that they are socially constructed and changing paradigms for explaining reality. They are no different in status or character from the discourses of the students' communities of primary socialization. If students can understand that these discourses are of equal status, they will have fewer inhibitions using them. Students should then be encouraged to adapt to these discourses in the manner of codeswitching—that is, when they communicate with their native community members they will use the conventions preferred by them; when they communicate in the academy, they will take on the disciplinary conventions. Social process scholars believe that discourse analysis can help describe and critique the conventions of diverse communities and discover commonalties from the students' backgrounds in order to ease their transition to academic discourses.

Conventions that are common in the society could be used
as bridges between different discourse communities—for
example, to ease the transition into the academic discourse
community for students who come from discourse communities far removed from it. . . . Through discourse analysis we might offer them an understanding of their school
difficulties as the problems of a traveler to an unfamiliar
country—yet a country in which it is possible to learn the
language and the manners and even "go native" while still
remembering the land from which one has come. (Bizzell
1982, 218, 238)

In attempting to practice this model in my courses, I have
faced some significant problems (see Canagarajah 1997a,
1997b). Despite the demythologization of discourses, minority students find it hard to accept that these discourses are dif-
ferent-but-equal. They know that academic discourses are
unequal and antithetical to the interests of their communities.
So using the academic discourses—albeit with some critical
detachment—would still give life and power to their dominant status. Furthermore, students are uncomfortable with
representing their identities through academic discourses.
They see that they are adopting voices and subjectivities that
they abhor and have been trained historically to suspect or
mock. What they seem to want is to take their identities, values, and interests with them as they communicate in the academy. It appeared to me (although they didn't articulate this explicitly) that students would like to creatively complicate the
academic discourse by adopting a "multivocal" approach that
fuses their native discourses with the conventions valued by
the academy.

Such a perspective gains a lot of respect in the postmodern
culture, where identities and discourses are not perceived in
dichotomous terms. All individuals claim hybrid subjectivities. Similarly, discourses and texts show considerable fusion
deriving from histories of contact. It is possible then for students not to use academic discourses in the academy's terms
but to construct mixed discourses and identities that take

their own interests into account. Such communicative acts may serve to democratize and broaden academic discourses. Vivian Zamel (1996, 1997) has proposed a model of *transculturation* in L2 circles to theorize that moving between discourse communities is quite natural for students who enjoy multicultural backgrounds. Her position is motivated by the postmodernist notion that essentialization, classification, and categorization of any kind are rigid and deterministic. Using terms like "transcending boundaries" and "transculturation model," she argues that academic discourses are so heterogeneous and ESOL student cultures so diverse that many different outcomes are possible. She cites radical minority scholars like bell hooks, Min-Zhan Lu, and Gloria Anzaldúa to make her case for student agency.

The pedagogical space Zamel creates for perceiving multilingualism and multiculturalism as a resource is welcome. She thus opens a view of L2 writing as additive, not subtractive, for literacy competence. However, the prefix *trans* in her language raises suspicions about Zamel's eventual direction. What is lacking is a critical orientation to this boundary-crossing process. It is made to appear that this movement between communities is unrestricted and unhindered (except perhaps by ill-advised teachers). As we discussed earlier, in addition to the academy being an exclusive and hegemonic community, the students themselves experience conflicts of identity and allegiance. They also come with histories of oppression and discrimination, which sets up a conflictual relationship with the academy. More importantly, the notion of hybrid identities shouldn't be used to remove subjects from their specific location in society and history. Despite processes of postmodern fusion and hybridity, minority communities still occupy a marginalized status in society, their discourses don't constitute cultural capital, and stereotypes are imposed on them to exert domination. They cannot move outside discourses and cultures to achieve a neutral, free position, as the prefix *trans* may suggest to some. So students do have to struggle against the imposition of negative identities and statuses in order to achieve a space of advantage for themselves. Multilingual students' struggle for voice is more *counter*discursive than *trans*discursive.

A perspective on the academy that takes into account the struggles and conflicts in conducting critical literacy is Pratt's notion of *contact zones*. She considers the postcolonial world as comprising many domains of cultural and ideological contact of diverse social groups, giving rise to new genres of literacies and communication. Though she adopts a postcolonial orientation that is congenial to the hybridity of subjects and the fluidity of discourses, she defines the academy as "social spaces where cultures meet, clash, and grapple with each other, often in contexts of highly asymmetrical relations of power" (1991, 34). Thus Pratt reminds us that heterogeneity shouldn't be taken to mean that the academy is an egalitarian domain. The cultural contact here takes place under asymmetrical relations of power. Because of this situation, minorities adopt many subtle and creative forms of communication to construct their oppositional forms of knowledge and discourses. Autoethnography, transculturation, critique, collaboration, bilingualism, mediation, parody, denunciation, imaginary dialogue, and vernacular expression are among the few such forms Pratt lists. Students cannot just cross boundaries as Bizzell argues, or merge boundaries as Zamel encourages, but they can appropriate discourses in order to gain voice. This means that students shouldn't adapt to the academy's conventions one-sidedly. The academy has to be, and is to some extent, permeable to alternate/oppositional discourses. Through discursive conflict, students adopt creative strategies to fuse their interests and values into the academic conventions.

How such a critical perspective differs from the social process school is important to understand. From the contact zones perspective, the academy is by definition a meeting point of disparate discourses (although under the unequal relationship set by the expert/professional scholars). For social process, the academy has a distinct discourse, in which the discourse of minority students does not have a place—though it has a legitimate place in vernacular settings. Furthermore, the motif of *crossing*, which occurs frequently in the writing of Mike Rose (1989) and Bizzell (1992), assumes students moving from one zone to the other. But the notion of *contact* considers these students as coming with their discourses to engage or negotiate with the discourse of the academy to construct texts of various levels of mediation or fusion. The motif of the contact zones perspective is one of expanding boundaries. This model therefore takes into account the resistance students may have in shifting to academic discourse in its own terms. It orientates to this process of switching codes or shuttling between communities as a process of struggle and conflict.

What teachers have to attempt is to get students to engage with the academy, not necessarily be inducted into it. It is not crossing over into the academy but shuttling between communities that might be ideologically desirable for students. Students then shouldn't give up their own experiences, values, and interests as they engage with academic discourse. While engaging with academic scholars, texts, and activities, they should do so with the consciousness that they are partial outsiders. They don't have to become insiders in the sense that they go fully "native" in the academic domain (as spelt out by Bizzell). As Bartholomae and Petrosky (1986) point out in their reading/writing pedagogy (discussed in chap. 5), there is an advantage in students maintaining their outsider status. The resulting discursive tension provides a critical detachment toward the academic community that can lead to creative text construction. Prior (1998) theorizes how members may participate in the specific discursive activities of the community with the full consciousness of their histories—that is, their experiences, values, identities. It is in this way that they can adopt a relative detachment toward the academic discourses, critique them, and develop new perspectives.

How does the native (or primary) discourse of the member play a role in his or her orientation to the academic discourse? Adopting terminology from Bakhtin, Prior argues that this may happen by a process of *lamination,* where the *authoritative discourse* of the institution merges with the *internally persuasive discourse* of the student. Both may exist in parallel for some time (or even in a state of tension) before they begin to inch toward each other with subtle modifications. Prior shows through his ethnographies on graduate students how their experiences and relationships outside the academy contribute to their appreciating the positions presented by their professors. There are some points on which the students' positions don't correspond to those of the experts in the discipline. Through time and constant negotiation between the advisor and student, both move toward a position that satisfies both of them while leaving their original positions slightly altered. Thus the authoritative discourse of the expert gradually becomes the internally persuasive discourse of the student, just as the former itself slightly changes in light of the new experiences introduced by the student. This is a creative and critical orientation to literacy. By bringing their own histories into their writing projects students are empowered, not paralyzed or confused. Therefore students have to make a sincere attempt to engage with members of the academic community and infuse their insights into the authoritative discourse.

Contact Zone Text Construction:
An Example

How does the life of shuttling between discourse communities shape literate products? How do contact zone engagements get represented in texts? The membership of bilingual writers in competing and conflicting communities can turn out to be a resource for critical literacy. These writers can bring to play the discourses and conventions from alternate communities to develop an independent and critical position in their communicative and knowledge-construction practices. What I see a Sri Lankan professor doing in his research writing is a model that ESOL students may aspire to. Following, I present excerpts from two of his essays—both written in English but for different discourse communities. The first paper was presented in a local academic forum, while the other was published in an international scholarly journal (published in the United States).

The opening of the first paper, "English in Our Tamil Society: A Sociolinguistic Appraisal" (Suseendirarajah 1992), is somewhat narrative and relaxed. The author sets the scene well before beginning his sociolinguistic analysis. Though this opening resembles that of many of his papers written in Tamil (as in Suseendirarajah 1991), his tone is a bit more objective in this paper in deference to the English-speaking local audience. The paper begins with an announcement of his research objective (move 3/step 1a according to the Swalesian moves).

[Move 3/step 1a]: An attempt is made in this paper to present briefly the status and functions of English in the modern Sri Lankan Tamil society and to discuss the attitudes of different categories of people in the society towards English. As a preamble, a brief historical view of the position occupied by English during the past, especially before the independence of Sri Lanka is presented.
[Move 1/step 1]: Generally, the status and functions of English in the Sri Lankan society have been and are governed by the language policy of the government. The societal attitudes too have been responsible for the position of English to date.
[Move 1/step 2]: [The author distinguishes sociolinguistic tendencies of different Sri Lankan communities.]

Though the paper adopts a narrative flow throughout and develops views on bilingualism through anecdotes and casual observations (i.e., without empirical data), the author adopts a formal researcher-like prose in the conclusion.

[Concluding paragraph]: A separate detailed study of the status and functions of English in our universities both in academic as well as administrative sections will be a desideratum. A comparison of language use among universi-

ties may be useful to understand language trends and problems in our universities.

The greater level of formality in this paper (compared to the more narrative and personal papers generally submitted in this forum in Tamil—see Canagarajah in press) is motivated by a need for instilling a more disciplined and objective stance in local academic discourse. The author has written elsewhere of the need to adopt an empirical approach in research activity, especially for those close to the interests of the local culture, as monolingual Tamil scholars tend to be too emotionally involved and tradition affirming in their scholarly work (see Suseendirarajah 1991). The writer is therefore constructing a somewhat hybrid text for the local academic context. Though the paper conforms to the largely narrative structure preferred in local forums, it is not wholly so. The more objective and analytical sections insert a new feature into local discourse. Thanks to his proficiency in English and research training in the West, the author is able to negotiate an independent footing and voice in the local academic discourse. The paper therefore makes a critical contribution in attempting to shift local conventions of knowledge making in new directions.

But consider a paper written for the Western academic community. The paper, titled "Caste and Language in Jaffna Society," was published in the mainstream journal *Anthropological Linguistics* (Suseendirarajah 1978). The introductory paragraph is uncharacteristically brief.

> *[Move 3/step 1b]:* The purpose of this paper is to correlate caste and language in the Jaffna Hindu Tamil society.
> *[Move 1/step 2]:* This study is mainly based on data collected from a few sample villages in the Jaffna peninsula where the political and economic ascendancy of the VeL-LaaLas (landlords) was very dominant in the recent past.

The author has to first adopt some discourse strategies to circumvent the problems he faces in meeting the typical requirements of Western journals. Since he is unable to perform a thorough literature review pertaining to his subject because of his limited resources, he begins directly with an announcement of his research. Unlike in his previous paper, where the introductory section runs to about five paragraphs, in this paper there are only two sentences for introduction. Based on observations from other RAs written locally, I have labeled this strategy "the least said, the better"—as the writer doesn't want to display the gaps in his knowledge by indulging in extended discourse. The writer is also cognizant of the fact that the relaxed and personal tone of local discourse may not be appreciated by the more focused Western academic audience.

The second sentence in the opening paragraph is another move of accommodation to the Western RA structure. But this too is achieved in a manner that is suitable to the needs of the writer. Not adopting a separate section for methodology, the writer provides some information on the fieldwork carried out in the introduction. The reason why periphery scholars are reticent in discussing methodology is that they don't enjoy the resources to employ the high-tech equipment or elaborate procedures used by scholars from the center. They also have a different valuation regarding the use of empirical methods. Not making a fetish of scientific approaches, they hold that findings deriving from lengthy periods of informal observation and disciplined study may constitute valid research. Therefore, they make a mere gesture to satisfy the Western expectations of methodology in articles written for such forums. (In fact, in the paper for the local audience, discussed earlier, there is no statement of methodology. The local audience takes for granted that the author has adopted a reasonably acceptable research procedure within his means and doesn't scrutinize methods closely.)

In the introductory section, then, the paper seems to accommodate the Western conventions of RAs in its matter-of-factness, objectivity, and restraint (although this is done in the author's own terms and in light of the constraints he faces). The paper continues in this vein till the concluding section.

In the final paragraph, however, some aspects of the writer's discourse seem peculiar.

[Concluding paragraph]: In concluding, it may be said that man has awakened. He has a sense of human equality and humanity. He is for better change. Sooner or later we may miss most if not all of the sociolinguistic correlates recorded herein. They are on the verge of dying out.

The writer indulges here in a moralizing/moralistic discourse. Statements of this nature are often freely interspersed in local academic writing. It is possible therefore that the writer is reacting here against an excessively depersonalized discourse that suppresses his voice. Though indulging in this discourse in other high-visibility sections of the paper—like the introduction or methodology—may prejudice the referees against publishing the paper, the writer strategically makes a space for it in the innocuous section of the conclusion. Perhaps he is assuming that the editor/referees may be less critical of this discourse when it appears in this context.

There are other minor ways in which the writer diverges from Western RAs. Western scholars may have chosen to have a greater sense of closure in the final paragraph by summarizing the paper or identifying future areas of research (in fact, the writer does precisely this in his paper to the local audience). Belanger (1982) prescribes such moves, following an empirical study of conclusions in RAs. The author also refuses to give in to other moves that are standard in the introduction. He doesn't include move3/step 2 (announcing principal findings) or move 3/step 3 (indicating RA structure), which are key components of Western academic texts. Local scholars have reservations with "front-weighted" structures that spell out the argument and findings in the very beginning of the paper, as they tend to prefer a more implicit development. What we see then is that the writer is making critical adjustments as he writes for different communities—"critical" because he wants to infuse his desired oppositional discourse into the established conventions of the Western academy. In fact, by using the discourse of the alternate communities he enjoys membership in, he is able to challenge each community strategically. This is precisely the advantage of our multiple memberships in discourse communities. And such are the hybrid texts that emerge from the intercultural negotiations in the contact zone.

The author may appear too bold in adopting these rhetorical modifications in the more rigorously refereed (compared to local journals) Western journal. Perhaps his confidence stems from a good understanding of the nature of the journal and the relevance of his subject matter. Sociolinguistic aspects of Jaffna society have rarely appeared in Western scholarly journals. Also, *Anthropological Linguistics* is more open to foregrounding linguistic data (in an empirical fashion), rather than demanding excessive theoretical or interpretive discussions (as done, e.g., by *Language in Society*). These reasons may explain why the paper did get published despite its violation of some of the standard moves expected in Western RAs.

We have to be careful, however, not to give the impression that this process of shuttling between communities is a free-floating movement that is easily achieved. The author's rhetorical switches are not free of commitment to ideological biases and social principles. What we see in Suseendirarajah is a movement to Western academic communities from the angle of his local community (and vice versa). He uses commonalties to move across boundaries but inserts his personal biases to adopt a critical perspective and oppositional stance. Thus he uses his local values and discourses for critical possibilities. As I argued earlier, it is difficult if not impossible to jettison one's native discourses and become native in a different community. The author engages with the Western academy with a solid grounding in his local discourses and knowledge. The fact that Suseendirarajah could get published in a mainstream journal, despite failing to fulfill all the established moves of the RA and in fact adopting certain peculiar moves, shows that oppositional forms of communication are not impossible in the academy.

Alternate/Oppositional Communities

Though the shuttling between communities that we see in Suseendirarajah is fascinating in its textual realization, it is not achieved easily. For minority students to bring their own preferred discourses into the classroom, to challenge the dominant academic discourses, and to creatively reconstruct genres takes a lot of courage and imagination. For this reason, students need the space to negotiate and experiment with discourses/texts without inhibition. The classroom and the educational institution sometimes don't provide for students the freedom and flexibility to negotiate discourses. Students are too intimidated by the power of their teachers (and other academic authorities) to express discourses and identities that are not institutionally desired. Examinations and institutional reward systems impose restrictions on the extent to which students can resist the discourses desired in the school. Also, the often rigidly structured school environment doesn't provide the space for creativity and play. In interacting with students from a variety of backgrounds (some from more privileged backgrounds), students are under pressure to conform to the dominant discourses and identities preferred in the classroom. Even in contexts where there is relatively more freedom, minority students tend not to challenge established discourses openly, as they fear that this would hinder their ability to score good grades and succeed educationally (see Canagarajah 1993, 1997b).

In such situations, minority students seek out and collaboratively construct alternate sites in the classroom where they can freely practice their preferred modes of communication and develop oppositional discourses. Though these hidden sites could seem divorced from the directly pedagogical happenings in the classroom and suggest negative outcomes for educational success, they may function as a site of "legitimate peripheral participation" (Lave and Wenger 1991).[2] From the slightly detached and indirect vantage point of the separate community life they enjoy, minority students develop resources, strategies, and discourses that enable a critical and creative appropriation of mainstream ways of thinking and communicating. Not only are the hybrid forms of contact zone literacy practiced here, but students also develop strategies that lead to critical writing. It is important therefore for teachers to understand the possibilities inherent in such student underlife behavior. The typical teacherly approach of suppressing these surreptitious activities of student culture, or of treating them as signs of disobedience, deviance, and dysfunction, needs to be reconsidered.

I call these hidden sites in the academy *safe houses* (see Canagarajah 1997b). They are for me sites that are relatively free from surveillance, especially by authority figures, perhaps because these are considered nonofficial or extrapedagogical by them. Domains of time as well as space may serve as safe houses in educational institutions. Of course, students can make other normal/routine sites in the educational environment free of surveillance by colluding in constructing a culture of underlife behavior (such as speaking an in-group language that cannot be understood by the teacher). Though there is considerable fluidity in the boundaries of these sites then, some locations still tend to favor the construction of safe houses. Figure 6 (on the next page) provides a list of sites I have uncovered as safe houses in my research.

Before we discuss the ways in which these sites help in the development of literacy, we have to note their significance for minority students. It appears that their classroom culture may draw from traditions of underlife resistance practiced by their communities for generations. There is historical and anthropological documentation that minority communities have always collaboratively constructed sites of community underlife where they can celebrate their suppressed identities and develop subversive discourses and identities that inspire resistance against domination. Members of my own Sri Lankan

In the classroom
Spatial domains: asides between students, passing of notes, small-group interactions, peer activities, marginalia in textbooks and notebooks
Temporal domains: transition from one teacher to another, before classes begin, after classes are officially over

Outside class: the canteen, the library, dorms, playgrounds, computer labs

In cyberspace: email, online discussions/chat

Fig. 6. Sites of pedagogical safe houses

Tamil community adopted the double-faced behavior of pretending to be Christians outwardly but maintaining a vigorous life as Hindus in their in-group circles in order to qualify for better jobs and higher education from the British during the colonial period.[3] Such behavior has often led colonial rulers to call their subjects lying, inscrutable, undependable, hypocritical, shifty, and cunning. But these are the *weapons of the weak*—to borrow the title of a book by James Scott (1985), who articulates the politics of this strategy by peasants in Malaysia. For the disempowered, who realize the difficulties of challenging the might of dominant groups directly, these are simple acts in their everyday life for gaining a measure of control over their lives. The acts of stealing, foot-dragging, cheating, and noncompliance are partial and "safe" ways of resisting the power of the master and gaining some relief in material terms for one's survival. Even the jokes, parody, sarcasm, name-calling, and veiled threats are disguised forms of resistance. These are acts through which the oppressed retain their dignity and develop hidden ideologies that explain the injustice of the situation or work out spiritual alternatives that give them hope. Over time, these communities develop a shared understanding of their oppression and ways of coping with the hostile environment. There is an expanding body of ethnographic literature that shows lower-caste groups using safe houses against upper-caste groups, women against men, and serfs against landowners.[4]

In a more general sociological sense, almost everyone seeks such spaces in the cracks between institutions and discourses to develop a sense of self. As Goffman (1961) argues, "The practice of reserving something of oneself from the clutch of an institution . . . is not an incidental mechanism of defence but rather an essential constitution of the self" (319). Goffman studies underlife behavior in what he calls "total institutions" (e.g., mental asylums, prisons, etc.). While the inmates conform to the restrictive selves demanded by the institution in the official eyes (primary adjustment), they take up a range of alternate practices and identities in the underlife to develop a more qualified/independent conformism (secondary adjustment). Goffman sees more possibilities of conformity rather than resistance to the system in such behavior. However, the notion of legitimate peripheral participation helps us to see how the qualified conformity and subtle distancing may form a paradoxical process of participating in academic discourse in one's own terms, negotiating and appropriating the dominant conventions to suit one's personal interests.

So how do safe houses in the academy help develop academic literacy for minority students? Let me quickly discuss an example in detail before I summarize some of the other ways in which safe houses help in literacy. Consider the following interaction in an ESOL class in Sri Lanka where the use of L1 is prohibited.

> T: [reads] . . . it is our duty to look after trees and replace them through reforestation. [to class] Reforestation means replanting trees and vegetation. [continues reading]

> S1: [whispering] Reforestation *enRaal ennappaa?* (What does "reforestation" mean?)

> S2: *umakku teriyaataa? kaaTaakkam.* Social science-*ilai paTiccam.* (Don't you know? Reforestation. We studied about that in "social science.")

> S1: *enna? kaTukalai aLikkiratoo?* (What? Destroying forests?)

S2: illai appaa. marankalai tirumpa naTukiratu. (No, man, replanting trees.)

While the teacher reads a passage for listening comprehension, the students are engaging in an aside to interpret a difficult word. In switching to Tamil to unpack the meaning of the English text, students display how the L1 may become a resource in L2 literacy. Their interpretation is collaborative, as they muster the resources and information each possesses to interpret the text. Here they are drawing from what they have learned in a social science course to help decode a text in the English classroom. We may also note here that using translation methods to understand texts is looked down upon in language-teaching circles. However, such unorthodox and non-institutionalized methods still have value for people at the local level and are often used to interpret texts. Barton and Hamilton (1998) call them *vernacular literacies* (defined as unorthodox practices developed in everyday contexts outside formal institutions). Safe houses therefore enable students to bring in to the classroom reading/literacy strategies they practice outside in their community and in-group contexts.

I have found other situations where students situate the classroom text in a wider social and cultural context that has more meaning to them. Thus they appropriate the academic texts to interpret them according to their own frames of reference. Such practices sometimes help students read oppositional—or at least independent—messages that differ from the interpretations of the teacher. For instance, the graffiti in the margins of textbooks reveal an attempt to understand the narratives and situations in different terms. The many symbols from Tamil nationalism that occur in the serialized detective story in one book reveal that the innocent man fleeing the agents of law to prove himself has inspired students to think of many Tamil resistance fighters who were (in the local ethnic conflict) unfairly incarcerated by the state although they were perceived as selfless and noble fighters for the rights of their community. Even the Tamil clothing and appearance provided for American characters might be an attempt to understand some of the situations in terms of local life. It is through such interpretative strategies that students seek connections to their cultural and social context from visuals and narratives that lack local relevance. The graffiti also suggest how students are engaging in a process of resistant reading in terms of alternate frames of reference.

Note also the practice of codeswitching in the earlier example. Students are mixing languages in their conversation. In fact, the use of L1 is usually prohibited in ESOL classrooms in Sri Lanka—as it was in this class. As we know, schools don't teach mixed codes or multivocal literacy, as such forms of communication are considered "nonstandard" or "impure." However, codeswitching is a widespread communicative practice in bilingual societies. Though the school doesn't teach these hybrid codes, students are developing much-needed competence in this medium in their own way. In shuttling between the vernacular and English, students develop hybrid codes and get important practice in using them. They are thus learning discourse strategies that are of help in practicing a multivocal literacy. In this manner, the infusion of subversive languages and discourses can challenge the values and interests behind the dominant codes.

Furthermore, safe houses provide a space where students can practice vernacular discourses, communicative genres, and speech acts. My ethnographic studies show that safe houses are a busy and colorful site of mixed discourses and heterogeneous speech acts. Though the surface life in the academy may pressure students to abandon their native discourses in favor of the powerful "mainstream" conventions, the safe house provides a space where the vernacular may be retained. The linguistic repertoire of the students remains intact, thanks to safe houses. In order to engage in the critical literacy of reconstructing dominant conventions according to oppositional discourses, it is important for students to retain their vernacular.

Though some pedagogies (influenced by the crossing model) let students practice their vernacular in their home context (while adopting the mainstream codes for formal classroom purposes), there is something lost in students not being able to practice vernaculars at school. But the engagement with competing discourses and languages in safe houses enables implicit comparisons between vernacular and academic discourses that help develop a metadiscursive awareness among students. Thus the safe house fulfills the need for a place where such comparisons can be carried out effectively. One might say that the safe houses compel students to develop a comparative awareness of the discourses they are shuttling between. There were other conversations I detected where students discussed the differences between academic and vernacular discourses more explicitly (see Canagarajah 1990). Through this process, students are able to develop a reflective and critical language usage. Such comparative understanding is invaluable for negotiating conflicting discourses in literacy and moving toward hybrid text production.

Furthermore, safe-house communication helps students resolve some of the conflicts they face in their identity and group consciousness as they engage in academic literacy. Students have often told me in interviews that using English or academic registers in their communication came into conflict with their other preferred identities. Sometimes students who scored good grades on academic assignments were excluded and stigmatized by their fellow students. But note in the codeswitching example cited earlier how students present themselves through their vernacular discourses. They have to collude in constructing this site where they can practice codes that are suppressed in the classroom. This practice develops subversive identities, as students position themselves oppositionally against the norms and rules of the institution. The safe houses thus provide a space where they can manage the conflicts for their identity in practicing academic literacy. Students are in effect saying to each other that they will play the academic game in public sites where they are evaluated, but in their in-group circles they celebrate their vernacular identities and assure each other of their grounding in the community ethos. Thus compartmentalizing the public sites and safe in-group sites, students also develop some important coping strategies to engage in academic literacy. They free themselves to live a dual life—engaging in academic discourse in one site but retaining the vernacular ethos in the other. The safe house also helps them encourage each other against the stresses of an "alien" environment, inspire each other for continued engagement, and provide a source of solidarity and sustenance for the development of oppositional literacy practices.

Apart from the more direct connections to the development of critical academic literacy, we mustn't ignore some larger contributions of safe houses. In negotiating these conflicting discourses and adopting coping strategies, students are finding ways of constructing a creative and independent voice in literacy. Voice, as we know from poststructuralist discourses, emerges as subjects position themselves in the cracks between discourses and institutions. The hybrid identities formed through safe-house practices go a long way in developing a critical voice for the students in academic literacy. Note also how these strategies help students experiment with safe ways of expressing critical positions in academic discourse (as I exemplified with Viji's and Donnie's essays in chap. 5). These practices develop a strategic "footing" that will help them enter the academic conversation to infuse their own messages according to their own frames of reference.

Such literacies don't develop in a single day. Students need a space to try out new forms of communication and develop new discourses through a process of trial and error. I did find examples of safe houses where students experimented with discourses. Consider another series of graffiti found in the margins of an ESL textbook.[5]

> I love all of the girls peautiful in the Jaffna University.
> Reader: I love you. Bleave me.
> I do not love you because I do not believe you. You are terrible man.

Each of these lines was written in different ink, presumably by different students. Though students are usually reluctant to use English in in-group communication, here they are play-fully using it for a discourse—romance—that calls for English. (Since the messages are not signed, the students are not being serious in uttering these declarations.) The Tamil language has a conservative ethos and favors the expression of love only in more formal terms. While playfully adopting these identities in a language that they have clearly picked up by themselves outside the classroom, the students are also en-gaging in text construction. Each clause used by the previous students gets embedded in a larger, more complex sentence in the hands of the third student. The safe house therefore fur-thers play and learning in a very paradoxical way.

Peripheral Apprenticeship

The literate and social life of safe houses shows that appren-ticeship into the academic community doesn't have to be a di-rect or unilateral process of teachers mentoring students into the discourses and relationships of the academy. Nor does it have to be undertaken through teacher instruction. Though there is a legitimate place for teachers and faculty members to gradually initiate students into the practices of the academy and socialize them into its values and norms (as we will dis-cuss in the next section), we should envision more indirect and even seemingly oppositional ways of participating in the knowledge-making activities of the academy. There are good reasons why safe houses may constitute an effective form of acculturating into academic practices. Students enjoy a healthy detachment from the experts to process the disciplin-ary discourses in their own terms. They are able to draw from their other community memberships to bring a critical per-spective on academic discourses. They muster their collective resources and develop a practice of negotiating competing discourses. In fact, the best way to gain recognition from the academy is to develop one's own agendas in the framework of the ongoing academic conversation. Direct mentoring by teachers may involve excessive dependence on their author-ity that can stifle the individuality of novices.

We are beginning to see more complex orientations to disciplinary enculturation emerging in recent research. Though many of these studies are related to the apprenticeship of graduate students, we can draw lessons from these case studies for college-level students as well. Casanave (1995) reacts against faculty-centered enculturation and encourages a diversified process of socialization involving multiple actors and activities. The academy is treated as an "intellectual village," rather than a rigidly stratified and self-contained community. Students are called upon to immerse themselves in a rich context of academic culture, rather than limit themselves to pedagogical assignments. These studies show that academic initiation involves a complex socialization into the community's practices of reading, writing, talk, and even everyday communication through the many literacy events that occur outside the classroom—that is, special lectures, seminars, conferences, ceremonies, and performances. Even in the case of traditional processes of enculturation, Belcher (1994) goes on to show that the more successful of the student/faculty relationships she studied were based on collaborative and consensual relationships, rather than hierarchical, one-way relationships.

Prior (1998) distinguishes between different typologies of participation in the academic community, exemplifying them through his case study of two ESL graduate students. *Passing* represents an institutionalized regiment of work in the academy, tabulated by credit hours, grades, and other bureaucratic requirements. Prior feels that this is the dominant mode of participation found in the academy. Students do experience tensions between passing and learning, as one doesn't necessarily imply the other. But often students tend to resolve the conflict in terms of passing, as it is an easy way of displaying academic engagement and achieving success. *Procedural display* is more relational, based on cooperative and responsive encounters between the teacher and the student, as they jointly accomplish the educational activity through practices of *alignment* and *coordination*. The latter practices involve aligning oneself to the positions of the mentor and collaborating in his or her research and theoretical activities. But effective forms of participation in communities "are diverse, multiple, always peripheral . . . [and] there is no core to such communities" (Prior 1998, 102). Also, complementing the mentor's projects may not help the student achieve a critical and independent position in the disciplinary circles. For these reasons, even procedural display cannot fully undertake the initiation into academic communities. To move to the third model then, *deep participation* is "a form of centripetal participation marked by rich access to, and engagement in, practices" (Prior 1998, 103). It is those students who have relatively unrestricted access to the genres, sites, and events of the community who develop mature levels of membership. They should enjoy their relative freedom to acculturate to academic discourses in their own terms, in relation to their values and interests. Of course, this outcome depends not only on the motivation, attitude, and creativity of the novice to gain access and understand the established discourses. To some extent, the academic community itself should make available its sites and genres for engagement with diverse groups of members. Comparing two ESL graduate students, Mai and Teresa, Prior finds that Mai's participation was limited by the range of people she came into contact with and by her attitude to texts as authoritative wholes with limited transparency. Teresa, on the other hand, developed dynamic relationships with others, who helped her in a multichannel engagement with academic practices, and thereby appropriated texts with confidence and clarity. The different patterns of socialization therefore have implications for why one student (Theresa) is eventually more successful than the other (Mai) in her research work.

What emerges from such research is that socialization into the disciplinary communities is a complex, multichannel activity. It is also collaborative in the sense that socialization occurs when students interact with others in meaningful, focused activities. This doesn't necessarily mean engaging in theoretical and research paradigms in the disciplines and becoming stodgy academics. There are other activities that are meaningful for undergraduate students and can enable them to undertake research and produce useful knowledge. For example, many instructors have used community-oriented projects in which students study and report on issues confronting the local people. Studying the attitudes of people to police brutality in an effort to improve the community/police relationship, recommending ways in which delays in the transit system can be solved, researching ways of reducing pollution in the city, and explaining the resistance of homeless people to getting help in shelters—these are projects that are meaningful for students in New York City. There are research reports on how similar projects carried out by high school students have been used for serious purposes by policy makers. Cole and Zuengler (2000) report about a hands-on, community-based, district- and state-supported project by a group of high school students, labeled the Asthma Project, which involved surveys and multidisciplinary collaboration. The study was eventually commended by the state legislature. Projects of this nature involve fieldwork, interviewing techniques, archival research, Internet searches, and the writing of case reports that integrate the different skills of reading, speaking, listening, and writing. Furthermore, students seek information and literature from a range of fields—sociology, economics, the news media, and psychology—that can facilitate engagement with experts from those fields and their own content-based courses. Increasingly, ESOL scholars feel that it is such project-based pedagogy that will prepare students for the new economy and the Internet-based work environment, which requires efficient knowledge workers (see Warschauer 2000; Gee 2000).

The university environment can also be used to engage students with the talk and texts of academics. Analogous to the "immersion" pedagogy for language acquisition, students can be involved in the workings of the academic community in order to develop a familiarity with its communicative genres and practices. In my freshman writing classes I ask students to attend special events in the college—public lectures by visiting scholars, seminars on special topics, conferences, et cetera—and produce a report for the class. This exposure lets them see the academic community in action. Also, this is a nonthreatening way in which they can participate (passively or peripherally) in the workings of the academy.

We have to also ask discipline-based faculty members to take their interaction with students seriously. Making a rigid distinction between language teaching and content teaching, professors sometimes overlook the ways in which both of these are interrelated. They have to consider their interaction with students as a process of mentoring into the discourse of their discipline. When students follow courses in the various disciplines, even when they are introductory ones, faculty members have to work hard on developing a meaningful relationship with them. Apart from the time they give for conferences and informal meetings with students, faculty members have to take seriously their attitude to the written work of the students. Are these assignments meaningful in enabling students to grapple with the established scholars and texts in the discipline? Do these assignments enable students to construct new knowledge, information, or perspectives of value to at least their peers and the instructor? How do instructors read, grade, and comment on the papers of their students? Some researchers point out that there is little meaningful response given to the written assignments submitted by their students (Braine 1988). It is equally limiting to comment only on mechanical concerns or the information embodied. Faculty members must be encouraged to provide a more holistic evaluation of papers, as the communicative conventions are as important as the knowledge produced in academic contexts of writing. In this way, faculty members communicate to students the conventions that matter in the discipline. They can pose the types of questions and concerns that are raised in other professional contexts by journal editors, thesis committees, and grant agencies. Students thus get an orientation to the tenor, relationships, and practices that govern academic interactions.

The Writing Classroom

We have to finally consider how we in the writing classroom may provide resources and opportunities for the socialization of students into the disciplinary communities that matter to them. After all, we ESOL teachers, too, represent the academic community! Often, we are the unacknowledged mentors who initiate our students into the disciplinary discourses. How pedagogies like the linked program, reading/writing courses, and content-based collaborative work can help orient students to the knowledge-producing activity of the scholarly community was discussed in the previous chapter. Here we will consider how some routine pedagogical activities, like grading/evaluating practices and peer-review activities, may contribute to initiating students into the literacy conventions of the academic community.

Teacher Response

What are our patterns of grading and commentary on students' papers? Recently there has been a spurt of research activity into this matter. Studies generally show that response practices are unsystematic, meaningless, and unproductive. Zamel (1985) notes that findings about teacher-response patterns in the L2 pedagogical scene agree with research in L1.

> ESL writing teachers misread student texts, are inconsistent in their reactions, make arbitrary corrections, write contradictory comments, provide vague prescriptions, impose abstract rules and standards, respond to texts as fixed and final products, and rarely make content-specific comments or offer specific strategies for revising the texts. (86)

Given the tradition in L2 pedagogy of using written work to develop grammatical competence, teachers overwhelmingly view themselves as language teachers rather than rhetoricians. This mode of teacher response has many negative consequences for the literacy development and critical thinking of students.

It fails to engage students in negotiating content and discourse with the audience; students begin to focus only on an error-free final product.

It reduces the significance of writing as meaningful communication as students get the impression that the teacher is not interested in what they are saying; they thus lose motivation for taking original and independent perspectives on their subject.

Students are denied chances of developing skills of critical textual negotiation with the teacher; literate negotiations and interactions are important for their own sakes, as they are conventional in many academic and professional communities of writing.

Writing fails to be collaborative, as students don't get an opportunity to engage with the multiple views and perspectives of others and critically appropriate them for their purposes.

Students are deprived of the rich exposure to the academic register and professional discourse that may be represented by the meaningful commentary written by composition teachers on their essays.

All this encourages "passing," as students assume that the activity of writing is for an institutional requirement of a grade or to display participation (which, according to Prior [1998], leads to a limited initiation into the academic community).

Recent research into teacher response, student attitudes to corrections, and effectiveness of teacher intervention in the revision process suggest the following practices as constituting better teacher feedback (see Ferris and Hedgcock 1998).

Whereas direct correction of errors by teachers is ineffective, indirect self-discovery techniques can help students learn to monitor and self-correct their errors (Ferris 1995; Hendrickson 1978; Lalande 1982).

In place of criticism alone or praise alone, a combination of praise and criticism is more effective (Cardelle and Corno 1981).

Content-related comments should be the focus of initial drafts (with some general hints about grammar), while mechanics are corrected in later drafts.

Teachers should write personalized comments, provide guidance or direction, and make text-specific comments (see Bates, Lane, and Lange 1993).

Although there is no conclusive evidence about whether marginal or terminal comments are more effective (see Leki 1990a), a combination of text-specific marginal comments and more elaborate end comments is a sensible balance (Ferris and Hedgcock 1998, 137).

These recommendations and research findings have to be modified by an awareness of the students' cultural backgrounds and their styles of learning. It has been noted by many researchers that students from certain Asian communities expect more feedback on their grammar (Leki 1991b). They also expect more explicit correction, rather than directions for self-discovery. It has been said that these expectations derive from the pedagogical cultures at home. But in some cases, they may follow from the tradition of the grammar-translation method introduced in these countries earlier by Western professionals themselves. Delpit (1995) makes a more serious point when she argues that students who are strangers to the codes and discourses of the mainstream expect more direct help. A student must bring with him or her a basic level of linguistic and rhetorical competence to understand the teacher's subtle hints and veiled questions. So it is important for the teacher to respond to the individual needs of the students, while leading students to address more complex issues of rhetoric. But we don't have to be at the mercy of student expectations. Students can be coached to appreciate the different kinds of response teachers provide and gradually be led to address critical issues in writing. As the definition of writing and writing pedagogy moves toward process-oriented paradigms, students are beginning to see the importance of content-based and rhetorical feedback (see Hedgcock and Lefkowitz 1994). In a sense, student expectations are a construct of teacher/teaching strategies.

A more troubling concern is the potential for teacher response to appropriate the student's work, imposing the teacher's own thoughts on the essay. Even in cases where teachers are sensitive to this problem or are liberal-minded enough to accept diverse approaches, students experience the temptation to accommodate the teacher's views unthinkingly. Displaying features of *passing,* students may tailor their work to the interests of the institution in order to qualify for a good grade, rather than risking all this with the uncertainties of an individualistic approach. In a context of heightened concern over the dangers of appropriation, we have teachers flip-flopping between either of two possible extremes—be so humble as to stop being critical and merely "serve as a sounding board" to clarify students' intentions (Brannon and Knoblauch 1982, 162) or assert their teacherly right of authority (Ferris and Hedgcock 1998, 133). From the perspective of critical practice, both strategies are unsound. Imposing the teacher's authority is inimical to the development of the student's voice. Writers need the space to try out their own interests and styles. On the other hand, the mentoring role requires a critical contribution. The teacher does have to represent the voice of institutional authority in an effort to acquaint students with the "authoritative discourses" they are dealing with in their educational and professional life. In publishing, for example, one must deal with many critical respondents—editors, referees, reviewers—in order to achieve one's interests. The right footing emerges through negotiation. Therefore, teachers should critique essays frankly, while encouraging students to work out their own perspectives and interests within the parameters established by institutional discourses. As exemplified through Prior's (1998) case studies on mentor/graduate student relationships, both teacher and student may modify their original position, learning from each other—with the paradoxical possibility that the authoritative discourse becomes an internally persuasive discourse.

In terms of mentoring, we shouldn't forget the function of teacher/student conferences in achieving this objective. While written feedback on papers may be too detached and cursory, conferences enable a more personal and extended interaction over the writing of the student. The teacher can provide information on other matters of academic discourse and institutional culture outside the immediate bounds of the text. Students can also negotiate the appropriate footing in relation to the teacher's expectations during conferences, whereas in written feedback they can only guess their proper stance (see Zamel 1985, 97). The possibility of following up on the written feedback from the teacher—to clarify his or her comments, challenge his or her position, or discuss alternatives—is especially useful in developing the student's critical attitude to writing. We must also keep in mind the finding from ethnographies of science that personal/background information that provides a rich context for meaningful academic literacy is often passed down orally (Geisler 1994). Students may develop the relevant schemata for academic texts through these one-on-one conversations with the teacher more effectively. We also mustn't exclude the benefits of the student witnessing the teacher as a practicing academic and active writer during these visits. I have found that it is in personal conferences that I get a chance to discuss my own research and provide samples of my writing (to suit the individual interests of students). The difficulties I face in representing my perspectives in writing against the commercial and ideological interests of my publishers is a frequent topic that conveys how we all have to negotiate conflicting positions in writing.

There are of course many practical difficulties in scheduling writing conferences. Teachers are so preoccupied with preparing for multiple courses and grading papers that they don't have the time to devote to individual conferences with students. Ferris and Hedgcock (1998) offer sound advice on the logistical and procedural aspects of conferencing. There are many ways in which teachers can resolve these conflicts.

Personalize conferencing strategies according to the different learning styles, motivations, and relationships of students. (Some students prefer an indirect discourse pattern, a less threatening and less individualistic interactional format, and a visual learning style—all of which may demand more written feedback than face-to-face oral conferences.)

Establish a range of organizational patterns, captured by the "Garrison method," for example, which includes permitting students to come up to the teacher in the classroom while other students are writing in the class, regularly scheduling conferences at consistent intervals, and/or requiring students to visit the teacher at least a couple of times during the semester in the office.

Adopt a more "nondirective" discourse pattern, so that students have the option of thinking for themselves and adopting more individual alternatives.

Build some kind of accountability and ask students to follow up by indicating how they negotiated the different options suggested by the teacher in the previous conference. (Perhaps they can write a journal entry after each conference to reflect on the meeting and evaluate the experience.) Such follow-up procedures can also help avoid miscommunication between the teacher and student, since teacher response may not always be clear.

While adopting these guidelines, we should consider how we can align the teacher/student relationship with findings on disciplinary initiation emerging from research. Teachers should see to it that they establish a relationship of collaboration on a common project. They should contribute to enhancing the student's work, cultivating the relationship of a team member, rather than imposing their own interests. They should acquaint students with the rich world of text and print by leading them to further reading suitable for their projects.

They should link students with relevant faculty members who do work connected to the interests of the students. They should provide information on other happenings and events in the academic community that will contribute to the student's project. There is even guidance needed for students to cope with the institutional culture and bureaucratic processes of the academy. More importantly, teachers should model classroom relationships that are cooperative yet critical, democratic yet authoritative, and intellectually engaged yet passionate, that inspire students to challenging social relationships outside the classroom. Composition teachers must consider their work as not merely limited to the close bounds of the text.

Peer Response

There are mixed evaluations on the effectiveness of peer collaboration in enhancing literacy development. Connor and Asenavage (1994) report that few of their students' revisions were based on peer commentary and that the majority of their changes were based on other sources such as teacher feedback and self-correction. Though Mendonca and Johnson (1994) report that their students adopted peer commentary for about 53 percent of their changes, we must remember that their subjects were graduate students (unlike the college-level students in the previous study). Also, their subjects received only peer feedback, unlike the multiple sources of response in the former study. This set of studies shows that the effectiveness of peer groups will depend on many contingent factors, such as student proficiency and pedagogical content. However, it is not fair to judge the usefulness of peer groups based purely on textual changes. There are other benefits for students. In reading and commenting on their peers' writing, students put into practice their passive rhetorical competence (though they may not demonstrate this in their writing performance). Students experience a nonthreatening context in which they can discuss and clarify rhetorical options in their small groups. They learn to negotiate multiple responses from their peers, based on the dif-

ferent cultural and rhetorical preferences each person brings
with them. To some extent, their peers simulate the response
of real readers "out there" who come with diverse expectations.
The way in which writers sift through the opinions of their
peers and adopt a personal stance for their revision teaches important critical skills of choice making in writing. The chance
to see the rhetorical efforts of their peers and discuss their rationale orientates students to diversity in rhetoric and communication. It is also interesting to see how students share information and knowledge among themselves in a manner that
contests or modifies established knowledge. Finally, students
may thus bring to the classroom "vernacular literacy practices"
that may help them negotiate institutional literacy better and
make an effective transition to academic communication (as I
demonstrated earlier in my research on safe houses).

There are of course many problems encountered in making
peer groups work. Questions have been raised about students'
competence to provide constructive comments. Leki (1990b)
reports from her research that students focused overly on surface-level issues of the text, provided vague and unhelpful
comments, sounded hostile and sarcastic in their feedback,
and lacked conviction that their peers' suggestions amounted
to much. In my recent ethnography on the attitudes of college-
level ESOL students to group work, a high-achieving Russian
student said: "You know I do everything, and I try to make
more active group or something, but nobody really can do this
and I am getting bored just because of that. Maybe because of
language and not everybody can express very well or something." Matters were complicated because these students
were doing this course in order to pass the WAT. Asked which
mode of instruction they preferred—given the choice of
teacher instruction, individual work, and group discussion—
twelve out of fifteen students rated group work the worst.
Asked which activity helped them most (among those listed,
e.g., computer-mediated communication, debates, oral presentations, and peer review), thirteen out of the fifteen students rated grammar exercises and essay writing higher than
other activities. We mustn't discount the influences of the

wash-back effect from a product-oriented uniform test on these uncomplimentary views of peer work.

Ferris and Hedgcock (1998) provide many constructive suggestions to overcome some of this opposition to peer work. Among their suggestions are the following: make peer response an integral part of the course; model the process (with teachers providing examples of how holistic, specific, constructive criticism can be provided); build response skills progressively throughout the term; structure the peer response task; hold students accountable for giving and using feedback; and preplan the logistics such as the size and composition of the groups (178). We have to note, however, that a preference for an overly teacher-managed peer response grouping can spoil the dynamism and diversity of the interaction. The peer response group shouldn't be turned into an alternate channel to undertake the teacher's agendas, expectations, and rhetorical preferences. The students should feel free to explore the diverse options among themselves. Although their views may sound shallow and unorthodox, there is also the possibility that they may develop oppositional perspectives. In the safehouse interactions I studied, I found that comments that I initially treated as irrelevant to the concerns of the course turned out to have subtle oppositional perspectives on classroom agendas. We must also be open to the possibility that—as in all collaborative communities—members may grow into expertise at their own pace, direction, and logic. Outside agents may hamper this natural development with their impatience. Therefore, it is important to let the peer respondents define their practice according to their logic after some initial guidelines and examples are given by the teacher on the objectives of this pedagogical activity. The secret of the peripheral participation reported in my data from safe houses is that students develop the solidarity and understanding to develop critical practices of literacy when they are given relative autonomy in pedagogical relationships.

More recalcitrant problems for peer groups have to do with cultural differences among students. Carson and Nelson (1994) raise the interesting issue that while collaborative learning may work effectively for students from different cultures, their objectives and interactional patterns may be different. For example, "collectivist cultures" may focus more on maintaining group harmony and solidarity; "individualist cultures" may focus on what benefits each individual member can get out of the activity. Students from different cultural groups also have different styles of voicing criticism: some leave it implied; others make it explicit. Even in collectivist cultures students may make their criticism—but in a manner that doesn't spoil the harmony of the group. In some cases, criticism takes second place to affirmation of the established perspective. In a comparison of peer groups formed according to different ethnic and gender memberships, I found a group of women—comprising two Japanese, a Korean, and a Russian—deferring to the opinions and leadership of a single member (the Russian student). The other students didn't initiate comments too many times, responded directly to the Russian student, didn't ask questions, and provided only monotoned tentative answers (see Canagarajah 1999a). The Japanese student wrote in her journal:

> I was in a group which had two Japanese and one Korean and one Russian. We often talked about subjects and some small talks. But we found one problem whenever we are together. We couldn't have one conclusion without compromise, not negotiation. And almost all conclusion we handed in to professor was Rossian classmate's idea. . . . She always had strong opinion, and I was often even impressed her ideas. But she would liked to pass the opinions every times, and we, Asian students who found it hard to strong discussion because it seemed like a quarrel, just feel tired to argue with her, and said "Okay, okay, whatever you want."

However, in an all-male group with students from Ghana, Pakistan, Bulgaria, and China, the students negotiated their differences better. Their group interactions were more equal and open. It is therefore difficult to generalize that all ESOL students may behave alike. Depending on the dynamics of the specific grouping—shaped by gender, ethnicity, learning style, linguistic proficiency—certain groups may establish constructive working relationships.

Zhang (1995) makes a broad cultural distinction between L1 and L2 students, opining that both come with different expectations of the types of intervention they desire in the writing process. Though it is unwise to generalize that non-Western students always come with passive and uncritical attitudes to learning, we cannot excuse these preferences as simply cultural. They have ideological implications too, displaying tendencies toward authoritarian and nonquestioning attitudes to life and society. It is in situations like this that teachers have to critically intervene to gradually pass down to students the significance of collaborative and critical learning. To some extent, these social relations can also be modeled by the way the teacher displays qualified leadership in the class. Furthermore, it is possible to accommodate strategies of critical learning (featuring questioning, contextualization, and exploration) within the different learning styles students bring with them. The teacher has to work individually to some extent to lead students to critical learning in ways that suit their personal learning styles.

The challenge in collaborative learning is to maintain the balance between teacher guidance and student autonomy. Our discussion of safe-house practices shows that student collaboration and in-group culture practiced away from the eyes of the teacher have immense educational value. Robert Brooke (1987) shows that even unauthorized interactions, which we may consider distracting or disturbing for classroom work, can show students orientating to educational discourses and literacy activities in their own terms. There are steps that can be taken to create more opportunities for safe-house interactions. While networked classes (in my research) provide immense possibilities for students to develop safe houses by themselves, teachers can consider other ways to nurture such sites in their classrooms. Small-group discussions, peer reviews/interactions, collaborative writing, and paired work assignments are simple ways in which safe houses can be constructed inside the classroom. Collaborative projects, guided fieldwork, and research activities (in libraries, dormitories, or outside the campus) enable students to practice safe-house pedagogy outside classrooms. A way to enhance such learning strategies is to use the texts constructed in the safe houses for discussion and analysis in the classroom. The transcripts of electronic conferences, verbal disputes in the mail, and drafts of essays can be used to non-threateningly analyze the ways in which student texts differ from the academic discourses and to explore the strengths and limitations they display as discourse/knowledge forms. Such strategies convey to students that their vernacular and peer group discourses are valued academically and that they don't have to be practiced in the secrecy of their safe houses. Similarly, the attempts students make to appropriate dominant discourses and construct hybrid texts are immensely useful for pedagogical purposes.

However, we must bear in mind that it is dangerous to romanticize the texts and discourses of the students. As noted earlier, students' behavior and discourses show a mixture of oppositional and accommodative tendencies that need to be critically unpacked for their hidden values and implications. There are also discourses such as ethnic chauvinism, sexism, and racism found in safe houses. Students must be encouraged, therefore, to adopt a critical attitude not only toward the academic discourses but toward their own—as we have often been reminded by critical pedagogues (see Freire 1970, 30–35; Giroux 1988, 183–85, 1992, 29; hooks 1989, 98–104; Willis 1977). Teachers therefore have the role of providing critical support. While encouraging students to collaborate in their own terms, they should help students adopt a critical attitude toward their preferred discourses and styles of learning.

Conclusion

The orientation to academic writing in terms of discourse communities develops certain important lessons on writing as a critical social activity. First, we realize that constructs such as form, genre, content, style, and register are not universal or value free. They are defined and valued differently by communities, in accordance with their needs, interests, and experiences. In this sense, writing is context bound and community specific. Students who are socialized into different patterns of communicative styles and versions of reality in their homes and native communities have to critically renegotiate the cultural and interactional patterns of the academy. In deciding the extent to which they can bring their own discourses into the academic community, students realize writing as conflict and struggle.

Second, we see the integrated nature of medium and message in semiotic terms. The notion of a discourse community means that the language valued by different people in their communicative activity embodies their ways of looking at the world. Similarly, aspects like form, genre conventions, register, and style are semiotic constructs informed by the values of the community. Therefore students have to understand that the discourse of the academic community cannot be acquired piecemeal. That is the approach of a novice. The more confident and successful students negotiate "the whole package" and use it in an integrated way—if need be, to provide a new coherence to the diverse elements of literacy in terms of their own interests and ideologies.

Third, we see that learning to write involves a process of socialization. One cannot learn to write by oneself. One cannot learn to write without close interaction with the communities that one is addressing. Simply knowing the form, content, and language of a specific community is not adequate. To use a construct from sociolinguistics, one must have the communicative competence to use grammar rules in the appropriate way. To develop such competence in the values, perspectives, norms, and practices of a community one has to intimately interact with the community concerned. Writing is social action, just as other activities in our life are tied to collective human life. For teachers used to providing instruction on the production of well-formed texts by isolated writers on made-up topics for the purpose of knowledge display and grades, this orientation provides a meaningful purpose for writing.

Finally, the discourse-community orientation implies that writers engage in knowledge production. Writing involves participating in the communicative and knowledge-producing processes of the relevant discourse communities. In getting socialized into the processes and practices of knowledge construction of the academic community, for example, students themselves become creators of new knowledge. At least, they get prepared for the processes required when they mature to the expert status of professionals. To stay apart from the relevant communities and simply learn the disembodied features of knowledge handed out to them in a mechanical way is to stay always dependent on the experts who call the shots. Multilingual students must realize that the effective way to become insiders in a discourse community is to enter the ongoing discourse and conversation in a relevant but critical manner where their contribution is valued.

Application

A. Students as Ethnographers of Communication

Recently many educationists have found that making students observe and describe the communicative norms of their community and the academy is an important pedagogical tool (see Heath 1983). Teachers can choose a discourse mode and provide a set of questions that will help students make disciplined observations. Students can also audiotape or manually write down typical interactions among themselves in order to develop a sensitivity to their own discourse conventions.

Here is a sample set of questions for describing the conventions of argumentation.

1. Observe arguments that typically take place among students in your ethnic/national community (e.g., Chinese, African American, Spanish).

2. Can you detect a progression in the argument?
3. Is there a structure for the ways in which individuals make claims, provide evidence, or draw conclusions?
4. What does it take for someone to win an argument? What are the characteristics of a winning argument?
5. What kind of evidence is valued/demanded by opponents?
6. What is the role played by the following in a winning argument—emotions, personality, tone, reasoning, character of the speakers, status, values, facts?
7. How is this style of argumentation influenced by the larger cultural traditions and social practices of your community?

Ask the same questions when you observe faculty members engage in debates or arguments in seminars and talks that you attend. What emerges as the differences between the faculty members' ways of arguing and students' ways of arguing? (Such questions can also be asked of disciplinary groups if students are interested in observing how faculty members belonging to a specific field conduct argumentation.)

B. Ethnography of Peer Groups
Capitalizing on action-research traditions, teachers should try to understand the participant frameworks, discourse styles, and pedagogical outcomes of peer response groups and other small-group activities. It is important in ethnographically motivated research to interpret the interactions and values of these groups in terms of students' own perspectives. Teachers are well situated for this kind of research, as we get to know our students closely during the span of the semester we are with them. We also observe them individually and collectively as they interact on pedagogical concerns. If we can only be disciplined about recording our observations textually (in notebooks), visually (by videotaping), and aurally (on audiocassettes) we will be able to study them with detachment and observe them repeatedly to make reliable generalizations. Some matters to be observed are the following.

1. We may observe students' attitudes to small groups—
   their objectives, their orientation to the group, their
   opinions relating to its pedagogical value, their styles
   of interaction, et cetera.
2. We may use Mangelsdorf and Schlumberger's (1992)
   discourse-based constructs. For example, students'
   stances toward their peers' drafts can be categorized as
   interpretive, prescriptive, or collaborative. (The researchers found a pattern of 23 percent, 45 percent,
   and 32 percent, respectively.) The type of responses
   displayed can be categorized as no comment, generic
   comment, critical evaluation, critical evaluation and
   suggestions, or critical evaluation and extended suggestions. Other interesting questions to ask are: Did the
   type of response relate to the discourse features in the
   text (e.g., thesis, paragraph organization, grammar, evidence)? Did the mode of comment relate to the commentator's or writer's class performance? What in the
   student's background motivated the type of interaction predominantly displayed?
3. We can also analyze peer responses/critiques according
   to the more socially motivated constructs of Villamil
   and de Guerrero (1996). They identify seven social-
   cognitive activities—reading, assessing, dealing with
   trouble sources, composing, writing comments, copying, and discussing task procedures; five mediating
   strategies—employing symbols and external resources,
   using the L1, providing scaffolding, resorting to interlanguage knowledge, and vocalizing private speech;
   and four aspects of social behavior—management of authorial control, affectivity, collaboration, and adopting
   reader/writer roles. Again, we should ask: Did these interaction patterns correlate to the type of revisions made
   and the grades obtained on the writing assignments?

Observe the effects of teacher-regulated and student-
formed peer grouping on the members' interpersonal
dynamics. We can describe the rhetorical and pedagogical consequences for both kinds of groups. Analyze

the language used in the groups, the extent to which they focus on classroom activities, and the possibilities of students discussing matters they dislike about writing and pedagogy.

C. The Discourse of Teacher Commentary

It is important to develop a reflexive awareness of the comments we make on students' essays. This will help teachers provide more constructive feedback to help students revise their papers better. Gather some of the drafts you have previously corrected for your students, or keep copies of the drafts submitted to you before you return them with your comments. Ask the following questions developed by Ferris and Hedgcock (1988, 149, 167–68). Their questions are modified by additional questions that encourage critical teaching.

1. To what extent is the feedback personalized?
2. Does the feedback provide adequate guidance and direction for the student writer?
3. To what extent is the feedback text specific?
4. Is there an appropriate balance of positive and critical commentary?
5. To what extent does the feedback lead the student to exploring the social implications of his or her claims, styles, and positions?
6. Does the feedback challenge the student to adopt positions and perspectives that are independent and critically examined?
7. How long is the feedback? For example, is it short (one to five words), average (six to fifteen words), long (sixteen to twenty-five words), or very long (over twenty-six words)?
8. What comment types predominate—requests, imperatives, questions, giving information, complements, criticism, grammar/mechanics observations?

Chapter 7
Teaching Multiliteracies

The teaching and study of writing have usually been disconnected from broader issues of literacy. Composition and literacy have fallen into different disciplinary camps in the academy, with different circles of scholars pursuing them. The former has been largely associated with the fields of rhetoric and English, while the latter has been the interest of educationists, social scientists, and applied linguists. It is important to emphasize that writing is part of a general pattern of literate behavior, involving a range of communicative skills. As we have already discussed in chapter 5, our reading influences in complex ways the things we write. Similarly, talking about something we have read increases our comprehension of the text, and the things we talk about inform the texts we produce. Today there are even more examples of how all the communicative skills are integrated in the act of writing. Literacy is getting radically redefined by contemporary media and communication technology so that we cannot continue to treat writing as an isolated and independent activity of merely inscribing alphabets on paper. Images, sound, and other symbol systems jostle with words in electronic texts. To be literate today involves multifaceted skills and competencies, forcing us to reconceive the nature of written media and the writing activity. Teaching writing as an independent skill may unfit our students for the new literacies out there in the real world.

Changes in Society and Communication

Before we consider the changing imperatives in the teaching of writing, it is important to consider the ways in which technology is forcing upon us new forms of communication. (Writing is already technologically predicated, even if we take into account the rudimentary instruments of pen and paper or chalk and slate.) Consider now the multimedia capability of CD-ROMs, the Internet, and the Web. Consider the access to different texts and graphics through the Internet. Consider the dynamic interaction enabled through real-time chat, email, and online discussions. Consider the digitized capabilities of storage and transfer of sound, speech, texts, graphics, and video. Consider the integration of resources like the computer, camera, video camera, audio recorder, speech synthesizer, text/speech converter, telephone, Dictaphone, presentation devices, and the printer. All these demand a literacy comprising multiple modalities, requiring the ability to decode and encode different symbol systems. To take reading as an example, we are now compelled to interpret visuals as we decode texts. Parallel to reading we also hear sound bites of famous personalities as narrators or newsmakers. The way space and time are manipulated in the presentation of these symbols demands different interpretive skills, not least of which is the ability to combine these different channels of information. This fusion of modalities has also led to the mingling of languages and discourses. Texts are becoming multivocal. For example, in a Web text describing the breakthrough in DNA (in an academic register) we will now simultaneously have a sound bite of scientist Watson (in a casual spoken register), a box on the side giving the legal uses of DNA (in legalese or the passionate oral rhetoric of Barry Scheck), with another link giving the testimony of someone who was released from the death penalty due to the evidence from DNA (possibly a sound bite in African American English or Spanish), concluding with a description of new uses of DNA by researchers in Germany or Japan (sound bites in their languages, captioned in English). Thus we now have the resources to present multiple discourses and languages within the boundaries of the same text. To capture the changes these features inspire in literacy, some scholars have recently coined the term *multiliteracies* (see Cope and Kalantzis 2000). The term suggests that to be literate today requires competencies in multimodal and multilingual forms of communication.

We must understand that these new texts and literacies are influencing and influenced by the changes in social life. Consider, for example, the changing nature of the workplace. In the Fordist industrial context of the "old economy"—characterized by a strict division of labor and hierarchies reflecting mental and physical work—literacy requirements and linguistic capital were divided unequally along the workforce. As Bernstein (1971) described it some time ago, the boss uses the expanded code (featuring relatively complex syntax and abstract vocabulary) and the worker the restricted code. But in the post-Fordist era of the computerized workplace in the new economy, all work involves engagement with knowledge, information, and communication (see Gee 2000). The division of blue-collar laborers and white-collar workers has become blurred, as everyone has to make informed decisions at work. Information technology has turned all of us into knowledge workers. The new workplace also requires a diversity of capabilities and aptitudes. Skills of planning and implementation are required of almost everybody. Computer literacy is also universally needed. Professionals have to move from one domain of work to another with ease, as and when they are required. Thus each worker has to deal with multiple textualities and discourses. Furthermore, in the globalized market of the new economy, there is greater interaction between communities and nations. A Canadian construction firm gets its plans drawn in Sri Lanka, imports its hardware from China, and employs immigrants from South America. There is communication between different language groups in this context of work. The transnational workplace and market in the contemporary information society require multilingual competencies from today's workers.

How are these technological, economic, and social changes altering ways of reading and writing? Are we only dealing with new media and/or content, while the processes of decoding and encoding texts remain the same? From the earlier description, we can infer some of the changes. In the new literacies, the place of language is reduced. Visual and sound symbols considerably complement, modify, and reconstruct the meaning of words (see Kress 2000). Second, we process texts not in the linear, top-to-bottom fashion we are used to. When we move from a page-based literacy to a screen-based one, processing takes place in different directions and on all sides of the text (e.g., if you think of a typical Web page). Furthermore, hyperlinks in all places of the text now lead us to other texts in other sites. We have to shift rapidly from one page to another to get a sense of the whole. Third, there is a disconcerting fluidity or hybridity in texts. The text is constructed with diverse (sometimes conflicting) discourses, codes, symbols, and channels. One needs competency in different genres to be literate. Finally, there is greater intertextuality today. This is not only in the sense that each text leads to other texts but in the sense that texts from diverse sources can be accessed and reproduced easily, eliminating all traces of the "original text." In fact, we don't know what the text is anymore—with one text leading to another or embedding another in endless ways.

In the light of such changes in textuality, Warschauer identifies some specific skills needed for reading on the Internet:

finding the information to read in the first place (i.e., through Internet searches);

rapidly evaluating the source, credibility, and timeliness of information once it has been located;

rapidly making navigational decisions as to whether to read the current page of information, pursue links internal or external to the page, or revert to further searching;

making on-the-spot decisions about ways to save or catalogue the information on the page;

organizing and keeping track of the electronic information that has been saved (see Warschauer 2000, 522).

Similarly, there are new challenges confronting writing. To begin with, many prefer the term *authoring* to writing because one doesn't have to compose a fresh text all the time. What is involved is the putting together of chunks of text and other symbolic media (sometimes from disparate sources and locations). Some of the skills required for Internet-based writing are

> integrating texts, graphics, and audiovisual material into a
>   multimedia presentation;
> writing effectively in hypertext genres;
> using internal and external links to communicate a message
>   well;
> writing for a particular audience when the audience comprises unknown readers on the World Wide Web;
> using effective pragmatic strategies in various circumstances
>   of computer-mediated communication (see Warschauer
>   2000, 523).

In addition to these differences in skills, computer-mediated-communication (CMC) is generating new genres of literacy. Denise Murray (2000) considers CMC as falling somewhere between orality and literacy in the dichotomy we use to analyze communication. CMC shares features of both oral and written language and their related degrees for formality. Murray points out that writers may negotiate the level of formality in different rhetorical contexts (two professors writing as academics vs. writing as colleagues, discussing a research project vs. discussing their upcoming vacations), moving closer to the oral or literate conventions of communication as needed. The simplified register that is developing in CMC can also pose the need for new genre knowledge among users. Consider the use of abbreviations (e.g., "IMHO" for "in my humble opinion"), simplified syntax (e.g., subject or modal deletion), acceptance of errors in mechanics (e.g., spelling), use of symbols to express emotional meaning (e.g., emoticons like the happy face), and formulaic phrases (e.g., emotes).

The conversation rules in CMC are also different from those in everyday face-to-face interaction or classroom discourse. I found several differences between online classroom discussions (CMC) and traditional classroom discourse (CD) in courses I taught (see Canagarajah 1990). For example, in CD the basic structure of conversation is shaped by the IRF sequence (i.e., initiation, response, feedback). That is, the teacher initiates a question, the student responds, and then the teacher evaluates the submission of the student before moving on to another IRF cycle with other students. According to this convention, for every single turn taken by the student, the teacher takes two; thus teacher talk is two-thirds of the quantity of classroom discourse. This explains why the traditional classroom is typically teacher centered. In CMC, however, the IRF sequence cannot operate. The medium doesn't lend itself to any one person (leave alone the teacher) exercising control over the flow of discussion. The turn-taking conventions of both everyday conversation and CD don't apply here. Therefore, there is potential for student talk to be in greater quantity and for students to enjoy greater freedom in managing the discussion. In fact, in CD it's the teacher who regulates turn-taking, permitting students the right to speak according to the teacher's discretion. But in CMC, there is unregulated turn-taking. The same person can take multiple/ consecutive turns; also, multiple students can take simultaneous turns (which means that students can all write their comments at the same time, though the screen will display their comments chronologically according to who clicked the "send" button first). Furthermore, in CD the teacher initiates questions for students to answer. The right for students to pose questions is severely constrained. Also, the teacher's questions are largely display questions—posed to check if the student knows what the teacher knows. There is little consideration for generating new information or constructing new knowledge through these questions. In CMC, on the other hand, the possibility for the teacher to monopolize question posing or to pose display questions is reduced because the question/answer routine doesn't apply. The contributions may be a series of declarative statements, building gradually toward a collaboratively constructed argument or persuasively achieved consensus. Finally, while the teacher sets the agenda for discussion and holds the power of initiating new topics (i.e., topic shifting) in CD, students can initiate and change topics with greater freedom in CMC. Students can set up their own subconferences on topics that interest them. All this means that there is no closure for the lesson in CMC. It is very open-ended, evolving, and collaborative. In this forum there is greater scope for negotiating themes/ meanings/interpretations by students. They have to discover the coherence behind the discussion and find the "answers" for themselves through negotiation with others. Though this characterization of CD is somewhat stereotyped (as formulated in sociolinguistic studies—see Mehan 1985; Stubbs 1976), the comparison reveals some interesting differences. In general, while there is greater scope for expression for students in CMC, there is also the need to do more interpretive work to find the progression and coherence in the lesson.

Such changes in technology and communication complicate some of the pedagogical assumptions motivating ESOL composition. Consider, for example, how the ESP approach may be misdirected in the present context. The ESP/EAP pedagogy is motivated by the Fordist industrial assumptions of specialization, as competence in a specific discourse or genre is considered important if one is to be functional in one's professional domain. But in the new economy, one has to be multivocal. In the same context (or text) students are compelled to use a diversity of discourses and registers. This doesn't mean that we expect ESP practitioners to teach all the discourses and languages under the sun. The new requirement is to develop the creative, reflexive, and intuitive communicative/interactional approaches that will help students move between discourses, developing relative degrees of competence according to their need. Students also need the competence to codeswitch or style shift. That is, they have to sense the difference in discourse demanded in different contexts and change their styles and strategies accordingly. They furthermore need the ability to transpose to new contexts and domains the communicative styles they have used in a different context. The rigid, one-to-one fit between genres and contexts doesn't hold anymore. Additionally, students require some competence in the new media and technologies of

communication. They have to exploit the rich resources af-
forded by these media for their purposes.

Adopting a Critical Perspective
on Multiliteracies

Some scholars now go to the extent of considering the contemporary multimodal/multilingual communication as liberating in itself (see Rheingold 1994). The Internet (in its unregulated form) is claimed to have expanded access to texts and
intellectual resources for everyone—without class, race, or
gender distinctions. Cyberspace becomes a virtual democracy
where people can relate to each other without traditional identities and statuses. Multiliteracies are treated as having broken
the dominance of particular codes, discourses, and genres,
providing legitimacy to many previously nonstandard codes.
The fluidity in rules of social interaction and communication
is considered to have democratized social relations. In fact, the
hybridity in texts is often perceived as inspiring egalitarian
textual conventions that break down the cultural capital required for literacy in the past. All hierarchies, restrictions,
structures, and institutions of social and communicative life
having been deconstructed, postmodern communication provides opportunities and possibilities for everyone.

This orientation considerably exaggerates the implications
of multiliteracies. Though changes in literacy are certainly
under way, they are not radical, and their ramifications are not
always empowering. To consider the notion of multimodality
first, there is considerable resistance to opening up the channels of communication to previously suppressed social
groups. The recent example of the National Institutes of
Health attempting to broaden scholarly research and publishing by proposing a new Internet-based publication (*E-biomed*) is a case in point. Scientists could not only access all the
research information available here free of charge but could
also post their own findings for others. In a two-tier publishing format, one set of papers would be published with the
usual blind review, while a second set would be posted after

a more flexible refereeing procedure. The director has proposed a wide set of referees, amounting to a thousand scientists, two of whom would have to approve a paper that was to be posted in *E-biomed*. This arrangement would enable a larger range of scholars (especially from the periphery) to publish their research work. Though not everyone in the periphery has a computer or has access to the Internet to take advantage of this publishing forum, this project does hold possibilities for democratizing academic communication.

However, these creative proposals have come under attack from other center-based scholars who are bent on maintaining the status quo. Their opposition exposes the economic and ideological interests motivating knowledge production. The editors of many of the existing medical journals have been the first to voice their opposition to *E-biomed*. The prestigious *New England Journal of Medicine* has stated, "*E-biomed* could have a disastrous effect on clinical journals. . . . [S]ubscribers would have no reason for subscribing" (see Pear 1999, F1). The American Society for Microbiology, which publishes ten scholarly journals, and the American Physiological Society, which publishes fourteen, have expressed similar opposition based on marketing considerations. It is sad that such economic motivations should stand in the way of democratizing knowledge production. Others express fears that publishing without rigid screening procedures would lead to the dissemination of "junk science." But these critics are ignoring the ideological implications of denying access to perspectives that don't meet the approval of a narrow band of referees. Research that doesn't meet the approval of a closed circle of like-minded scholars doesn't have to be junk science. It may simply constitute oppositional knowledge emerging from alternate perspectives. It is clear therefore that there are vested interests of economic and ideological considerations that militate against the establishment of alternative journals and academic literacies that benefit from new technologies.

We also know that multilingualism is quite restricted in academic publishing circles, despite the claim of many that a large range of languages have been empowered by the new media (Warschauer 2000). Scholarly publications are still dominated by the English language (for statistics on how journals in diverse disciplines are overwhelmingly in English, see Swales 1990 and Canagarajah in press). Furthermore, despite the accommodation of a certain amount of flexibility in style and tone, referees still insist on a narrowly defined set of conventions and discourses as constituting research writing (see for a study of reviewer commentary Canagarajah in press). To a large extent, then, disciplinary communities gatekeep access to membership by wielding standardized forms of language and discourse. To give the impression to our students that "anything goes" in multiliteracy is to mislead them.

Terms like *multilingualism* and *multiculturalism* sometimes mask other inequalities in language contact situations. What we see in the hybrid discourses of contemporary communication is the mixing of registers and dialects in a single language—English. As for mixing non-Western languages, there are strict constraints on how much of that will be appreciated. Similarly, in cases of multilingual competence, what is valued in Western communities is competence in economically profitable languages—that is, other European languages or those of commercial/technological advantage in East Asia. This is a kind of *elite bilingualism* that is selective and exclusive. As for developing competence in the languages of economically disadvantaged groups—like those of Native Americans or Hispanics in United States and South Asian or African languages at the global level—not many are interested. We have to then consider the hybridity we see in the dominant institutions and media as not going far enough. What is practiced is a form of multidialectalism (involving variants within the same language—i.e., English) rather than multilingualism (involving divergent languages). Thus English still dominates the new media (see Murray 2000; Luke 2000; Lo Bianco 2000).

We must also take note of the newly created digital divide when we consider the democratizing possibilities of computer literacy. The access to computers is still stratified according to class, race, and nationality. (By nationality, I mean that the United States and certain Western European communities enjoy greater access to computers and Internet connection than those in the third world do—see Murray 2000 for recent statistics.) In addition, having a computer doesn't suffice anymore; we now realize the need for high-speed modems to really take advantage of the resources in cyberspace. To make matters worse, even in the United States, there are so many communities living far from telephone connections that they cannot participate in virtual communities. For such reasons, many in the periphery still get their work done orally. I have reported an ethnography on academic communication in Sri Lanka, where local scholars and institutions still give importance to oral interactions and knowledge production (see Canagarajah 1996). Of course, this is not a "pure" oral community; it features its own multiliteracies. But the literacies of the periphery community are largely based on oral modes of interaction. This leads to inequalities, as those with more literate-based communication monopolize institutional discourses and symbolic resources.

More importantly, the resources of the new media may be used differently by different communities. The uses of these technologies are influenced by the preferred thought processes and styles of communication of the respective communities. Narasimhan (1991) argues that South Asian communities are used to manipulating literate symbols only in the temporal dimension, as in their valued oral modes of communication. (By temporal, Narasimhan means the linear, sequential processing of symbols and codes, as in face-to-face interaction.) For this reason, some periphery communities fail to manipulate the multidirectional spatio-temporal possibilities of the new media. This is not because of inherent cognitive deficiency but because literacy is influenced by the attitudes and histories of different communities. We must note in this context that some communities have a history of domination by literacy and technology—as the Lao of Vietnam (see Duffy 2000) and Native American tribes in the United States (see Cazden 2000). For them multiliteracy is suspect.

If the infrastructure for the new media of literacy is controlled by a specific social group, then we have to examine how the medium influences the message. The discourses and ideologies represented in cyberspace may favor the limited interests of the dominant groups. It is not difficult to do a semiotic analysis of the icons displayed in different computer programs to realize the biased nature of the media. Carmen Luke (2000) provides a fascinating interpretation of the commonly used symbol of "trash" for deleting unwanted files. She notes that for many communities, especially those residing around garbage-disposal areas and making a living from recycled products (e.g., in Central America, India, and Russia), "trash" doesn't have the same connotations as for those in the West. Garbage, for the former, is life, home, and vocation. It's a gold mine of unexpected treasures.[1] Other disadvantaged groups, like women, also feel discriminated against by the discourses of cyberspace. Herring (1996) argues that a male discourse style—characterized by adversarial argumentative stances, agonistic styles of interaction, and an aggressive negotiation of speaking rights—creates conflicts and disadvantages for women.

The implications of all this are quite paradoxical. The contemporary communication media of diversity and pluralism are controlled by a small social circle. Do the fusion, hybridity, multimodality, and multilingualism only mask the limited interests of the dominant groups? Consider, for example, the monopoly of Microsoft in the software industry. We are faced with the irony of a capitalistic, aggressively profit-oriented enterprise churning out programs that encourage intertextuality and multiliteracies. I am pointing out contradictions like this not to argue that students should not be made proficient in the emergent communicative practices. What is important is to make them also aware of the implications and ramifications of new literacies. The liberating and democratizing powers of current technology should not be taken for granted. Students have to go beyond developing a simple functional literacy in the new media and new genres. They have to still adopt a critical literacy for expanding the possibilities of the new resources, appropriating the available media for their oppositional purposes, and democratizing the cyberworld for broader participation. In terms of literate practices, we must observe that while some changes have occurred in encoding and decoding texts (as outlined earlier), other more fundamental processes of reading and writing haven't changed. Readers still face the need to observe the text closely, interpret it in the light of the broadest possible social context, and adopt a questioning attitude toward the message and the medium. Similarly, writers have to actively negotiate the values undergirding genre conventions and text structure to represent their interests better. If anything, these "old" strategies of reading and writing have become even more urgent than ever before, as the knowledge explosion, ready accessibility to texts/information, and conveniently formatted production/reception media seem to lull us into complacency. Also, the disembodied and dislocated texts in the new media increasingly obscure the contexts and purposes of texts so that we have to be alert readers.

Computers in Writing Instruction

Computer-assisted language learning (CALL) is quite fashionable these days, being lauded as a revolutionary mode of learning that boasts collaborative and process-oriented composing possibilities.[2] Many teachers of writing have greeted the introduction of computers in writing instruction with great enthusiasm and expectation. Before we rush into this fad, we need to distinguish between the different pedagogical uses of computers and adopt a critical orientation toward their contribution.

At the most basic level, we see the use of computers for word processing. Many composition instructors teach word-processing skills in their writing classes. They are obviously influenced by the widely held assumption that word processing benefits composing processes—that is, that students feel encouraged to revise at will without fearing the tedium of rewriting the whole draft each time (as they would do if they wrote manually); that they experiment with all kinds of changes, emboldened by the advantage of having the draft saved electronically; that they compose different sections of the essay in a nonlinear way and experiment with paragraph organization and text structure, aided by the ease of cutting and pasting the text; that they employ the time saved from mechanical aspects of production on rhetorical fine-tuning; that they learn that nothing is written in stone and adopt the healthy attitude that each draft is tentative; and that they gain affectively (deriving pleasure and confidence) from composing electronically.[3]

But word processing can also be detrimental to the composing process. I have found that word processing develops a false sense of confidence and convenience, making students begin composing without a clear plan or objective. As a consequence, the final products are less coherent and effective. I have myself experienced this difference in my personal composing experience. The papers I published from hand-written drafts in Sri Lanka (where there were no electronic resources for composing and limited stationery for use) were much better planned. The realization that I couldn't write too many drafts made me plan the whole essay carefully before I started writing. When I came to the United States after that, I tended to compose hastily, with the expectation that I would "discover" my structure and purposes as I composed. On many occasions, my rambling and disorganized initial drafts hampered the extent to which I could adopt radical revisions at later stages.[4] Furthermore, instructors have mentioned that students who are slow in typing or are intimidated by technology experience motivational problems in composing on the computer (see Taylor, Jamieson, and Eignor 2000). Word processing, at any rate, is a mixed bag of blessings. One shouldn't encourage students to treat computers as a shortcut to the complex process of composing.

A second area of computer use in composition comprises grammar pedagogies and editing programs. Students can do self-paced exercises to improve their grammatical competence. They can also put their draft through a grammar- or spelling-check program for automated editing. Here, again, we should teach students to use this resource critically and thoughtfully. Students have to be judicious in choosing the suggested word or spelling, sensitive to the full textual context. As we have all found often, corrections by such programs are sometimes misleading and ambivalent as there is a limited orientation to context. (My spelling- and grammar-check program flagged that very sentence as wrong, prompting that I needed a comma after the word "ambivalent"!) Students may abdicate their ownership of the text to the computer by relying too much on its ability to correct and perfect their writing. Furthermore, students may develop a product-oriented attitude to writing as they conceive of composition as a matter of getting their spelling and syntax right. Their ability to develop their own voices and to experiment with style can be severely curtailed. Grammar and spelling correction should be used only as a last resort to spot any unexpected mistakes in the final stages of the finished product.

Third, there are integrated writing programs featuring online discussion, email, and brainstorming/revising heuristics. Some of the networked programs enable students to exchange/share their drafts and comment on them to enhance peer review. Compared to the previous two functions (which are largely product oriented), the latter is more attuned to the rhetorical process of writing. In fact, there are many instructional programs like Daedalus that come packaged with a variety of pedagogical functions, sometimes having the power to supplant the traditional classroom and the role of the teacher. I like to illustrate the challenges involved in teaching writing as a computer-assisted course through my experience with Daedalus. Of course, we have to keep in mind that if there are complications in adopting this program effectively they don't necessarily mean that the programmers are at fault. We will see how the students' expectations and other institutional constraints can shape the way the medium functions. The software program is simply a resource that calls for the agency of teachers and students for meaningful results.

Of course, it is important for the software developers to be cautious in marketing the virtues of their product. Integrated writing programs are usually touted as helping practice the latest pedagogical fashions or delivering unconditional success. The instructor's guide to Daedalus, for example, says: "DIWE [Daedalus Integrated Writing Environment] integrates two powerful and highly successful approaches to writing instruction. . . . These are the process approach described by Flower and Hayes on the one hand, and on the other the collaborative approach popularized Bruffee and others. . . . The electronic classroom becomes a student-centered learning environment, in contrast to the teacher-centered environment of the traditional classroom. . . . You'll have to help your students learn to accept their new freedoms and responsibilities" (Daedalus Group 1993, ii). We get the sense that students are magically transformed into talkative/interactive members! These "new freedoms" derive from a student-centered, process-oriented, socially collaborative pedagogy. These are of course the fashionable labels that attract teachers to use this program. In their enthusiasm, the publishers use a language that suggests that these wonders are automatically realized by the program. One cannot deny that in certain pedagogical contexts and among motivated student groups these virtues can be realized quite well. Some of my composition classes for native-speaking students confirmed the possibilities of this program for new classroom relations and literacy practices (see Canagarajah 1997b).

However, I faced some special challenges in an ESOL writing class.[5] The students in this class were from diverse ethnic groups. There were twelve Chinese, two Koreans, three Russians, one Haitian, one Peruvian, one Guyanese Indian, and one Greek. Since these students didn't belong to a single ethnic group (even the Chinese-speaking students came from different Southeast Asian communities), we cannot relate their pedagogical practices to anyone's "native culture." We should also be careful not to generalize their attitudes and strategies as typical of all ESOL students. What is perhaps common to all these students are their struggles for survival in a new setting. These are newcomers to New York City—poor, marginalized, and therefore motivated to be goal-oriented overachievers. We should also keep in mind the institutional culture. Students in this public university are far more exam oriented, as they have to do a common writing assessment test, the WAT (which I introduced previously). A lot of anxiety is generated by this test among immigrant students as this fifty-minute writing assessment on an unseen topic, featuring common topics and evaluation standards for both native-speaking and ESOL students, helps determine if the students can continue their college education.

The online discussions in this class (called InterChange in the Daedalus program) diverged from the possibilities envisaged by the programmers in significant ways. The transcript in the appendix to chapter 7 represents the lengthiest and most involved discussion in the whole course. The assignment is to interpret and apply to their own contexts an essay on the benefits of living in an ethnically diverse neighborhood. We first see the students answering my opening series of questions in a single contribution. Alex, in fact, numbers his comments according to my questions. After their single posting, some students ask me what else they should do. A few answer a follow-up question posed by me to generate more discussion. In general, each student interacts only with the teacher. Some said they had finished the assignment after their single response to the question, perhaps waiting for the teacher's response to their "answer." It appears that the students are gravitating toward a teacher-led classroom discussion, adopting the IRF structure. Their submissions display an attitude of providing the "correct answer" to the question, rather than exploring the topic collaboratively. Some write their answer in one long contribution, implying that they are considering this a complete response to the question and not contemplating an interaction with others in the class. It appears that the *display* of knowledge is more important than a collaborative *discovery* of knowledge. Many students are not reading the contributions posted by others or engaging them in a discussion. After their own posting, some sat idling without doing anything. Some moved to other tasks that were more product oriented—such as computer-based grammar exercises. It is clear that despite the possibilities in the program and the deep personal relevance of the subject matter, the students conducted the discussion in a product-oriented manner.

The attitudes of the students were also not always favorable toward participation in computer-assisted learning. In the final survey at the end of the course, the students expressed that they considered the time spent in the computer-mediated class a waste. The benefits they found were largely related to increased opportunities for socialization and relaxation (which they considered unimportant for their learning needs and objectives). Therefore, there were frequent cases of student absence whenever we met in the computer-mediated classroom. During the class meetings students always grumbled and asked questions like the following: "What is the point of this activity?" "How do online discussions and email help language learning?" "Will these activities help me pass the WAT?" It was clear, however, that the students were quite adept at using computers: they talked about using computers in other courses; they were quite creative and confident in solving glitches in the program; and they used computers for personal communication outside the college. Their resistance, therefore, was not motivated by computers per se; it had to do with pedagogical conflicts in the course.

As we try to account for their attitude, consider some of the views expressed by the students in interviews and surveys with me. When asked, "What is your impression of Inter-Change discussions? Did you enjoy this? Why/why not?" Stephanos gave an unqualified answer.

> NO. Because we are taking a class that is going to give the WAT at the end of the semester and instead of writing as many essays as possible we are loosing one day per week on the computer lab doing nothing important at least for me.

It was clear from the comments of many others in the class that they were more concerned about the final writing test. Since the

WAT demanded product-oriented writing, students failed to perceive any usefulness from a process-oriented pedagogy. We must take note here of the "wash-back effect" (discussed in chap. 4). Rather than being an unconnected appendix to the course, the test shapes the pedagogy and classroom relations from the very beginning. We have to take seriously, therefore, the mismatch between the curriculum/pedagogy and the assessment procedure. The effectiveness of the computer-assisted pedagogy seems to lie in the extent to which it is complemented by the other institutional requirements and policies.

Interestingly, the positive things students stated had to do with the product-oriented and utilitarian functions of the program. They didn't seem to appreciate the playful, creative, and pleasure-giving aspects of the computer-mediated pedagogy. When asked, "Did you gain anything by using the computer program for this course?" Wu answered:

> Yes, I gain a lot in my ability to quickly turn my thoughts into writing via doing the mail and interchange, which is very helpful when taking writing tests.

Maria answered:

> I learned to think a little more clear, when I talk I tend to use slang, but with this method; I write what I feel and make the proper corrections. I think it helps my gramar.

Others appreciated the revision and editing heuristics, as these came close to the concerns they had about developing a grammatically correct final product. Soo said:

> I like the editing of others' essays the most. It is because I think that it is a good way to practise grammar. A student also need to understand the idea of the author before he or she can correct the grammar.

In explaining this desire for formal, ritualistic, structured learning, we shouldn't resort to treating it as a cultural influence of ESOL students. In addition to the punitive test, we should also keep in mind the immigrant drive for success and other anxieties that come with such a social positioning. The students are tense, goal oriented, and achievement driven. They don't have any time or concern for play. They want to get things done right—and quickly—in order to pass the final standardized test. As far as their confusions about the relevance of this pedagogy are concerned, it is important for the instructors to spend considerable time explaining the value of the learning strategy. Furthermore, teachers shouldn't immediately assume that a process-oriented, student-driven pedagogy is always effective or empowering. Certain students work better in a more structured environment.

It is interesting that in the traditional classroom, where we met on alternate days, students enjoyed working in an environment where the teacher was in control, with texts, questions, and tasks clearly defined and the purposes and outcomes made explicit. I constantly showed the relevance of the tasks to grammatical proficiency and writing tests in order to ensure student participation in readings and discussions. Readings on gun control, drugs, or mercy killing were prefaced by the explanation that students are assigned topics of contemporary social/cultural relevance for the WAT and that it was important for them to develop a good background knowledge on these subjects and formulate an independent position. Paradoxically, while students found more relaxed/collaborative work boring, they enjoyed "utilitarian" work. They demanded activities that were clearly functional, produced immediate results, and developed their individual aptitudes and proficiencies.

Ironically, once these conditions were guaranteed, students were prepared to participate actively and display signs of critical thinking. Though the classroom environment was teacher led and formally structured, students were prepared to challenge my interpretation often and provide alternate ways of reading the texts. My usual strategy was to challenge their responses, confront their assumptions, and provoke them to engage in an involved discussion. With this prodding, students were prepared to explore at depth the linguistic and rhetorical choices of the texts we discussed. Compared to the silence of collaborative learning, there was more production of language with the teacher in the traditional classroom. This pedagogy did help writing in some ways. Students were prepared to debate the statements given as the prompts for their writing assignments, to look at them from different points of view, and to provide stronger support for their claims. The awareness that their claims could be challenged made students more objective and critical in their writing.

We have to acknowledge then that in certain contexts a teacher-led, structured learning environment can generate critical learning. Critical practitioners like bell hooks (1989) have argued in other contexts that a direct confrontational teaching style has served them better in making students examine their hidden biases and engage with others in the class in critiquing commonsense assumptions. A far too open-ended "process pedagogy" can make students complacent, in addition to lacking direction or focus. It can also mislead them about the world outside the classroom, where relationships are not that egalitarian. It is mistaken, therefore, to go along with the widespread view that critical learning can be practiced only in a collaborative, student-led learning environment. We have to consider the social and pedagogical contexts in adopting a teaching practice that will realize the principles of critical learning and writing.

In understanding the surprising outcome of my course, we have to keep in mind the larger policy considerations that impinge on classroom relations and student attitudes. This is a time when CUNY and the city of New York are turbulent with debates about failing standards in language and literacy among urban/immigrant students. Open admission is under attack. English-only bills are being proposed at the national level. In the face of all this, educational objectives and standards are being made more rigid. ESOL students are pressured increasingly to attend nonacademic service centers to develop their communication skills before registering for academic courses at the university. Those who fail the proficiency tests more than a couple of times are put on stringent probation or dropped from college. Standardized tests are becoming the final measure of a student's proficiency. When we devise critical pedagogies—whether the courses are computer mediated or not—we cannot ignore the subtle ways political realities outside the walls of the classroom affect learning processes.

The textual and linguistic hybridity we find in postmodern communication has created the myth that forces of imperialism and discursive control have all but disappeared, or at least been neutralized. Combined with the poststructuralist notion that structures of power are upheld by microsocial linguistic and discursive processes, enabling students to discern textual and discursive patterns of ideological mystification is treated as empowering. In fact, deconstructing texts is treated as an act amounting to bringing the related social institutions crashing down. Similarly, adopting multivocal writing is treated as a liberating act of finding a social space in conditions of inequality. Also, democratic relations in the classroom are exaggerated as equaling the creation of egalitarian institutions in society. I am inclined to view such pedagogical approaches as creating a state of "happy idiocy." We have to adopt a pedagogy that doesn't ignore larger social conditions in favor of textual or pedagogical reconstruction. As we saw in the classroom experience described earlier, society has a way of exerting its own pressure on learning styles and educational outcomes. The material conditions of work, poverty, immigrant status, and racism need to be addressed if students are to engage in a holistic educational and literate experience.

Classroom Practice

The experiences in the writing course reported earlier are unusual because of the mediating influences from the unique pedagogical context. There are other ESOL teachers who have reported more positive outcomes from CALL-based pedagogies. Eva Lam (2000), for example, finds that the Internet empowers her Chinese-speaking subject Almon to explore alternate identities, interact with a wider range of speech communities through English, develop writing proficiency in diverse discourses, and feel empowered to use the language in his terms.[6] The first purpose of reporting my study is to alert teachers not to take CALL complacently or turn technology into a fetish. The second purpose—a larger concern beyond the use of computers—is to break the myth that critical pedagogy involves a set of "politically correct" practices. In their effort to systematize and popularize their pedagogy, critical practitioners have themselves defined this orientation into a set of neat axioms or preferred strategies from time to time (see Giroux 1992). But we have to understand that the pedagogy has to be shaped in constant negotiation with students, in relation to the specific cultural and social forces that impinge on the teaching situation.

Furthermore, there are many issues relating to classroom practice where critical pedagogues differ. How can interactions between teachers and students be fashioned to prepare students for egalitarian social relations? Should a critical learning environment involve abdicating the teacher's authority and responsibility and letting students define the pedagogy? Not necessarily. This is not to say that teachers should consider themselves ideologically more enlightened, having the power to dictate the curriculum and pedagogical practice to students. The authority of the teacher can be negotiated with students in relation to their preferred interests and values (see Grossberg 1994). Teachers should be humble enough to recognize their own ideological limitations, through a reflexive engagement with students in the classrooms. The diverse histories represented by communities of minority students, constituting experiences of both marginalization and empowerment, are of personal educational value to instructors.

Should classroom relations be based on an attitude of sympathy or confrontation? Though critical pedagogues have taken polarized positions on this question as well, the approach need not be exclusive. Both attitudes may be called into play in different contexts. Schenke (1991) talks of adopting a nurturing attitude to tap the suppressed memories of her nonvocal ESL students. She has to adopt a gentle approach to tapping the critical thinking of students who have gone through traumatic experiences in their countries. hooks (1989), however, talks of confronting the ideological blinders of her African American students. Paradoxically, even minority students may acculturate into the dominant community's values and need to be exposed at times.

Though I have warned earlier that we shouldn't mistake textual or discursive critique at the micropedagogical level for social change, we mustn't underestimate the power of classroom processes to change social relations outside the walls of the school. In this sense, changes initiated in the classroom can serve to reconstruct wider social and political conditions from the ground up. The classroom is in itself social, often mirroring the inequalities and hierarchies found outside. The challenge for teachers is to help students make the transition from critical thinking in the classroom context to critical social practice in life outside. Different social domains—texts, classrooms, school, society—have relative autonomy, even though there are clear interconnections. So teaching students to critique the discourses that are dominant in one domain doesn't necessarily mean that other domains are challenged as well. Students should be encouraged to see the way power pervades diverse social institutions and to translate their critical insights made in one domain to the other.

To undertake these pedagogical challenges, teachers should focus on the attitudinal changes required to practice radical education, rather than seeking techniques and methods that implement critical principles. Hitherto teachers have largely separated themselves from researchers, policy makers, and theoreticians. For example, teachers sometimes mistakenly assume that their task is to simply implement materials, curricula, and techniques developed by scholars and policy makers outside the classroom (sometimes with little classroom experience). We have to resist these divisions of labor and relations of dependence. Teachers should be more independent and creative to devise practices that respond to the conditions in their own classrooms. Depending on generic activities and materials prepared by others will not serve our students well. Pedagogy should in fact be a continuing process of developing creative practices that build on the changing situations in our unique classroom relations and student competence.

In order for this to happen, we have to resist another separation that has been made in our fields—that teachers are not researchers. To develop suitable pedagogical practices, teachers have to reflect on and analyze their classroom conditions. There are some interesting research methods that have gained legitimacy among research circles that enable teachers to study their classrooms with greater confidence. Ethnographic methods like participant observation, collaborative research (with students and other instructors), and action research are ways in which teachers can engage with their students and develop a critical orientation to their everyday classroom life.[7] In fact, the teacher's familiarity with the classroom and personal empathy with students provide a vantage point that generates useful research insights. Similarly, the reflective engagement as a researcher provides deeper imaginative involvement suitable for teaching. It is not impossible therefore to marry teaching and research. It is with this concern in mind that I have suggested some research questions and activities at the end of each preceding chapter.

What this book envisions is the new status of the teacher as a *transformative intellectual*—to use Giroux's coinage (which I introduced in chap. 2). Teachers are not mindless practitioners but informed intellectuals. They are not conformists who simply implement the agendas of others but transformers of social and educational conditions. The teaching of writing, like pedagogical activities in other contexts in the academy, calls for critical interventions by teachers so that their mission isn't confined to the narrow bounds of the text but encompasses the social life of their students. We have to realize that teaching, writing, and social practice are all deeply interconnected. Uncritical writing is not just ineffective communication but unreflective and disempowering social practice.

Appendixes

Appendix to Chapter 3

Text 1 (in L1 for local Publication): "YaaLpaaNa camuukaTai viLanki koLLal—aTan uruvaakkam asaiviyakkam paRRiya oru piraarampa usaaval" (Understanding Jaffna Society: A Preliminary Inquiry into its "Formation" and "Dynamics") (Sivatamby 1992)

> *[Move 1/step 2]:* One of the features about Jaffna culture that is always visible but never discussed is a realistic depiction of the society. We don't speak or even attempt to speak about culture, which is always in front of our eyes besides regulating and controlling our social practices.

> *[Move 1/step 1]:* Since this silence hampers the healthy development of this society, I am undertaking this analysis to overcome this at least academically. At a period when our community is facing a serious crisis in its history, and when it is undergoing radical changes, it is the duty of the social sciences to at least provide some preliminary thoughts and data on our community's fundamentals and assumptions.

> *[Move 1/step 3?]:* Research relating to Jaffna society from anthropology and sociology is poor indeed. There are only a few foreign scholars working in this field (Bryan Pfaffenberger, Kenneth David, Skjonberg). Tamil scholars who have earned international prestige in these disciplines—like S. J. Tambiah—themselves do not give full attention to anthropological and social scientific research relating to the concerns of Tamil Eelam people.

> *[Move 3/step 1b]:* In a situation like this, doing research on the nature of the social changes taking place here is the duty of academics at the University of Jaffna. I have been drawn to this subject from the experience of reviewing the tradition of Tamil literature from the disciplinary perspectives of social history, sociology, and anthropology. This article is being written from that academic background.

> *[Concluding paragraph]:* If I have troubled anyone's mind with the manner in which I have presented this subject or the data, please forgive me. [The author quotes a religious verse that confesses his weakness and invokes God to use him as an instrument for knowledge and human progress.]

Text 2 (in L2 for local publication): "Towards an Understanding of the Culture and Ideology of the Tamils of Sri Lanka" (Sivatamby 1984)

> *[Move 1/step 1]:* The Tamils of the Jaffna peninsula of Sri Lanka constitute the dominant Tamil group in the island. It is largely their experience at the national level and their perceptions of the Sinhalese and their moti-

vations that have defined the Tamil grievances and decided the pattern of the struggle to redress them.

[Move 3/step 1b]: An attempt is made here to understand the Jaffna man in relation to two of the most important ideological perceptions he has of himself: a) the preserver of the great Saiva-Tamil tradition, and b) the heir to the liberal traditions of the West and the reformist tradition of Gandhi symbolised by the Jaffna Youth Congress Movement.

[Move 1/step 2]: The Sri Lankan image of the Jaffna Tamil as . . . The relevant census figures of the Jaffna district for 1971 were . . .

[Concluding paragraph]: The quantitative and qualitative changes that have taken place in the evolution of Tamilian nationalism, should be seen in the perspectivity of the liberal Youth Congress tradition. That would provide the nationalist ideology with a continuity and possibility of development on social democratic lines.

Text 3 (in L2 for foreign publication): "The Ideology of Saiva-Tamil Integrality: Its Social Historical Significance in the Study of Yalppanam Tamil Society" (Sivatamby 1990)

[Move 1/step 2]: The current ethnic crisis . . . has brought about an overall unity and solidarity among the Tamils of Ilankai. However, in terms of social formation—the social structure and relationships, the modes of production at the peasant level—we could easily see that there are three discernible Tamil formations. . . . [The author provides historical background.]

[Move 1/step 1]: So, any study of the history of the Tamil demands within the Ilankai context should necessarily focus on the nature and role of the importance of Yalppanam Tamil society, the type of problems it faced, how it expressed and formulated them as its political grievances, and the type of solutions it put forward. . . . The pre-eminence of Yalppanam has been brought up by many factors.

[Move 3/step 1b]: Amidst the social and political challenges which it had to confront, the Yalppanam Tamil society developed two ideologies which have been the main source of its social, intellectual, cultural, and political sustenance. Those are:

a) the Saiva Tamil ideology propounded by Armuka Navalar, and
b) the reformist liberal ideology of the Youth Congress.

They are in fact contradictory to each other, but in the manner they have been coalesced into that society and its political articulations, one finds the specific characteristics of the Yalppanam society emerging. A full scale intellectual history of Yalppanam would be the apt academic way one could see how these two strands have been woven into one whole. [A footnote refers to another article by the author titled "An Ethnography of the Sri Lankan Tamils".]

[Move 3/step 1a]: In this paper an attempt is made to present in a preliminary manner the formation and the subsequent history, in outline, of the continuity of the Saiva Tamil ideology.

[Concluding paragraph]: But to say that the Saiva Tamil ideology has been weakened or is no more effective is to run to hasty conclusions. It should be remembered that the social base of this ideology at the place where it really rises—the rich peasantry—has not yet been changed in any effective sense. The possibilities of this ideology slowing down the social radicalization of the militants is not improbable.

Appendix to Chapter 7

Transcript of class discussion—26 October

The names of the students are fictional. All grammar and spelling is per the original class discussion.

Msg. 1. Suresh Canagarajah

We will interpret today's reading. Those who wish can begin discussing by considering the following questions: 1. Which type of neighborhood do you think provides a better environment for a newly arrived immigrant to learn to live in a different culture? 2. What advantages/disadvantages do immigrants have in living in the type of neighborhood described by Galarza? 3. What advantages/disadvantages do they have in living in a neighborhood that is mainly composed of people from their own country?

Before going to those questions, some of you may like to consider a general question: consider what the writer is trying to say through this essay about his boyhood in this kind of neighborhood. (I hope everybody will express their views.)

Msg. 2. Maria Suarez

I think that newly arrived immigrants should not seclude themselves from a new culture, but try to interact with people from that culture, so it won't be hard and take too long to adjust to a new culture. I think if an immigrant comes here and puts him/herself in an enviroment as in their country, they might feel more comfortable and not homesick. But, then again they won't be able to adapt to a new enviroment, or learn about the people if they only move around a certain enviroment.

I think the only advantage that you may have is that, you will be around people who are in the same situation as you are. From there it might be hard to move up or interact with other people.

Msg. 3. Rina Khan

I think that a neighborhood that have a multi-culture society would provide a healthy environment for immigrants coming to america.The neighborhood that Earesto is living in is perfect for immigrant to learn the diversity of the american culture. In fact this will help immigrant to become more understand to other culture. I am not saying that you should not live with people from your home country, but the mixed community will help you to live better.

The advantages of living in the type of neighborhood that Ernesto live in are enormous. You get to have hand on understand of all the different culture within your surrounding.

Msg. 4. Mike Yang

When people first come to this country, most of them do not know how to speak engilsh, or speak very little. When they live in a neighborhood where there are a lot of their own countrymen, its is better for them to fit into the society more easier. They would feel more comfortable, and feel more like home rather than feeling like in a strange place. If people live in a neighborhood where there are many races, people can learn many cultures. I think it is better to live in such enveionment only if they how to speak english or the language which most people speak.

Msg. 5. Viktor Weinstein

The most important thing for anyone who just entered a new country is to overcome culture shock and language barrier. It is not always easy, for some people it is the most difficult time of their immigration.

I personnaly believe that the best way to quickly overcome difficulties of immigration is to dive fully into a new environment. It helps your language learning, and adjusting to new sphere of influence.

Some people believe that slow transition is most useful. They can't just forget their language and their motherland. Those people will be sruggled by nostalgia before they become Americans, and that is not good. I think it greatly depends on the age of an immigrant. Older people are very hard to adjust.

Msg. 6. Ben Baruch

1. I live in italian-russian heighborhood. It's called Bensonhurst. Actually, as long as it's save, I don't really care about neiboghrhood. I believe that older people prefer their own culture, language neighborhood. Young people, like me, prefer mix neighborhoods.

2. I think that Galarza's neighborhood has a lot of advantages, like opportunity to explore different cultures, traditions and customs. However, there are few disadvantages too. People from different countries have different mentalities, traditions and costums. So, people might misunderstand each other.

3. People, who are living in the neighborhood that is mainly composed of
    people from their own country, have many advantages. People fill them-
    self safer than in the mix neighborhood. They don't have communica-
    tion problems. From the other side, People like that will never be part
    of American community, and the reason for that is language.

Msg. 7. Suresh Canagarajah

Ben, Viktor, is it possible to find the type of neighborhood Ernesto describes here in NYC? It looks like most neighborhoods are segregated according to specific ethnic groups.

Msg. 8. Soo Cheng

I think that it is better for the immigrants to live in neighborhood which is
composed of people from many different countries. Especially in America.
For the American population, it consists of many people that come from
different countries. They have different types of culture. So that it is much
easier for a new immigrant to adjust into this country if his or her neighborhood is composed of people from different countries. He or she can
know different types of culture in the same area. As the result he or she will
has the basic idea to deal with the people who have different types of culture. It will make his life in America more flourished.

Msg. 9. Suresh Canagarajah

Mike, what do you think of Chinatown? Are the people living there missing a lot culturally? What is your opinion of the children growing up in
these neighborhoods?

Msg. 10. Viktor Weinstein

It probably is possible, somewhere on the border of two neighborhoods.
And its a shame too. In this country, and especially in this city we people
of all different nationalities have to stay together.

Msg. 11. Suresh Canagarajah

It does look as if the society Ernesto describes is quite old—that is, of the
past. Nowadays parents won't let their children to go out with outsiders
like Ernesto's parents do. They probably didn't have missing children and
child abuse those days!

Msg. 12. Wu Wang

I think it depends on what you objective is to choose which neighborhood
to live in. For some immigrants, it's better to live with people of your own

culture, because it would provide the necessary transition and buffer zone. On the other hand, some immigrant would prefer to live in author's environment, meaning away from your culture, because they think a little "growing pain" is necessary for them to join the main stream.

I would choose the latter in the case of myself. Because I have some English background, as well as my mother, and I am still very young, it is not very hard for me to melt into the culture here. And if I chose to stay in China Town, I would simply delay the process of transition and waste my time.

Yet while the latter one applies to my family, there are a lot of other immigrant need the first environment, too. Because many new immigrants have no knowledge of English, and may be too old to catch up, they would be better off living in a environment of their own culture, and have many fellows to help them when needed.

All things being said, it is up to every person to decide which environment they should choose according to their situation.

Msg. 13. Sau Zang

It is better to live in small town than city because it is more easier to know each other or get togather. The author had a deep relationship with every one who lives near him. Although, everybody has different culture, language, they still live peacefully and lovely because they help each other.

Msg. 14. Ging Zen

I think the type of neighborhood that provides a better environment for a newly arrived immigrant is to live in a neighorbood that contain some of their own people. It will be better for them because when they just came here, they know nothing about it. So there will be someone who they can talk to when they don't understand what is happening. The advantages of living in the type of neighborhood described by Galarza is that the immigrants tend to know a lot of different peoples. The disadvantage is that they may not get comfortable with it because of the difference of culture and values. The advantage of living in a neighborhood that is mainly composed of people from their own country is that they are comfortable because it seem like they are back to their hometown. The disadvantage is that they won't learn to live in a different culture.

(End of transcript)

Notes

Chapter 1

1. While the first few terms here are well known, the final three—especially those that concern our profession relatively more closely—may sound strange. For publications that employ these labels, see Fowler and Kress 1979 for *critical linguistics;* Fairclough 1995 for *critical discourse analysis;* and Kumaravadivelu 1999 for *critical classroom discourse analysis.*
2. For a perspective on the need to reconsider these traditional distinctions, see Nayar 1997.
3. The new realizations about linguistic identity create a need for new terminology. In referring to students and teachers in second-language programs, I will use the term *ESOL* except when I make a specific point about the ESL/EFL situation or the L1/L2 distinction. Though this label is awkward, especially when it is used as an adjective to qualify teachers and students, it has been used in these contexts in the professional literature for a long time (see Canagarajah 1993; Harklau 2000). The term *ESOL* enables me to side step the question of whether the subjects are balanced bilinguals or not and of whether they are using English as a second language, a foreign language, or a nativized language.
4. For a debate on this issue in the pages of the *ELT Journal,* see Rajagopalan 1999 and Canagarajah 1999b.
5. These are culled from a review article on L2 writing research by Silva (1993). We must note that Silva is only reporting the findings of studies made by others and is not personally responsible for the findings represented in the article.
6. Since Fox adopts this view specifically in the case of Japanese students, see Kubota 1999b to understand why such generalizations fall short of capturing the complexity of Japanese cultural thought processes.
7. See Canagarajah 1997a for an ethnographic study where minority students (consisting of bilingual and bidialectal students) resist the notion of switching identities in different communities. They negotiate ways of infusing their values into mainstream discourse.
8. See Phillipson 1992 for an articulation of the linguistic imperialism thesis. For debates that slightly modify Phillipson's thesis, without

denying the power of English, see Pennycook 1994 and Canagarajah 1999c.

9. See Ngugi 1986 for a forceful argument favoring this position.
10. See Achebe 1975 for an articulation of this position.
11. See Kachru 1986 for the notion of English as "an unmarked code" in formerly colonized communities. Crystal (1997) too presents the position of English as a value-free global language.
12. See Canagarajah 1999c for a detailed exposition of this approach.
13. There are of course many intermediary positions on ideology, as I will discuss later. For example, Santos (1993) in composition scholarship and Rajagopalan (1999) in ELT pedagogy argue that power is real but that it can be kept out of writing activity or the classroom. In saying this, they excuse teachers from having to commit themselves to any ideological position.
14. See Bizzell 1982 and Rose 1989 for progressive compositionists who have articulated this position.

Chapter 2

1. Matsuda 1998 presents findings from a survey of teacher-development programs to substantiate this point.
2. This is not to deny that there are "privileged ESL students" (see Vandrick 1995) who come from countries like Hong Kong, Taiwan, or Japan and are materially well endowed. Even the students who come from poorer countries like India or Ghana are often children of the elite in their communities. But these factors shouldn't make us ignore the fact that these students still face linguistic and cultural marginalization in the dominant academic discourses.
3. For an introduction to these research approaches, consult the following publications. Auerbach 1994 and Nunan 1990 are good introductions for action research. Auerbach et al. 1996 is a good demonstration of this method in a literacy classroom. Hornberger 1994 introduces the idea of participant observation and other ethnographic methods.
4. I am trying to distinguish here between the apolitical American version of structuralist linguistics, identified with scholars like Bloomfield, Hockett, and (less obviously) Chomsky, from the more radical French version, associated with Saussure and his European followers. See for a discussion of this difference Hodge and Kress 1988, chap. 1.
5. I demonstrate this connection extensively in Canagarajah 1996.
6. I treat content- and reader-focused approaches as related orientations, influenced by similar intellectual movements, with the proviso that the former adopts a more product-oriented and the latter a somewhat process-oriented emphasis on academic discourse. For other scholars who treat these schools as related movements, see Shih 1986, 635–40; Spack 1988, 34–36.

Chapter 3

1. For sample exercises, see Brown 1994; Frodesen 1991.
2. *Essentialize* comes from the root *essence*. Such constructs are based on the assumption that the characteristics described of a community are intrinsic and natural to them. In making such assumptions, ethnocentric scholars also identify unique characteristics of a community, derived from broad generalizations.
3. See Kubota 1998 for this argument. Kubota demonstrates the advantages of this approach by comparing Japanese students writing in Japanese and Canadian students writing in English. Similarly, Indrasuta 1988 compares Thai students writing in Thai and American students writing in English.
4. Connor (1996, 164) discusses the need to compare writers of similar levels of proficiency and offers examples of studies that control for authorship. Taylor and Chen (1991) make a case for comparing texts of similar genres (e.g., academic writing) and of specific content focus within a genre (e.g., writing in economics, botany, or philosophy).
5. Hinds (1987) shows the ways in which culturally based expectations about the differential responsibility of readers and writers may create differences in the text. For example, Japanese readers assume they have to work hard to interpret the text, while American readers assume it is the responsibility of the writer to communicate clearly. Japanese writers therefore use less cohesive devices because they expect readers to do more work in order to get the text to mean. (See Kubota 1998 for a more complex explanation of these differences.)
6. For a sample of these different modes of process-oriented approaches to contrastive rhetoric, see Connor 1996, chaps. 4 and 10.
7. There are of course some studies that compare the writing in L1 and L2 of the same set of students (see Indrasuta 1988; M. Cook 1988; Dunkelblau 1990; and Kamel 1989). But the large subject pool and quantitative modes of analysis don't permit the researchers to ask the questions related to individual strategies of negotiation that I pose in this chapter.
8. We may chart the relationship between these schools in the following way:

9. Although it is important to describe the range of genres in each discipline, this is beyond the scope of this book. Studies of this nature have just begun.

10. Dwight Atkinson (1996) samples articles in the *Philosophical Trans-actions of the Royal Society* from 1675 to 1975 to show the multiple factors motivating rhetorical change through a period of three centuries.

Chapter 4

1. Such values were championed by the Romantic movement in European literary history at the beginning of the nineteenth century as individuals reacted against the intellectualism and conventionality of Enlightenment writing. Many critics would contend that Romantic values still play a dominant role in creative writing and textual reception.

2. For example, Susan Sontag (2000) in her contribution states, "Writing is finally a series of permissions you give yourself to be expressive in certain ways. To invent. To leap. To fly. To fall. To find your own characteristic way of narrating and insisting: that is, to find your own inner freedom" (E2).

3. We have to be careful in generalizing from Silva 1993, as the review combines studies of different kinds—those comparing ESL writers with "native-speaker" writers and those comparing writing in L1 and L2 by writers of different language groups.

4. It must be acknowledged that when he discusses theoretical implications, Silva (1993) argues for the need to develop unique theoretical models to explain L2 writing. It is not clear, however, if the models would radically deviate from the "comparative fallacy" informing the studies in the article.

5. The wash-back effect is defined as "the effect a test has on the teaching environment which has preceded it" (see Hamp-Lyons 1991, 337).

6. Vai Ramanathan has told me recently that her coauthors are not against the critical practice version described here; they are only critical of the critical thinking version and of its imposition in ESOL classes (Ramanathan, personal communication, 29 August 2001). But in their paper they implicate critical thinking with scholars like Freire, Shor, and Aronowitz and Giroux, whom they associate with "critical/radical pedagogy" (see Ramanathan and Kaplan 1996). Therefore readers may get the impression that the position of these scholars is also criticized. In other words, it appears that in their paper Ramanathan and Kaplan don't make the distinction I am making here but in fact lump both approaches together. As for the second point, though imposing the thinking practices of Western logical thinking in the guise of critical thinking is evil, it is equally biased to consider ESOL students as alienated from critical thinking or to believe that they won't have any advantages negotiating it for their educational advancement. My position in this book is that there are advantages for multilingual students in negotiating with disparate cultures and languages.

7. For a review of the literature that develops such a perspective on the self, we need to understand developments in postmodernism (Foucault 1990), poststructuralism (Spivak 1990), postcolonialism (Hall 1990), and feminism (Butler 1990). A simpler—that is, more readable—introduction to some of these movements is provided by Belsey 1983 or Coward and Ellis 1977. A more critical review of theories on identity is found in Smith 1989.

8. A version of this framework was originally provided by Kramsch 2000. I have considerably modified and reinterepreted her model in order to suit my theoretical biases.

   Though language and discourse are interconnected, I define discourse as more macrosocial. Discourses are socially patterned ideological paradigms. Language is defined as the sign system at its most basic (or microsocial) level, characterized by irrepressible heterogeneity, conflict, and creativity (see Kress 1985).

9. I borrow this distinction from Giroux (1983), who warns that "the concept of resistance must not be allowed to become a category indiscriminately hung over every expression of 'oppositional behavior'" (109). Giroux distinguishes between *resistance,* which he sees as displaying ideological clarity and commitment to collective action for social transformation, and mere *opposition,* which is unclear, ambivalent, and largely passive.

Chapter 5

1. I am synthesizing here views articulated by many poststructuralist and postmodernist theorists. Those who wish to grapple with the primary texts should read Kuhn 1962; Foucault 1972; Derrida 1981; Haraway 1989; and Harding 1991.

2. For EAP-oriented textbooks that display a pragmatic, normative, and skills-based approach to writing, see Bogel et al. 1988; Bowen, Madsen, and Hilferty 1985; Brinton, Snow, and Wesche 1989; and Carrell, Devine, and Eskey 1988.

Chapter 6

1. From this perspective, Joseph Harris (1989) is correct to point out that the term *community* connotes notions of harmony, fellowship, solidarity, unity, and uniformity that may mislead us about the conflictual relations between these social groups. We will continue to use the term in this book for convenience, keeping in mind the qualifications.

2. According to this influential orientation to education, learning always takes place through community-oriented activity, especially when members relate to the group in terms of their diverse interests and values, despite some measure of detachment. From this perspective,

multilingual students who enjoy separate community identities and interactions may still participate in an indirect way in the larger educational processes of the mainstream community.
3. Chelliah (1922), in passing, mentions such behavior by local Hindu Tamil students in Christian missionary schools in Sri Lanka.
4. Consider the following publications for masked forms of resistance in these communities: Abu-Lughod 1986; Adas 1992; Guha 1983; Khare 1984.
5. These lines are quoted as they were in the original. The spelling and grammatical peculiarities have not been edited out.

Chapter 7

1. Selfe and Selfe (1994) perform an interesting analysis of many other icons in the computer media to show the cultural biases behind them.
2. For examples of such claims, see Warschauer 2000; Bernhardt, Edwards, and Wojahn 1989; Bernhardt, Wojahn, and Edwards 1990.
3. For research on these advantages, see Pennington 1993a, 1993b.
4. See Cmejrkova 1996 for similar observations.
5. Note that this class was not held completely as a computer-assisted course as there was limited time given for each class in the computer lab. The class alternated between the traditional classroom and the computer lab for an equal number of class meetings.
6. See also Murray 2000 and Warschauer 2000 for other discussions on the benefits of Internet-based language learning.
7. For introductions to these research approaches, see Auerbach 1994; Hornberger 1994; Nunan 1990.

Works Cited

Abu-Lughod, L. 1986. *Veiled sentiments: Honor and poetry in a Bedouin society.* Berkeley: University of California Press.

Achebe, C. 1975. *Morning yet on creation day.* London: Heinemann.

Adas, M. 1992. From avoidance to confrontation: Peasant protest in pre-colonial and colonial Southeast Asia. In N. Dirks, ed., *Colonialism and culture,* 89–126. Ann Arbor: University of Michigan Press.

Allaei, S. K., and U. M. Connor. 1990. Exploring the dynamics of cross-cultural collaboration in writing classrooms. *Writing Instructor* 10 (1): 19–28.

Appadurai, Arjun. 1996. *Modernity at large: Cultural dimensions of globalization.* Minneapolis: University of Minnesota Press.

Aronowitz, S., and H. Giroux. 1985. *Education under siege: The conservative, liberal and radical debate over schooling.* South Hadley, Mass.: Bergin Harvey.

Atkinson, D. 1996. The *Philosophical Transactions of the Royal Society of London,* 1675–1975: A sociohistorical discourse analysis. *Language in Society* 25 (3): 333–72.

———. 1997. A critical approach to critical thinking in TESOL. *TESOL Quarterly* 33 (1): 71–94.

Auerbach, E. R. 1994. Participatory action research. *TESOL Quarterly* 28 (4):693–97.

Auerbach, E. R., with B. Barahona, J. Midy, F. Vaquerano, A. Zambrano, and J. Arnaud. 1996. A*dult ESL literacy from the community to the community: A guidebook for participatory literacy training.* Mahwah, N.J.: Lawrence Erlbaum.

Bakhtin, M. M. 1981. *The dialogic imagination.* Austin: University of Texas Press.

Bartholomae, D., and A. Petrosky. 1986. *Facts, artifacts and counter-facts: A basic reading and writing course for the college curriculum.* Pittsburgh: University of Pittsburgh Press.

Barton, D., and M. Hamilton. 1998. *Local literacies: Reading and writing in one community.* London and New York: Routledge.

Bates, L., J. Lane, and E. Lange. 1993. *Writing clearly: Responding to ESL compositions.* Boston: Heinle and Heinle.

Bazerman, C. 1988. *Shaping written knowledge: The genre and activity of the experimental article in science.* Madison: University of Wisconsin Press.

Beach, R., and L. Bridwell. 1984. Learning through writing: A rationale for writing across the curriculum. In A. D. Pellegini and T. D. Yawey, eds., *The development of oral and written language in social contexts,* 183–98. Norwood, N.J.: Ablex.

Belanger, M. 1982. A preliminary analysis of the structure of the discussion sections in ten neuroscience journal articles. Mimeograph.

Belcher, D. 1994. The apprenticeship approach to advanced academic literacy: Graduate students and their mentors. *English for Specific Purposes* 13:23–34.

———. 1997. An argument for nonadversarial argumentation: On the relevance of the feminist critique of academic discourse to L2 writing pedagogy. *Journal of Second Language Writing* 6 (1): 1–21.

Belcher, D., and U. M. Connor, eds. 2001. *Reflections on multiliterate lives.* Clevedon, U.K.: Multilingual Matters.

Belsey, C. 1983. *Critical practice.* London: Methuen.

Benesch, S. 1993. ESL, ideology and politics of pragmatism. *TESOL Quarterly* 27 (2): 705–17.

Bernhardt, S. A., P. R. Edwards, and P. G. Wojahn. 1989. Teaching college composition with computers: A program evaluation study. *Written Communication* 6 (1):108–33.

Bernhardt, S. A., P. G. Wojahn, and P. R. Edwards. 1990. Teaching college composition with computers: A timed observation study. *Written Communication* 7 (3):342–74.

Bernstein, B. 1971. *Class, codes and control.* Vol. 1. London: Routledge and Kegan Paul.

Bizzell, P. 1982. Cognition, convention and certainty: What we need to know about writing. *PRE/TEXT* 3:213–43.

———. 1992. *Academic discourse and critical consciousness.* Pittsburgh: University of Pittsburgh Press.

Bogel, F. V., P. Carden, G. H. Cox, S. Davis, D. P. Freedman, K. K. Gottschalk, J. Hjortshoj, and E. E. Shaw, eds. 1988. *Teaching prose: A guide for writing instructors.* New York: Norton.

Bowen, R., H. Madsen, and A. Hilferty. 1985. *TESOL techniques and procedures.* Cambridge, Mass.: Newbury House.

Braine, G. 1988. A reader reacts. *TESOL Quarterly* 22 (4):700–702.

Brannon, L., and C. H. Knoblauch. 1982. On students' rights to their own texts: A model of teacher response. *College Composition and Communication* 33 (2):157–66.

Brinton, D., M. A. Snow, and M. B. Wesche. 1989. *Content-based second language instruction.* Boston: Heinle and Heinle.

Brooke, Robert. 1987. Underlife and writing instruction. *College Composition and Communication* 38 (2):141–53.

Brown, H. D. 1991. TESOL at twenty-five: What are the issues? *TESOL Quarterly* 25 (2): 245–60.

———. 1994. *Teaching by principles.* Englewood Cliffs, N.J.: Prentice-Hall.

Butler, J. 1990. *Gender trouble: Feminism and the subversion of identity.* New York: Routledge.

Canagarajah, A. S. 1987. *Contrastive rhetoric: A critique and a proposal.* Monograph B 171. Duisburgh: Linguistic Agency, University of Duisburgh.

———. 1990. Negotiating competing discourses and identities: A sociolinguistic analysis of challenges in academic writing for minority students. Ph.D. diss., University of Texas, Austin.

———. 1993. Critical ethnography of a Sri Lankan classroom: Ambiguities in opposition to reproduction through ESOL. *TESOL Quarterly* 27 (4): 601–26.

———. 1996. Non-discursive requirements in academic publishing, material resources of periphery scholars, and the politics of knowledge production. *Written Communication* 13 (4): 435–72.

———. 1997a. Challenges in English literacy for African-American and Lankan Tamil learners: Towards a pedagogical paradigm for bidialectal and bilingual minority students. *Language and Education* 11 (1): 15–36.

———. 1997b. Safe houses in the contact zone: Coping strategies of African American students in the academy. *College Composition and Communication* 48 (2): 173–96.

———. 1999a. Comparing teacher-facilitated and student-constructed safe houses: The coping strategies of bilingual students in academic literacy. Report submitted for National Council of Teachers of English grant-in-aid, Baruch College. Mimeograph.

———. 1999b. On EFL teachers, awareness, and agency. *ELT Journal* 53 (3): 207–14.

———. 1999c. *Resisting linguistic imperialism in English teaching.* Oxford: Oxford University Press.

———. 2000. Understanding L2 academic writing as codeswitching. Paper presented at the thirty-fourth annual TESOL Convention, 14–18 March, Vancouver.

———. In press. *A geopolitics of academic writing.* Pittsburgh: University of Pittsburgh Press.

Cardelle, M., and L. Corno. 1981. Effects on second language learning on variations in written feedback on homework assignments. *TESOL Quarterly* 15 (2):251–61.

Carrell, P. L., J. Devine, and D. Eskey, eds. 1988. *Interactive approaches to second language reading.* Cambridge: Cambridge University Press.

Carson, J. G., and G. L. Nelson. 1994. Writing groups: Cross-cultural issues. *Journal of Second Language Writing* 3 (1): 17–30.

Casanave, C. P. 1995. Local interactions: Constructing contexts for composing in a graduate sociology program. In D. Belcher and G. Braine, eds., *Academic writing in a second language: Essays on research and pedagogy,* 83–110. Norwood, N.J.: Ablex.

Cazden, C. B. 2000. The limits of indigenous literacies. Paper presented at the annual American Association for Applied Linguistics convention, 12–14 March, Vancouver.

Chelliah, John V. 1922. *A century of English education.* Vaddukoddai: Jaffna College.

Cmejrkova, Svetla. 1996. Academic writing in Czech and English. In A. Ventola and A. Mauranen, eds., *Academic writing: Intercultural and textual issues,* 137–52. Amsterdam and Philadelphia: John Benjamins.

Cole, K., and J. Zuengler. 2000. Positioning in a science classroom: Appropriating, resisting, and denying "scientific identities." Paper presented at the annual American Association for Applied Linguistics convention, 12–14 March, Vancouver.

Connor, Ulla. 1996. *Contrastive rhetoric: Cross cultural aspects of second language writing.* Cambridge: Cambridge University Press.

———. 1999. Learning to write academic prose in a second language: A literacy autobiography. In G. Braine, ed., *Non-native educators in English language teaching,* 29–42. Mahwah, N.J.: Lawrence Erlbaum.

Connor, U. M., and K. Asenavage. 1994. Peer response groups in ESL writing classes: How much impact on revision? *Journal of Second Language Writing* 3 (3):257–76.

Cook, M. 1988. The validity of the contrastive rhetoric hypothesis as it relates to Spanish-speaking advanced ESL students. Ph.D. diss. Abstract in *Dissertation Abstracts International* 49 (9):2567A.

Cook, V. 1999. Going beyond the native speaker in language teaching. *TESOL Quarterly* 33 (2): 185–210.

Cope, B., and M. Kalantzis, eds., 2000. *Multiliteracies: Literacy learning and the design of social futures.* London and New York: Routledge.

Coward, Rosalind, and John Ellis. 1977. *Language and materialism: Developments in semiology and the theory of the subject.* London: Routledge and Kegan Paul.

Crystal, David. 1997. *English as a global language.* Cambridge: Cambridge University Press.

Cummins, J. 1991. Interdependence of first- and second-language proficiency in bilingual children. In E. Bialystok, ed., *Language processing in bilingual children,* 70–89. Cambridge: Cambridge University Press.

Daedalus Group. 1993. *Daedalus integrated writing environment: Instructor's guide.* Austin, Tex.: Daedalus Group.

Delpit, Lisa. 1995. *Other people's children: Cultural conflict in the classroom.* New York: New Press.

Derrida, Jacques. 1972. Structure, sign and play in the discourse of the human sciences. In Richard Macksey and Eugenio Donato, eds., *The structuralist controversy: The languages of criticism and the sciences of man,* 249–67. Baltimore: Johns Hopkins University Press.

———. 1981. *Positions.* Trans. Alan Bass. Chicago: University of Chicago Press.

Duffy, J. 2000. Never hold a pencil: Rhetoric and relations in the concept of "preliteracy." *Written Communication* 17 (2): 224–57.

Dunkelblau, H. 1990. A contrastive study of the organizational structure and stylistic elements of Chinese and English expository writing by Chinese high school students. Ph.D. diss. Abstract in *Dissertation Abstracts International* 51 (4):1143A.

Eisterhold, J. C. 1990. Reading-writing connections: Toward a description for second language learners. In B. Kroll, ed., *Second language writing:*

Research insights for the classroom, 88–101. Cambridge: Cambridge University Press.

Elbow, Peter. 1981. *Writing with power: Techniques for mastering the writing process.* New York: Oxford University Press.

Emig, Janet. 1971. *The composing processes of twelfth graders.* Urbana, Ill.: National Council of Teachers of English.

———. 1977. Writing as a mode of learning. *College Composition and Communication* 32 (3):365—87.

———. 1983. *The web of meaning.* Upper Montclair, N.J.: Boynton/Cook.

Faigley, Lester. 1986. Competing theories of process: A critique and proposal. *College English* 48 (6):527–42.

Faigley, Lester, and Kristine Hansen. 1985. Learning to write in the social sciences. *College Composition and Communication* 36 (1):140–49.

Fairclough, Norman. 1995. *Critical discourse analysis: The critical study of language.* London: Longman.

———. 2000. Multiliteracies and language: Orders of discourse and intertextuality. In B. Kope and M. Kalantzis, eds., *Multiliteracies: Literacy learning and the design of social futures,*162–81. London and New York: Routledge.

Ferris, Dana. 1995. Can advanced ESL students become effective self-editors? *CATESOL Journal* 8:41–62.

Ferris, Dana, and John S. Hedgcock. 1998. *Teaching ESL composition: Purpose, process, and practice.* Mahwah, N.J.: Lawrence Erlbaum.

Flower, Linda, and John R. Hayes. 1981. A cognitive process theory of writing. *College Composition and Communication* 32 (3):365–87.

Flower, Linda., V. Stein, J. Ackerman, M. Kantz, K. McCormick, and W. Peck. 1990. *Reading-to-write: Exploring a cognitive and social process.* New York: Oxford University Press.

Foucault, Michel. 1972. The discourse on language. In *The archaeology of knowledge,* 215–37. Trans. A. M. Sheridan Smith. New York: Pantheon.

———. 1990. *The history of sexuality.* Vol. 1. Trans. Robert Hurley. New York: Random House.

Fowler, Roger, and Gunther Kress. 1979. Critical linguistics. In Roger Fowler, B. Hodge, G. Kress, and A. Trew, eds., *Language and control,* 185–213. London: Routledge.

Fox, Helen. 1994. *Listening to the world: Cultural issues in academic writing.* Urbana, Ill.: National Council of Teachers of English.

Freire, Paulo. 1970. *Pedagogy for the oppressed.* New York: Herder.

———. 1985. *The politics of education.* South Hadley, Mass.: Bergin and Garvey.

Frodesen, J. 1991. Grammar in writing. In M. Celce-Murcia, ed., *Teaching English as a second or foreign language,* 2d ed., 264–76. Boston: Heinle and Heinle.

Fulwiler, Terry. 1982. Writing: An act of cognition. In C. W. Griffin, ed., *Teaching writing in all disciplines,* 15–36. San Francisco: Jossey-Bass.

Gaies, Stephen. 1980. T-unit analysis in second language research: Applications, problems, and limitations. *TESOL Quarterly* 14 (1):53–60.

Gardner, R. C., and W. E. Lambert. 1972. *Attitudes and motivation in second language learning.* Rowley, Mass.: Newbury House.

Gee, J. P. 2000. New people in new worlds: Networks, the new capitalism and schools. In B. Cope and M. Kalantzis, eds., *Multiliteracies: Literacy learning and the design of social futures,* 43–68. London and New York: Routledge.

Geisler, Cheryl. 1994. *Academic literacy and the nature of expertise: Reading, writing, and knowing in academic philosophy.* Hillsdale, N.J.: Lawrence Erlbaum.

Giroux, Henry A. 1983. *Theory and resistance in education: A pedagogy for the opposition.* South Hadley, Mass.: Bergin and Garvey.

———. 1988. *Teachers as intellectuals: Toward a critical pedagogy of learning.* New York: Bergin and Garvey.

———. 1992. *Border crossings: Cultural workers and the politics of education.* New York: Routledge.

Goffman, Erving. 1961. *Asylums: Essays on the social situation of mental patients and other inmates.* New York: Anchor.

Grabe, W., and R. B. Kaplan. 1996. *Theory and practice of writing.* London: Longman.

Green, J. M., and R. Oxford. 1995. A closer look at learner strategies, L2 proficiency, and gender. *TESOL Quarterly* 29 (2): 261–98.

Grossberg, Lawrence. 1994. Introduction: Bringin' it all back home: Pedagogy and cultural studies. In Henry Giroux and Peter McLaren, eds., *Between borders: Pedagogy and the politics of cultural studies,* 1–25. New York: Routledge.

Guha, Ranajit. 1983. *Elementary aspects of peasant insurgency.* Delhi: Oxford University Press.

Hairston, Maxine. 1982. The winds of change: Thomas Kuhn and the revolution in the teaching of writing. *College Composition and Communication* 33 (1):76–88.

Hall, Stewart. 1990. Cultural identity and diaspora. In J. Rutherford, ed., *Identity, community, culture, difference,* 222–37. London: Lawrence and Wishart.

Halliday, M. A. K. 1985. *An introduction to functional grammar.* London: Arnold Edward.

Halliday, M. A. K., and R. Hasan. 1976. *Cohesion in English.* London and New York: Longman.

Hammond, J., and M. Macken-Horarik. 1999. Critical literacy: Challenges and questions for ESL classrooms. *TESOL Quarterly* 33 (3): 528–43.

Hamp-Lyons, L. 1991. *Assessing second language writing in academic contexts.* Norwood, N.J.: Ablex.

Haraway, Donna. 1989. *Primate visions: Gender, race, and nature in the world of modern science.* New York: Routledge.

Harding, Sandra. 1991. *Whose science? Whose knowledge? Thinking from women's lives.* Ithaca: Cornell University Press.

Harklau, Linda. 2000. "From the 'good kids' to the 'worst'": Representations of English language learners across educational settings. *TESOL Quarterly* 34 (1):35–68.

Harris, Joseph. 1989. The idea of community in the study of writing. *College Composition and Communication* 40 (1):11–22.

Heath, Shirley Brice. 1983. *Ways with words.* Cambridge: Cambridge University Press.

Hedgcock, J., and N. Lefkowitz. 1994. Feedback on feedback: Assessing learner receptivity to teacher response in L2 composition. *Journal of Second Language Writing* 3 (2):141–63.

Hendrickson, J. 1978. Error correction in foreign language teaching: Recent theory, research, and practice. *Modern Language Journal* 62:387–92.

Herring, S. C. 1996. Posting in a different voice: Gender and ethics in computer-mediated communication. In C. Ess, ed., *Philosophical perspectives on computer-mediated communication,* 115–45. Albany: SUNY Press.

Hess, David J. 1995. *Science and technology in a multicultural world.* New York: Columbia University Press.

Hillocks, G., Jr. 1986. *Research on written composition.* Urbana, Ill.: National Council of Teachers of English.

Hinds, J. 1987. Reader versus writer responsibility: A new typology. In R. B. Kaplan and U. M. Connor, eds., *Writing across languages: Analyzing L2 texts,* 141–52. Reading, Mass.: Addison-Wesley.

Hodge, Robert, and Gunther Kress. 1988. *Social semiotics.* Ithaca: Cornell University Press.

hooks, bell. 1989. *Talking back: Thinking feminist, thinking black.* Boston: South End Press.

Hornberger, Nancy. 1994. Ethnography. *TESOL Quarterly* 28 (4): 688–90.

Howard, Rebecca Moore. 1995. Plagiarisms, authorships, and the academic death penalty. *College English* 57 (9):788–806.

Hunt, K. 1965. *Grammatical structures written at three grade levels.* Urbana, Ill.: National Council of Teachers of English.

Indrasuta, C. 1988. Narrative styles in the writing of Thai and American students. In A. C. Purves, ed., *Writing across languages and cultures: Issues in contrastive rhetoric,* 206–26. Newbury Park, Calif.: Sage.

Johns, Ann M. 1990. L1 composition theories: Implications for developing theories of L2 composition. In B. Kroll, ed., *Second language writing: Research insights for the classroom,* 24-—36. Cambridge: Cambridge University Press.

———. 1993. Reading and writing tasks in English for Academic Purposes classes: Products, processes, and resources. In J. G. Carson and I. Leki, eds., *Reading in the composition classroom: Second language perspectives,* 274–89. Boston: Heinle and Heinle.

Johns, Ann M., and Tony Dudley-Evans. 1991. English for Specific Purposes: International in scope, specific in purpose. *TESOL Quarterly* 25 (2):297–314.

Kachru, Braj B. 1986. *The alchemy of English: The spread, functions and models of non-native Englishes.* Oxford: Pergamon.

Kamel, G. 1989. Argumentative writing by Arab learners of English as a foreign and second language: An empirical investigation of contrastive rhetoric. Ph.D. diss. Abstract in *Dissertation Abstracts International* 50 (3):677A.

Kaplan, Robert B. 1966. Cultural thought patterns in intercultural education. *Language Learning* 16:1–20.

———. 1976. A further note on contrastive rhetoric. *Communication Quarterly* 24:12–19.

———. 1986. Culture and the written language. In J. M. Valdes, ed., *Culture bound,* 8–19. Cambridge: Cambridge University Press.

Khare, R. S. 1984. *The untouchable as himself: Ideology, identity, and pragmatism among the Lucknow Chamars.* Cambridge: Cambridge University Press.

Knorr-Cetina, Karin D. 1981. *The manufacture of knowledge: An essay on the constructivist and contextual nature of science.* Oxford: Pergamon.

Kramsch, Claire. 2000. Linguistic identities at the boundaries. Paper presented at the annual AAAL convention, 12–14 March, Vancouver.

Kramsch, Claire, and W. S. E. Lam. 1999. Textual identities: The importance of being non-native. In G. Braine, ed., *Non-native educators in English language teaching,* 57–72. Mahwah, N.J.: Lawrence Erlbaum.

Kress, Gunther. 1985. Ideological structures in discourse. In Tuan van Dijk, ed., *Handbook of discourse analysis,* 4:27–42. London: Academic Press.

———. 2000. Multimodality. In B. Cope and M. Kalantzis, eds., *Multiliteracies: Literacy learning and the design of social futures,* 182–202. London and New York: Routledge.

Kubota, Ryuko. 1998. An investigation of Japanese and English L1 essay organization: Differences and similarities. *Canadian Modern Language Review* 54 (4): 475–507.

———. 1999a. An investigation of L1-L2 transfer in writing among Japanese university students: Implications for contrastive rhetoric. *Journal of Second Language Writing* 7 (1): 69–100.

———. 1999b. Japanese culture constructed by discourses: Implications for applied linguistics research and ELT. *TESOL Quarterly* 33 (1): 9–35.

Kuhn, Thomas S. 1962. *The structure of scientific revolutions.* Chicago: University of Chicago Press.

Kumaravadivelu, Braj. 1999. Critical classroom discourse analysis. *TESOL Quarterly* 33 (3): 453–84.

Kuriloff, Peshe. 1996. What discourses have in common: Teaching the transaction between writer and reader. *College Composition and Communication* 47 (4):485–501.

Lado, Robert. 1957. *Linguistics across cultures.* Ann Arbor: University of Michigan Press.

Lalande, J. F. 1982. Reducing composition errors: An experiment. *Modern Language Journal* 66:140–49.

Lam, Eva Wan Shun. 2000. L2 literacy and the design of the self: A case study of a teenager writing on the internet. *TESOL Quarterly* 34 (3): 457–82.

Latour, B., and S. Woolgar. 1979. *Laboratory life: The social construction of scientific facts.* Princeton: Princeton University Press.

Lautimatti, L. 1987. Observations on the development of the topic of simplified discourse. In R. B. Kaplan and U. M. Connor, eds., *Writing across languages: Analysis of L2 texts,* 87–114. Reading, Mass.: Addison-Wesley.

Lave, J., and E. Wenger. 1991. *Situated learning: Legitimate peripheral participation.* Cambridge: Cambridge University Press.

Leki, I. 1990a. Coaching from the margins: Issues in written response. In B. Kroll, ed., *Second language writing: Research insights for the classroom,* 57–68. Cambridge: Cambridge University Press.

———. 1990b. Potential problems with peer responding in ESL writing classes. *CATESOL Journal* 3:5–19.

———. 1991a. Building expertise through sequenced writing assignments. *TESOL Journal* 1:19–23.

———. 1991b. The preferences of ESL students for error correction in college-level writing classes. *Foreign Language Annals* 24:203–18.

———. 1995. Coping strategies of ESL students in writing tasks across the curriculum. *TESOL Quarterly* 29 (2): 235–60.

Li, Xiao-Ming. 1999. Writing from the vantage point of an outsider/insider. In G. Braine, ed., *Non-native educators in English language teaching,* 43–56. Mahwah, N.J.: Lawrence Erlbaum.

Lo Bianco, J. 2000. Multiliteracies and multilingualism. In B. Cope and M. Kalantzis, ed., *Multiliteracies: Literacy learning and the design of social futures,* 92–105. London and New York: Routledge.

Lu, Min-Zhan. 1994. Professing multiculturalism: The politics of style in the contact zone. *College Composition and Communication* 45 (4): 442–58.

Luke, C. 2000. Cyber schooling and technological change: Multiliteracies for new times. In B. Cope and M. Kalantzis, ed., *Multiliteracies: Literacy learning and the design of social futures,* 69–91. London and New York: Routledge.

Mangelsdorf, K., and A. L. Schlumberger. 1992. ESL student response stances in a peer review-task. *Journal of Second Language Writing* 1 (3):235–54.

Marcus, G., and M. M. J. Fischer. 1986. *Anthropology as cultural critique: An experimental moment in the human sciences.* Chicago: University of Chicago Press.

Matsuda, Paul Kei. 1998. Situating ESL writing in a cross-disciplinary context. *Written Communication* 15 (1), 99–121.

Mauranen, Anna. 1993a. Contrastive ESP rhetoric: Metatext in Finnish-Economic texts. *English for Specific Purposes* 12:3–22.

———. 1993b. *Cultural differences in academic rhetoric.* Frankfurt am Main: Peter Lang.

McCrimmon, James M. 1984. Writing as a way of knowing. In R. L. Graves, ed., *Rhetoric and Composition,* 3–11. Upper Montclair, N.J.: Boynton/Cook.

Mehan, Hugh. 1985. The structure of classroom discourse. In Tuan A. van Dijk, ed., *Handbook of discourse analysis,* 3:119–31. New York: Academic Press.

Mendonca, C. O., and K. E. Johnson. 1994. Peer review negotiations: Revision activities in ESL writing instruction. *TESOL Quarterly* 28 (4):745–69.

Miller, Keith D. 1992. *Voice of deliverance: The language of Martin Luther King, Jr., and its sources.* New York: Free Press.

Mohan, Bernie A. 1986. *Language and content.* Reading, Mass.: Addison-Wesley.

Mohan, Bernie A., and Winnie Au-Yeung Lo. 1985. Academic writing and Chinese students: Transfer and developmental factors. *TESOL Quarterly* 19 (4):515–34.

Muchiri, Mary N., Nshindi G. Mulamba, Greg Myers, and Deoscorous B. Ndoloi. 1995. Importing composition: Teaching and researching academic writing beyond North America. *College Composition and Communication* 46 (2): 175–98.

Murray, D. 2000. Protean communication: The language of computer-mediated communication. *TESOL Quarterly* 34 (3): 397–422.

Myers, Greg. 1990. *Writing biology: Texts in the social construction of scientific knowledge.* Madison: University of Wisconsin Press.

Nandy, Ashish, ed. 1990. *Science, hegemony, and violence.* Delhi: Oxford University Press.

Narasimhan, R. 1991. Literacy: Its characterization and implications. In David R. Olson and Nancy Torrance, eds., *Literacy and orality,* 177–97. Cambridge: Cambridge University Press.

Nayar, P. B. 1997. ESL/EFL dichotomy today: Language politics or pragmatics? *TESOL Quarterly* 31 (1): 9–37.

Ngugi wa Thiong'o. 1986. *Decolonizing the mind: the politics of language in African literature.* London: Currey, Heinemann.

Nunan, David. 1990. Action research in the language classroom. In Jack C. Richards and David Nunan, eds., *Second language teacher education.* Cambridge: Cambridge University Press.

Oxford, Rebecca. 1990. *Language learning strategies: What every teacher should know.* New York: Newbury House.

Paul, Dannette. 1996. Introducing chaos into scientific discourse: A study of reception and effect of rhetorical devices in revolutionary science. Ph.D. diss., Pennsylvania State University.

Pear, Robert. 1999. N.I.H plan for journal on the web draws fire. *New York Times,* 8 June, F1, F6.

Peirce, Bonny Norton. 1995. Social identity, investment, and language learning. *TESOL Quarterly* 29 (1): 9–32.

Pennington, M. C. 1993a. A critical examination of word processing effects in relation to L2 writers. *Journal of Second Language Writing* 2 (3):227–55.

———. 1993b. Exploring the potential of word processing for non-native writers. *Computers and the Humanities* 27:149–63.

Pennycook, Alastair. 1994. *The cultural politics of English as an international language.* London: Longman.

———. 1996. Borrowing others' words: Text, ownership, memory, and plagiarism. *TESOL Quarterly* 30 (2):201–30.

Perl, S. 1979. The composing processes of unskilled college writers. *Research in the Teaching of English* 13:317–36.

Phillipson, Robert. 1992. *Linguistic imperialism.* Oxford: Oxford University Press.

Pratt, Mary Louise. 1991. Arts of the contact zone. *Profession* 91:33–40.

Prior, Paul. 1998. *Writing/disciplinarity: A sociohistoric account of literate activity in the academy.* Mahwah, N.J.: Lawrence Erlbaum.

Radecki, P., and J. Swales. 1988. ESL student reaction to written comments on their written work. *System* 16:355–65.

Raimes, Ann. 1985. What unskilled ESL students do as they write: A classroom study of composing: *TESOL Quarterly* 19 (2):229–58.

———. 1987. Language proficiency, writing ability, and composing strategies: A study of ESL college student writers. *Language Learning* 37:439–68.

———. 1991. Out of the woods: Emerging traditions in the teaching of writing. *TESOL Quarterly* 25 (3):407–30.

Rajagopalan, Kanavilli. 1999. Of EFL teachers, conscience, and cowardice. *ELT Journal* 53 (3): 200–206.

Ramanathan, V., and D. Atkinson. 1999. Individualism, academic writing, and ESL writers. *Journal of Second Language Writing* 8 (1):45–75.

Ramanathan, V., and R. Kaplan. 1996. Some problematic "channels" in the teaching of critical thinking in current L1 composition textbooks: Implications for L2 student-writers. *Issues in Applied Linguistics* 7:225–49.

Reid, J. M. 1989. English as a second language composition in higher education: The expectations of the academic audience. In D. M. Johnson and D. H. Roen, eds., *Richness in writing: Empowering ESL students,* 220–34. New York: Longman.

Rheingold, H. 1994. *The virtual community: Homesteading on the electronic frontier.* New York: Harper Perennial.

Rohman, D. Gordan. 1965. Pre-writing: The stage of discovery in the writing process. *College Composition and Communication* 16 (1): 106–12.

Rose, Mike. 1989. *Lives on the boundary.* New York: Penguin.

Santos, Terry. 1993. Ideology in composition: L1 and ESL. *Journal of Second Language Writing* 1 (1):1–15.

Schenke, Arleen. 1991. The "will to reciprocity" and the work of memory: Fictioning speaking out of silence in ESL and feminist pedagogy. *Resources for Feminist Research* 20:47–55.

Schneider, M., and U. M. Connor. 1991. Analyzing topical structure in ESL essays: Not all topics are equal. *Studies in Second Language Acquisition* 12:411–27.

Scollon, R. 1991. Eight legs and one elbow: Stance and structure in Chinese English composition. Paper presented at the International Reading Association, Second North American Conference on Adult and Adolescent Literacy, 21 March, Banff.

Scott, James C. 1985. *Weapons of the weak: Everyday forms of peasant resistance.* New Haven: Yale University Press.

————. 1990. *Domination and the arts of resistance.* New Haven: Yale University Press.

Selfe, Cynthia, and Richard J. Selfe Jr. 1994. The politics of the interface: Power and its exercise in the electronic contact zone. *College Composition and Communication* 45 (4):480–504.

Shapin, Steven. 1984. Pump and circumstance: Robert Boyle's literary technology. *Social Studies of Science* 14:481–520.

Shen, F. 1989. The classroom and the wider culture: Identity as a key to learning English composition. *College Composition and Communication* 40 (4): 459–66.

Shih, May. 1986. Content-based approaches to teaching academic writing. *TESOL Quarterly* 20 (4):617–48.

Silva, Tony. 1993. Toward an understanding of the distinct nature of L2 writing: The ESL research and its implications. *TESOL Quarterly* 27 (4):657–78.

Sivatamby, K. 1984. Towards an understanding of the culture and ideology of the Tamils of Sri Lanka. In *Commemorative Souvenir: Jaffna Public Library,* 49–56. Jaffna: Catholic Press.

————. 1990. The ideology of Saiva-Tamil integrality: Its sociohistorical significance in the study of Yalppanam Tamil society. *Lanka* 5:176–82.

————. 1992. YaaLpaaNa camuukaTai viLanki koLLal—aTan uruvaakkam asaiviyakkam paRRiya oru piraarampa usaaval (Understanding Jaffna society: A preliminary inquiry into its "formation" and "dynamics"). Prof. S. Selvanayagam Memorial Lecture 8, University of Jaffna, Sri Lanka.

Smith, Paul. 1989. *Discerning the subject.* Minneapolis: University of Minnesota Press.

Sommer, N. 1980. Revision strategies of student writers and experienced adult writers. *College Composition and Communication* 31 (3): 378–88.

Sontag, Susan. 2000. Directions: Write, read, rewrite. Repeat steps 2 and 3 as needed. *New York Times,* 18 December, E1–E2.

Spack, Ruth. 1984. Invention strategies and the ESL college composition student. *TESOL Quarterly* 18 (4):649–70.

————. 1988. Initiating ESL students into the academic discourse community. *TESOL Quarterly* 22 (1):29–51.

Spivak, Gayatri. 1990. *The post-colonial critic.* New York: Routledge.

Stubbs, Michael. 1976. *Language, schools and classrooms.* London: Methuen.

Suseendirarajah, S. 1978. Caste and language in Jaffna Society. *Anthropological Linguistics* 20:312–19.

————. 1980. Religion and language in Jaffna society. *Anthropological Linguistics* 22:345–62.

————. 1991. PantiTamaNiyin peerum pukaLum vanTa vaaRu (Accounting for the name and prestige of Panditamani). Paper presented at the Academic Forum, 22 March, University of Jaffna, Sri Lanka. Mimeograph.

————. 1992. English in our Tamil society: A sociolinguistic appraisal.

Paper presented at the Academic Forum, 28 October, University of Jaffna, Sri Lanka. Mimeograph.

Swales, John. 1990. *Genre analysis: English in academic and research settings.* Cambridge: Cambridge University Press.

Tannen, D. 1986. *That's not what I meant! How conversational style makes or breaks your relations with others.* New York: William Morrow.

Taylor, G., and T. Chen. 1991. Linguistic, cultural, and subcultural issues in contrastive discourse analysis: Anglo-American and Chinese scientific texts. *Applied Linguistics* 12 (3): 319–36.

Taylor, C., J. Jamieson, and D. Eignor. 2000. Trends in computer use among international students. *TESOL Quarterly* 34 (3): 575–84.

Truscott, J. 1996. The case against grammar correction in L2 writing classes. *Language Learning* 46:327–69.

Vandrick, Stephanie. 1995. Privileged ESL university students. *TESOL Quarterly* 29 (3):375–80.

Villamil, O. S., and M. C. M. de Guerrero. 1996. Peer revision in the L2 classroom: Social-cognitive activities, mediating strategies, and aspects of social behavior. *Journal of Second Language Writing* 5 (1):51–75.

Walcott, Derek. 1986. *Collected poems, 1948–1984.* New York: Farrar, Straus, and Giroux.

Warschauer, M. 2000. The changing global economy and the future of English teaching. *TESOL Quarterly* 34 (3): 511–36.

Widdowson, H. 1983. *Learning purpose and language use.* New York: Oxford University Press.

Williams, Raymond. 1977. *Marxism and literature.* London: Oxford University Press.

Willis, P. 1977. *Learning to labour: How working class kids get working class jobs.* Manchester: Saxon House.

Witte, S., and L. Faigley. 1981. Coherence, cohesion, and writing quality. *College Composition and Communication* 32 (2):189–204.

Zamel, Vivian. 1982. Writing: The process of discovering meaning. *TESOL Quarterly* 16 (2):195–209.

———. 1983. The composing process of advanced ESL students: Six case studies. *TESOL Quarterly* 17 (2):165–87.

———. 1985. Responding to student writing. *TESOL Quarterly* 19 (1):79–102.

———. 1996. Transcending boundaries: Complicating the scene of teaching language. *College English* 6 (2): 1–11.

———. 1997. Toward a model of transculturation. *TESOL Quarterly* 31 (2): 341–51.

Zhang, S. 1995. Reexamining the affective advantages of peer feedback in the ESL writing class. *Journal of Second Language Writing* 4 (3):209–22.

Subject Index

Page numbers in italics indicate figures.

abstract approach, 2, 3
academic community: center/periphery relationships, 167–68, 218–19 (*see also* marginalization); collaborative relationships in, 190–93, 199, 204–5; multiple discourse communities in, 164, 165; negative attitudes toward, 169, 171; passing vs. procedural display, 190–91, 195; passive and active pressure of, 134, 135; peripheral apprenticeship in, 189–93; power conflicts in, 38, 145–47, 167–68, 169, 173, 218–19; socialization into (*see* community, issues of); Western dominance of, 132–33, 218–20 (*see also* Western culture)
academic essays, five-paragraph, 68, 137
accommodation strategy, 112, 113, 115
African American culture: appropriation strategy, use of, 114–15, 118; and grammar instruction, 47
African languages, 220
alignment, 190–91
alternate/oppositional communities. *See* safe houses
American Physiological Society, 219
American Society for Microbiology, 219
Anglo-American culture. *See* Western culture
Anthropological Linguistics, 180
apprenticeship, peripheral, 189–93
appropriation strategy: in negotiating content, 135–37, 155; in negotiating RA form, 76–79, 115; in negotiating self, 114–15, 116, 118
Asthma Project, 192

attitudes toward difference, 11–14; deficit, 11–12, 13, 14, 63–64; estrangement, 13, 19; relativistic, 12–13, 14, 19; resource, 13–14, 16, 17. *See also* ESOL critical writing, approaches to
audience: as integral to writing process, 161–62; for RAs, and switching discourses, 78. *See also* community, issues of
authoring, 214–15
autonomous textuality, 145–47
avoidance strategy, 107–10, 113, 115–16

bidialectals, 8
bilateral process, 14, 26–27
bilingualism, 8; elite, 220

CALL (computer-assisted language learning), 223–32; grammar and editing skills, 224–25, 229; integrated writing software, 225–30; online discussion vs. classroom structure, 227–30; product-oriented writing, 225, 227; student attitudes toward, 228–30, 232–33; word-processing skills, 223–24. *See also* computer use
CD (classroom discourse). *See* classroom discourse (CD)
center-based scholars, 76
center/periphery relationships, 167–68, 218–19
Chinese culture, 90–91, 92, 94, 150, 151–54
classroom discourse (CD): CALL, compared to, 227–30; CMC, compared to, 215–17; IRF sequence, 216, 227–28; political considerations, 231–32

Name Index

Allaei, S. K., 92
Anzaldúa, Gloria, 172
Appadurai, Arjun, 10
Aronowitz, S., 29
Asenavage, K., 200
Atkinson, Dwight, 97, 100, 102, 151

Bakhtin, M. M., 155, 174
Bartholomae, D., 147–49, 174
Barton, D., 185
Bates, L., 196
Bazerman, C., 130, 134, 144
Beach, R., 32
Belanger, M., 179
Belcher, D., 76, 190
Benesch, S., 131
Bernstein, B., 100, 132, 133, 213
Bizzell, Patricia, 32, 90, 132, 170, 171, 174
Bourdieu, Pierre, 117
Boyle, Robert, 74–75
Braine, G., 140, 193
Brannon, L., 197
Bridwell, L., 32
Brinton, D., 137
Brooke, Robert, 204
Brown, H. D., 50–51, 117

Canagarajah, A. Suresh, 10, 74, 76–79, 93, 95, 102, 103, 111, 113, 132, 154, 156, 167, 171, 177, 181, 182, 187, 203, 215, 221, 226
Cardelle, M., 196
Carson, J. G., 92, 202–3
Casanave, C. P., 190
Cazden, C. B., 221
Cole, K., 192
Connor, Ulla M., 60, 91, 92, 112, 113, 118, 200
Cook, V., 89
Cope, B., 212

Corno, L., 196
Cummins, J., 145

Daedalus Group, 226
Delpit, Lisa, 47, 196
Derrida, Jacques, 155
Dudley-Evans, Tony, 32
Duffy, J., 221

Eignor, D., 224
Eisterhold, J. C., 144
Elbow, Peter, 35, 86
Emig, Janet, 32, 87

Faigley, Lester, 47, 60
Fairclough, Norman, 62, 65
Ferris, Dana, 49–50, 51, 132, 144–45, 195–96, 197, 198–99, 202
Flower, Linda, 31, 87, 90, 97, 126
Foucault, Michel, 127, 167
Fowler, Roger, 61
Fox, Helen, 13
Freire, Paulo, 98, 205
Fulwiler, Terry, 32

Gaies, Stephen, 58
Gardner, R. C., 117
Gee, J. P., 192, 213
Geisler, Cheryl, 70, 145–47, 198
Giroux, Henry, 29, 38, 98, 99, 205, 233, 235
Goffman, Erving, 184
Grabe, W., 58, 64
Green, J. M., 120
Grossberg, Lawrence, 99, 233

Hairston, Maxine, 31
Halliday, M. A. K., 58–59, 61
Hamilton, M., 185
Hammond, J., 101–2
Hansen, Kristine, 47